HANDBOOK FOR SUCCESSFUL URBAN TEACHING

Johanna K. Lemlech
University of Southern California

UNIVERSITY
PRESS OF
AMERICA

LANHAM • NEW YORK • LONDON

Copyright © 1977 by

Johanna K. Lemlech

University Press of America,™ Inc.

4720 Boston Way
Lanham, MD 20706

3 Henrietta Street
London WC2E 8LU England

Reprinted by arrangement with
Harper & Row, Publishers, New York.

Library of Congress Cataloging in Publication Data

Lemlech, Johanna Kasin.
    Handbook for successful urban teaching.

    Reprint. Originally published: New York : Harper &
Row, ©1977.
    Bibliography: p.
    Includes index.
    1. Education, Urban–United States. 2. Teaching. 3.
Minorities–Education–United States. 4. Urban schools–
United States. 5. Teachers–Training of–United States.
I. Title.
[LC5131.L39   1984]   370.19'348   83–21855
ISBN 0–8191–3373–6 (pbk. : alk. paper)

"To My Family"

Contents

1

An Introduction to the Urban School Environment   1

2

The Urban Specialist Teacher: Role, Decisions, Tactics   35

3

4

5

6

Mainstreaming: A Construct for Teaching All Children Humanely

Preface
to the Instructor

As an urban teacher educator I have participated in an unending debate with colleagues: Should the preservice teacher observe and participate in multicultural classrooms torn by strife, dissent, chaos, and inappropriate teaching in order to learn about "reality"? Or, should the preservice teacher observe and participate in "model" situations in order to learn "what ought to be"? Through the years I have responded negatively to both propositions because I do not believe that one learns to teach through the observation of a "nonteacher"; nor does one learn to assess, prescribe, and evaluate diverse learning interests, problems, and needs in a test-tube situation.

My continuing perspective has been to search out those teachers and schools in the urban environment that are successful and accomplishing noteworthy goals. I look for teachers who utilize flexible teaching strategies and adapt those strategies to the needs of their students. I look for individuals who are willing to adapt different organizational plans in order to test and accommodate students' learning approaches. I want my students to have experiences in using a variety of resources and working in resource centers. I expect my students to develop and evaluate curriculum materials, teaching strategies, teaching styles, organizational patterns, and teacher-parent and teacher-student relations.

To accomplish this, I place my students in many schools. I contact the appropriate personnel responsible for teacher preparation in the public schools, and assignments to schools are made with full knowledge and acceptance of the school districts. Principals and teachers seem to welcome the assistance of college students who will perform "teacher assistant" tasks such as the preparation of materials, tutoring, and leadership of small groups of students.

My own classroom at the university often becomes a forum where students debate what they do and see in terms of the purposes of education. To facilitate their understanding, I have found it necessary to offer some guidelines in terms of what to look for in order to assist them to interpret why it is happening. This book is the culmination of many years of classroom teaching in the public schools and in teacher education at the university, where I have attempted to define teacher competencies in terms of subject matter knowledge, pedagogy, and humanistic behaviors.

The greatest challenge facing teacher educators is the preparation of urban specialist teachers. Essential to that preparation is the development of a *minority perspective*. That perspective can be accomplished through appropriate teaching experiences, in-depth readings, and developmental tasks. Critical to the development of that perspective will be professional dialog that examines problems and issues which affect minority Americans. In this book a number of teaching suggestions have been offered; they are not to be construed as a suggested "cure-all" for urban education. Teachers must constantly reappraise teaching techniques and strategies in terms of what works.

The 1970 census revealed that 67 percent of the American population resides in what the census bureau defined as urban areas. Geographers characterize the growth and change of cities by describing urban sprawl or designating the multiple nuclei characteristic of large cities in the United States. Multicultural populations live in suburbs surrounding the city as well as in what has become known as inner city ghetto areas. In this book the term *urban schools* is defined by the the students who attend them. In some cities these schools may be 10 to 20 miles from the inner city. The students may be of low economic status and/or a multicultural heritage; the problems of these students and the ways in which teachers can confront them have similarities.

The intent of the substantive material in the text and the workshop format is to link the content of teacher education with the "practice" of teaching so that as the reader completes the book, he or she will have developed both knowledge and some developmental skills to prepare for the classroom. Although competence is developmental and college students differ in experiential background and in needs, most students using this book should be able to

1. Describe urban school facilities, environment, and personnel involved in urban education
2. List social agencies and institutions that affect and/or can respond to the urban community and the urban teacher
3. Develop a community profile describing culture, people, businesses, needs, and problems

4. Identify appropriate goals for multicultural education
5. Relate students' physical, sociocultural, and ecological needs with recommended practices for classroom teaching.
6. Describe a variety of teaching styles and match each style with the corresponding classroom environment
7. Discuss conceptual categories and learning styles
8. Debate correspondence of teaching style, learning style, and learning environment
9. Identify teacher and learner behaviors
10. Recognize a skill sequence
11. Recognize and write appropriate behavioral objectives
12. List curriculum materials available for use other than the basic textbook
13. Develop a simplified teaching lesson using a strategy in Chapter 5 as a model
14. Contrast the social system perspective of mental retardation and the clinical perspective
15. Identify children with exceptional needs
16. Identify selective factors that influence teachers to refer a child for psychological study
17. Debate the effectiveness of special classroom placement vs. mainstreaming
18. Identify teacher skills for mainstreaming
19. Discuss factors that affect the development and measurement of intelligence
20. Discuss forces that influence societal change

This book has been written for students enrolled in social foundation courses and for students in curriculum and methods classes. I have purposefully chosen classroom episodes to demonstrate a wide variety of teaching approaches, different grade levels, and typical teaching situations. The students and teachers' names used in the episodes are intended to be "universal" rather than to designate a specific cultural group. Throughout the book I have emphasized the individual nature of perception.

Since the teacher's minority perspective would be deficient without empathy for the minority experience with social discrimination, problems related to stereotyped thinking and prejudice have been emphasized in several chapters. Readers are directed to examine their own language patterns, mass media, curriculum materials, and classroom interaction. The role plays included in Chapters 1, 2, and 3 were intended for use in the college classroom as springboard situations to involve teacher education students in professional concerns and to impel the examination of stereotyped thinking and the nature of prejudice.

The unique feature of this textbook is the workshop section included in each chapter. Workshops have been organized in the following ways:

Workshop tasks have been planned at increasing levels of complexity as the reader progresses from Chapter 1 to Chapter 6. The activities in each workshop correspond to the chapter content and often suggest that the reader reflect upon and review pertinent information in the chapter. Although several of the activities have been designed specifically for individuals with access to public school classrooms, the majority of the workshop tasks can be performed in a variety of settings.

Each activity has one or more objectives listed at the beginning of the task. The objective(s) may be used as a competence measure for the reader's self-evaluation or the instructor's evaluation. Workshop activities may be used as evidence of student involvement and participation in the knowledge and practice of teaching.

Readings have been suggested in some chapters for the reader to gain in-depth knowledge and to call attention to areas of controversy. For instance, Chapter 3 offers only background information dealing with the urban experience of minority groups; it is not intended to be comprehensive. Additional readings are essential to the urban specialist teacher in order to engender the minority perspective.

The "correct answer" syndrome has been avoided in most workshop activities to facilitate the use of the activity as a springboard for college class discussions. Students should be encouraged when using the workshops to expand the scope of the activity instead of rigidly following the task outline.

Observation skills have been emphasized in each chapter, beginning with the observation of the organizational structure and environment of the school and its facilities in Chapter 1.

The community profile (Chapter 2) and team teaching (Chapter 6) are intended to convey to the student the nature of professional relationships and in the case of the community profile to provide an activity for a group report in the college classroom. For both activities the students designated as a group should be assigned to the same school community or the same recreational facility.

Use of the role plays in the college classroom is recommended, and suggestions for each are as follows:

"Bridgeport Unified School District" (Chapter 1): Rules for the open-structured role play in Chapter 5 should be followed.

The Bill Green incident (Chapter 2) can be effectively used with a small-group discussion format. After each group has discussed the questions and made decisions, it is interesting for the groups to compare their perceptions, decisions, and anticipated consequences. Debate among groups should be encouraged.

"Transitional Neighborhood" (Chapter 2): Use of the rules for role playing with a caucus group (to be found in Chapter 5) is effective with groups designated to represent parents, school board, Mr. Blaise, and Miss Jones.

"Local Control" (Chapter 3): Either the open-structured or the caucus group rules can be used. If caucus groups are desired, groups should be assigned specific roles, such as militant community group, moderate community group, principals, school board, and professional teachers' group.

"News Item—Free Press" (Chapter 3): This role play is effective using the caucus group rules. Designated roles may be as follows: parent group, police, school administrative staff, one or more student groups, one or more teacher groups. The student group(s) may represent the individuals involved or the student body at large accepting or rejecting the police action. The teacher groups may also represent conflicting opinions as to whether or not the principal was justified in calling the police on campus; one group may support the administrative viewpoint; another group may feel that there was much ado about nothing.

This book has been written with the hope that it will foster debate about the educative process for teaching in urban schools. It is my belief that successful urban teaching will be a reality because teachers are capable of creating diverse learning environments and capable of utilizing different teaching approaches in order to achieve school success for all students.

J. L.

Preface
to the Reader

Sal si puedes ("Get out if you can") has been a familiar theme not only of Spanish-speaking migrants and ghetto residents but of some teachers and administrators teaching in urban schools. Yet it does not have to be so. In many urban schools teachers have dared to dream the impossible dream and have sought to "right the unrightable wrong." These teachers are effective, competent, and successful; they are proud to teach in urban classrooms.

Some urban schools have budding young artists painting culturally significant murals on the exterior of their school buildings instead of the all too familiar graffiti. In some urban schools children and teachers laugh and learn together because teaching and learning can be joyful processes. For *most* children, learning is fun and natural, and for *most* teachers, teaching is pleasurable.

This book describes successful teaching. It is intended to be optimistic and enthusiastic. In the last decade the bookstores have been overloaded with books that denounce the urban school. Almost daily, the press recounts the errors made by the urban teacher and heaps scorn on the urban administrator. The track record of some teachers and the failure syndrome of some urban students certainly would shatter the most complacent professional. But one must remember that riots, failure, and calamity make headlines; successful teachers and teaching do not.

The accomplished urban teacher can be considered a skillful "tactician" because the essence of effective teaching in a specified environment is that of choosing specific techniques to achieve desired outcomes. The effective teacher is a precise professional; he or she is able to interpret students' learning requirements in terms of social, emotional, physical, and educational needs. The teacher analyzes community interests and utilizes the community in the classroom; the teacher chooses appropriate content and unites and controls teaching style and stratagems to meet the apparent needs of student and community. The effective urban teacher has been designated in this book an urban *specialist* teacher.

Successful schools have something special about them—things are happening and you can detect it as soon as you enter the school grounds. Usually it is a cheerfulness and "caring," along with a sense of authenticity. The use of the physical plant is supportive to the morale and purpose of the educational program. School-wide goals and objectives are clearly stated, and students, teachers, and community are cognizant of them. The successful school is characterized by a sense of commitment.

In the years to come it is expected that a stable school faculty will be a reality. There will be sufficient teachers to staff all classrooms. This reduction in teacher turnover should encourage schools to choose faculty members who will in essence be specialists in the accomplishment of specific tasks or goals. They will be committed to working as a professional team, the collegial team, and they will be oriented to the community in which the school is located. Perhaps like large industries, school districts in the future may overhire. In that way teachers will be encouraged to revitalize their professional preparation. A part of each school faculty could be released to develop school-oriented classroom materials, to attend in-service classes, and to accomplish the myriad small tasks that underlie successful teaching.

This book has been written for undergraduate and graduate students enrolled in teacher preparation courses who eagerly await their own classroom experiences as teachers. It has been designed to provide knowledge, skills, and affective understandings. In writing this book, my objectives were as follows:

To provide meaningful information about urban schools

To illustrate the classroom application of theoretical research

To facilitate the interpretation of interactional relationships between and among individuals and groups in the school setting

To provide springboards for college classroom and collegial group discussions

To provide practice suggestions to develop observation skills

To provide situations in which the reader can apply teaching skills

To provide ideas for teaching that are adaptable for different groups and to individualized needs

To illustrate flexible teaching strategies that are adaptable to varied teaching and learning styles

To suggest ways in which the reader can begin the development
of curriculum materials

Each chapter has two major goals: (1) to present information
about teaching in the urban environment within a practical framework, and (2) to provide workshop materials to facilitate the application and interpretation of that information. Each workshop activity has
one or more objectives specified at the beginning of the activity to
facilitate self-evaluation.

To use the book advantageously, the reader should be involved
with children. Although a school setting is ideal, it is not absolutely
essential. It is possible to study groups of children at after-school play
on school grounds and on the city streets, at Y activities, recreation
centers, camps, detention centers, religious schools, scouting activities,
and so on. In most cases it is wise to have your instructor arrange for
your visits; if you are to do it yourself, it is courteous to call in advance
to explain what you are studying and why it is important to you.

Access to observational settings for child or adolescent study is
rarely a problem, particularly if the observer is willing to become an
involved participant. Both school and recreational settings are in need
of extra hands to assist in tutoring, small-group leadership, or the
development and preparation of student materials. Having once gained
access to the community or school site, the observer is advised to be
tactful and to make judicious use of time. The following suggestions
may be helpful:

Your own understanding of student interests and leadership constraints will be enhanced if you become an active participant. If your
participation is *not* desired by the leader, then you have no choice but
to become a courteous observer.

It is discreet *not* to take notes in front of the group you are
observing. Note-taking tends to make people nervous; therefore, plan
your visit so that your participation and/or observation is purposeful.
(What are you looking for? What is happening? Why is it happening?
What will be the result? Was the result anticipated?) After your visit,
plan some free moments to reflect on your observations. Subject your
thoughts to analysis and *record* what happened. Some of the workshop
activities do require that you take notes while the activity is in progress.
Hold off on these observations until you are a familiar member of
the group. Data collection should not increase anxiety for you or for
the group you are observing. If you need information from the group
leader/teacher, be sure that you choose a moment when the leader is
free to discuss the activity. Usually this should not occur in front of
the students involved.

If you are to lead/teach an activity, plan it carefully. Suggestions
for team teaching can be found in the workshop of Chapter 6. Before
you commence the activity, be sure that you share your plans with the

leader/teacher. Obtain suggestions if they are forthcoming and an evaluation after you have completed the activity. If you lead/teach an activity, self-evaluate. Did you accomplish what you had anticipated? What evidence do you have? If you were to lead/teach the group again tomorrow, what would you do next? What would you do differently? If it is possible to taperecord an activity that you lead/teach, share it with a friend and evaluate it together.

Visits to the community setting should occur using a team approach. It is unwise for a student to develop a community profile alone. In some inner city areas, community groups have been subjected to continuous study, and as a result they sometimes do not receive student groups graciously. I would suggest the following:

1. If possible, tour the community with a resident or someone who is well known in the community.
2. A social agency in the community may welcome your assistance and be willing to take you on a tour.
3. If you do not have a guide, it may be better to take a driving trip through the community rather than a walking trip.
4. A great deal of information can be gained by interviewing business people in the community.
5. Do not tape an interview without first asking permission.
6. Do not photograph people in the community without their permission.
7. More will be gained by a community visit if you preplan your questions. (What are you looking for?)
8. As you study other peoples' cultures, think about your own cultural perspective. How would the person or groups you are studying study about you? What would they learn and how could they learn it?
9. Try to discover characteristic behavior (patterned ways of behaving). Talk to people; let them describe their life style to you. Treat your interviewee as an authority.

The book has been organized in the following way:

The focus of Chapter 1 is the school and its function in the urban community. Attention is given to the role of the school in responding to, initiating, and implementing change—in the urban community, in the development of strategies for school success, and in providing equal educational opportunities. Workshop activities emphasize the self-concept needs and goals of a multicultural society; observation activities focus on school facilities, school and classroom environment, introductory observation of student interaction. The final workshop activity can be used as a college class role play or as an individual activity for self-evaluation of personal values.

The emphasis of Chapter 2 is on the teacher—role, decisions, and tactics. The teacher's specific tasks, strategic options, tactical competencies, and teaching style are discussed. The "Community Profile," a team report, is included in the workshop for Chapter 2. Other activities emphasize teaching methods, teaching style, teacher-parent relations, student evaluation, and the analysis of special facilities, programs, and resources. Observation activities direct the reader to observe management techniques used in the school and in the classroom. The final workshop activities include role plays for group interaction or self-evaluation of objectivity and stereotyped thinking.

Concepts of community, culture, and social organization are discussed in Chapter 3, along with the problems of poverty and prejudice in the urban community. Information about multicultural groups is presented within a historical context. It is expected that the reader will use the bibliography at the end of the chapter to gain additional insights about a multicultural society. The author's perspective concerning "what educators should do" is presented with four major areas of adjustment and change suggested. Workshop III asks the reader to detect prejudice in language, in classroom behaviors, and in textbooks. School-community relations are to be observed. Two role plays are included in the workshop for self-expression and evaluation.

Chapter 4 examines students' learning characteristics, cultural influences that affect the learning process, and learning style differences. Developmental theories of Piaget and Kohlberg are presented, along with the classroom application of the theories. Urban teaching suggestions derived from the research are included. Workshop activities suggest observation of students' learning approaches. The reader is expected to become more proficient in observing student behaviors and is asked to identify areas of student competence as well as contributing and/or inhibiting factors. The reader/observer is expected to "prescribe" means to enhance or modify student behavior.

Strategies for success are illustrated in Chapter 5, with urban teaching priorities specified and school-success-oriented behaviors featured. The teaching strategies are intended as models, adaptable to varied situations and different grade levels. The exemplar strategies, particularly appropriate for the reader to use to gain experience in curriculum development, are the lessons for small-group research and discussion, role playing, and gaming. The workshop section for Chapter 5 emphasizes that competency in curriculum analysis and creation is developmental; to become proficient the reader must practice. Therefore, the reader is asked to analyze the models in the chapter and use them as examples for new strategy development.

Chapter 6 is intended as an introduction to special education. The concept of mainstreaming will have important effects on urban education as exceptional children are returned to the regular classroom and as children *erroneously labeled* exceptional are maintained in their regular classroom situation. Superior observation skills to perform an expanded assessment will be required of classroom teachers; these are discussed in Chapter 6. Teaching skills for mainstreaming, research, and innovative models, as well as new professional relationships, are explored in the chapter. The workshop section asks the reader to apply assessment skills at a higher level than that required in the earlier chapters. Integrating mainstreamed children requires personal awareness of teaching style and understanding of the environmental and learner behavior constraints imposed by the chosen teacher behavior. The reader is asked to review material presented in Chapter 2 and infer relationships between desired behavior and teaching performance. To demonstrate the concept of professional relationships, the final workshop activity directs the reader to join with colleagues in the development of a team strategy for small-group teaching. The information presented in Chapter 6 focuses on the concept of mainstreaming, but the skills involved in the workshop should serve also as a culmination for the reader to self-evaluate beginning pedagogical skills, knowledge about teaching, and professional awareness.

J. L.

Acknowledgments

I am indebted to many colleagues in the public schools and in the university who have influenced and encouraged me in preparing this book. Especially I need to thank the following individuals: Helen Jones for her many fine suggestions and for the final preparation of the manuscript; Dr. Theodore Alexander, principal of the Normandie School for personal experiences and insights; Linda Ellis and Joe Ferris, who continually demonstrate successful teaching strategies; Dorothy Washington for her fine suggestions; Barbara Kornblau, special educator, for her review of Chapter 6; and countless other colleagues who field-tested teaching strategies and invited my students to participate in successful multicultural education.

I am particularly grateful to my husband Bernie for his sensitive understanding and steady encouragement; I am also indebted to my daughters Donna and Margery for bestowing confidence, time and assistance in the many details of manuscript preparation.

An introduction
to the
urban school
environment

All individuals are entitled to equality of treatment by law and in its administration. Each one is affected equally in quality if not in quantity by the institutions under which he lives and has an equal right to express his judgment, although the weight of his judgment may not be equal in amount when it enters into the pooled result to that of others. In short, each one is equally an individual and entitled to equal opportunity of development of his own capacities, be they large or small in range. Moreover, each has needs of his own, as significant to him as those of others are to them. The very fact of natural and psychological inequality is all the more reason for establishment by law of equality of opportunity, since otherwise the former becomes a means of oppression of the less gifted.[1]

Expectations about a new experience often color an individual's perception or judgment. The description that follows of an initial encounter in an elementary school was neither necessarily accurate nor typical of the perception of other new urban teachers. But the size and complexity of some urban schools may be overwhelming (and thus appear chaotic) to the uninitiated student or new teacher, as they did to this student teacher.

The noise hit me first, then the mass of kids. I didn't know what to look at, or past; the hall was dimly lit and filled. It was eerie and I realized that I was in a near panic. Everybody ignored me; it was like I was invisible. I was assigned to observe in Room 22. It was a sixth grade class and they would be having language at 11:00 A.M. Inside the room the teacher was writing on the board. The kids stopped talking, momentarily, as they filed into the room and glanced at the chalkboard. The teacher asked the kids to describe anything that happened to them personally, or that they had witnessed over the previous weekend. As they began to talk, I realized that I couldn't understand them. I felt completely isolated.[2]

The average urban elementary school accommodates a population of 1,000 to 1,200 students. Junior high schools often have a student population of from 1,700 to 2,200 students; senior high schools may accommodate a student population that ranges between 2,000 and 3,500 students. Many urban schools with the advantage of federal funding offer breakfast, lunch, and snacks to the students and coffee, snacks, and lunch to the adults. Cafeteria workers often begin their day at 5 A.M. to accommodate the steady traffic in and out of the cafeteria area. To accomplish the gigantic task of feeding everybody and providing lavatory and play facilities, the urban school develops different schedules for different grade levels. To remind teachers and students of these schedules many schools use a bell system or squawk box designed to drive the acoustically sensitive individual out of his mind. It is little wonder that new teachers and first-time observers may find the urban experience overpowering.

The variety of people and jobs within the school also may seem formidable to the first-time visitor. The typical school consists of: a principal, one or two vice-principals, a nurse, a school counselor, clerical staff, sometimes an individual called a "welfare and attendance officer" (20 years ago he was called the "truant officer"), cafeteria workers, custodians, reading specialist teachers, mathematics specialist teachers, English as a second language teachers, a special teacher for the educationally handicapped (a pseudonym for children exhibiting behavioral problems), "regular" classroom teachers, community aides, instructional consultants, student teachers, assorted visitors, and at times a police officer or two. Coordinating this mass of people and learning who does what, when, and where is the major concern and task of the urban school administrator.

Some urban schools use their school plant environment to foster positive feelings and to develop the morale of their students, faculty, and community. In East Los Angeles, for example, where there is a high enrollment of Mexican American students, the school buildings are often decorated with murals depicting Mexican history and life in the southwestern part of the United States. With the assistance of community members, some schools repaint and refurbish lunch areas, litter cans, and doors to classrooms. Each is painted in a bright color to be attractive to the students. In many cases, changing the school plant environment has resulted in less vandalism, greater community involvement, and student pride in the school.

The Normandie Elementary School in Los Angeles provides an example of how community involvement and pride achieved a lowered crime rate. In Table 1.1, statistics for the school year 1975–1976 compare the Normandie School with neighboring schools. The secret

Table 1.1. Summary of specific types of crimes at individual locations

	Rob-bery	Assault, battery	Sex offenses	Bur-glary	Theft	Mal. mis.* van-dal-ism	Arson	Nar-cotics	Loiter-ing, tres-pass	Total crimes	Total student population	Black pop.
Elementary												
Budlong		1		23	2		1			27	1,425	95.3%
52nd Street				11	1	1				13	1,253	96.8
Menlo				10	8					18	1,050	87.8
37th Street				15	1					16	1,366	94.3
Normandie				6						6	1,253	95.4
Junior High												
Foshay	12	13		15	11	1	5	5	11	73	2,292	95.6
Muir	6	11	1	19	7	1	2	4	3	54	2,103	98.1
Senior High												
Manual Arts	12	20	1	31	29	6	4	7	2	112	2,642	96.9

* Malicious mischief.
SOURCE: *Security Section Annual Report 1975–1976.* Los Angeles, Los Angeles City Unified School District, p. 22.

of success at the Normandie School may be the philosophy of the school principal: Teaching people to care!

The 1970 census indicated that 67 percent of the population in the United States lived in urban areas. Educators have conflicting viewpoints about the meaning of urban education. Some educators believe that urban education signifies teaching *about* the city and the problems of people influenced by the megalopolis, such as transportation, health services, inflation, jobs, consumer education, and so on. Others believe that urban education refers to the population that resides in the city and particularly the inner city. Urban schools differ from rural schools in three significant ways

1. The size of the student body and adult staff
2. The multicultural population they serve
3. The diversity of student needs, interests, and abilities

A 1974 school census in Chicago[3] provides an example of the racial composition of that city's schools.

Summary of Chicago Schools'
Racial Balance, 1974

28.2%	Caucasian
57.9	Black
.2	American Indian
1.0	Asian American
12.7	Latin (total)
5.7	Mexican
5.8	Puerto Rican
.5	Cuban

In this text the term *urban education* refers to the students who attend urban schools. Primarily these students are of low socioeconomic status and/or a multicultural heritage. The majority of the students live in what we can refer to as "poor" neighborhoods, but at no time should the reader assume that this text characterizes the students with one set of criteria or conditions. Many poor families also live in suburban neighborhoods; their problems and the ways in which teachers can confront those problems will be similar to those of inner city neighborhoods.

The Structure of the School

The school exists in a social milieu side by side with other social institutions. Each social institution is a subsystem working independently, yet in a larger sense, dependent on all other systems. Each of the subsystems provides services to the community. Some of these systems include recreational facilities (parks, sport arenas), religious facilities (churches, temples), cultural centers (museums, libraries), social welfare facilities (social security, unemployment, family agencies), health facilities (clinics, hospitals, emergency services).[4] Each social institution plays a distinctive "role" in order to achieve its goals. The ability of a social institution to change or adapt its role (activities and services) to the needs of society is an indication of its viability.

Each institution also has its own distinctive organization. In the school, there is both a formal and an informal structure. The jobs, duties, time schedules, curriculum, rules (don't run on the playground; if you're not in your seat when the bell rings, you will be counted tardy) comprise the formal structure of the school. The formal organizational structure of the school can be defined as that pattern of actions and human relationships which are expected or can be predicted to exist in the everyday life of the school. The informal organizational structure comprises behaviors that arise as a result of the formal structure. Robin Williams described an informal organization in this way:

> In a certain college classroom, the teacher never assigns seats and roll call is never taken; there is no official or even explicit specification of seating arrangements. Yet within a few weeks the amorphous aggregate has become patterned; with high regularity the same individuals occupy the same seats day after day—an informal organization has emerged.[5]

It is the informal organization of the urban school that often seems to shock those who are inexperienced and sometimes inhibit the observer's ability to perceive reality. The following example illustrates:

> At Manning Junior High School the day begins at 7:55 A.M. Students are expected to be in their seats at 8:00 A.M., but in Ms. Randolph's class at 8:10 A.M. the students were still arriving. Ms. Randolph was sitting at her desk in the front of the room and successfully ignoring those students who were seated. The students were just as successfully ignoring Ms. Randolph as they chatted, exchanged insults, and slapped each other. Not until 8:20 A.M. did Ms. Randolph begin class by passing out some dittoed sheets. As she passed the sheets she punctuated the effort with "GET IN YOUR SEAT: STOP THAT RACKET: WHERE'S YOUR PENCIL? TUCK IN YOUR SHIRT." As the period progressed, Ms. Randolph would compliment some students and berate others. Although some explanation of the work would be given, students rarely seemed to understand and only a few would ask questions.

Analysis of the above excerpt indicates that a formal time pattern was ignored. Thus we see the emergence of an informal organization within Ms. Randolph's classroom that governed behavior in that environment. The students "learned" that punctuality was unnecessary and unvalued in that classroom. Ms. Randolph played at the "role" of teacher as she scolded and dispensed work assignments, but in reality she taught informally, and at times nonverbally, that she did not care about or respect her students.

An example in another classroom follows:

> Fifteen minutes were allotted to languaging, "show and tell," so that the first graders could share their out of school experiences. Although the students were only supposed to talk and take turns, William brought his pet lizard to class. As he spoke, the lizard jumped out of his pocket and the students, seated in a circle on the floor, jumped and then laughed delightedly. Then all eyes turned toward the teacher; the faces became rigid and quiet as they waited expectantly for the teacher's comment. Ms. Marsh smiled, then laughed and proceeded to fetch a jar to hold William's lizard. The teacher questioned William about the food and habits of his pet and the students relaxed and enjoyed the experience.

Here, a teacher's "formal" role pattern was expected by the students but did not materialize. Instead, the teacher used the situation to enrich and extend her students' language and science experiences. The teacher as the "leader" of the classroom changed the formal structure from an interactive expression of conflict to an interactive expression of cooperation.

Interaction may be described as human behavior that results in cooperation, conflict, or competition between individuals and among groups. Within the formal organizational structure of the school there is interactive behavior that can be anticipated and considered typical and normal: teacher talk—student response; teacher assignment—student performance and conformance to the task. But when teachers and students digress from their expected tasks, when there is an undercurrent, an underpinning or counterpoint within the social structure, then the inexperienced observer may find events puzzling and behavior distracting.

Each classroom provides a different environmental experience in terms of behavior. The physical setting also affects interactive experiences. Some classrooms are absolutely sterile, nothing but chairs, tables, and printed notices on the bulletin boards. In other rooms, one finds a variety of learning centers to attract students and entice them to learn. Some centers have science materials, others have music, artifacts, social studies, reading skills, mathematics practice materials, library books, games, and viewing or listening materials. Bulletin boards may direct student interest with questions about current events, happenings in the school, or exhibits of student work.

In some classrooms the tables and chairs are arranged neatly facing forward, curtailing discussion and interaction; in other rooms the tables and chairs are clustered in small groups to encourage students to look at one another, work together, and talk. In one junior high school English classroom, the teacher had grouped the chairs in a semicircle so that the students could see each other during a class discussion. The desks were abandoned in the back of the classroom.

In many elementary classrooms teachers find no need for a personal desk; the sometime visitor to the classroom often has difficulty determining the "front" of the room. The teacher seldom is seated, but instead gives assistance individually or to small groups of students as he strolls from one end of the room to the other. In some classrooms, observers feel relaxed; in others, they feel "edgy." One may only speculate how the student learner feels in these same environments.

Why Do We Have Schools?

Every society from prehistoric to modern has created some model of education. The model created has depended upon the needs of the society. The school is a social institution created to perform certain functions. The Educational Policies Commission of the National Education Association identified four major purposes for education in the United States: self-realization, human relationships, economic efficiency, and civic responsibility.[6] Educators have wholeheartedly accepted these purposes for education in a democracy, believing that they transcend time and place and are appropriate to the needs of all Americans, whether affluent or poor.

The function of school in its social setting and its goals may not be compatible. When we consider that the health of an institution is characterized by its ability to adapt to changing circumstances, the school which seems to mirror our society may not be adapting. If the urban school only reflects its physical setting, is it facilitating change in the urban environment? Is it the role of the urban school to modify values? Should the school be used as a setting for racial integration? If the school is *not* a setting for racial integration, is it providing equal opportunity for all students?

To consider the function of schools today, and specifically the goals of the urban school, the balance of this chapter will focus on the following questions:

- Does (can) the school facilitate change in the urban environment?
- Should the school modify group values?
- Does (can) the school provide equal opportunity for all children?

Can (Does) the Urban School Facilitate Change
in the Urban Environment?

The school functions as an independent institution, yet it is inextricably bound to the family and operates in conjunction with the family to "socialize" the child. In addition, the school is expected to develop literacy skills, prepare and motivate the child for adult roles, and develop loyalty and citizenship responsibilities.

Compulsory attendance laws operate to free the mother from the drudgery of child care so that she may work and perform another role in society or so that she may have more time to spend with her younger children or to enjoy leisure activities. As children grow older, they spend more and more time out of the home and conceivably in the confines of the school. Many institutions in society besides the family have a vested interest in compulsory school attendance. Labor needs to protect the job market; industry desires a skilled, technologically oriented labor force and a public that values both production and consumption; the government desires a "trained" and orderly citizenry; professional groups expect a public knowledgeable about and desirous and respectful of services.

In the school, the young child learns self-control. In some ways he loses his concept of individuality as he becomes a member of a new and larger group. Most children learn to subjugate their own wishes and inclinations as they experience group pressure from classmates and adult pressure from their teacher. They begin to experience the universality of the classroom. The emotional dependence upon family becomes somewhat abated. As children progress through the school years, society expects them to mature and develop independence.

Accommodation, adaptation, and change

To the extent that the urban school or any other institution participates and becomes involved in community (neighborhood, societal) problems, it will adapt to as well as influence its environment. As the urban school becomes involved in pre- and postschool day programs to accommodate the children of working parents, it is adapting to the needs of the community and in a sense "reshaping" that community. As the school opens its facilities for the use of the community during evening and weekend hours, it is serving its clients in a new and influential way. As parents become involved in advisory groups to set goals for their school, they are affecting change in the school and school personnel working with communty groups become "politicized." As school personnel develop work-study programs, work-experience programs, or remedial teaching programs, student dropouts will decrease and the school will be influencing the job market. As school systems develop health care programs utilizing diagnostic and treatment centers, health care in the urban environment will be affected. When social institutions cooperate in joint endeavors, community-oriented programs can be designed.

The school can only affect change as it works within the community and with other groups in society. A list of child care needs to improve the life of the urban child includes the following:

- Before and after school care and supervision for school-age children.
- Extended day care for preschool children.
- Hot meals for children of all ages.
- Health and dental care and instruction. (Toothbrushes could be available in the school setting with time provided and encouraged.) A dentist and doctor should be available so that parents do not spend three to four hours of time for each clinic visit.
- Adults who "model" a variety of occupations and skills.
- Entertainment (plays, films, clowns, puppets) provided after school hours—and even before school to encourage school attendance.
- Club programs for all ages (dance, sports, dramatics, exploration, chess, checkers, vocal and instrumental music).
- Home management skill development including sewing, cooking, dietetics, auto mechanics, plumbing, wallpapering, plastering, carpentry.
- Economic skills such as managing a budget, using a checkbook, comparing "bargains," buying on credit.

Suggestions for improving the life of the community include the following:

- The use of school facilities: playgrounds, libraries, auditorium, gyms (and showers), sewing machines, shops. These facilities should be open during evenings and weekends.
- Special classes for mothers and daughters, fathers and sons.
- Home management skill development for adults.
- Entertainment for adults.
- The use of adults and teenagers in the community as resource personnel to teach specific skills, to tutor, to supervise. (Both boys and girls should work in nursery and preschool facilities.)
- School acknowledgment, concern, and planning for cultural holidays and customs.
- Work experience programs for teenagers offering school credit for industrial and business training.

- Encouragement of multi-aged classes during the day and evening so that students and adults may make up what they have missed without the stigma of being considered dumb.
- Child care and nursery training for teenagers and adults.

Some of these suggestions have been tried in the form of crash programs and have been found to be quite effective. Financial support for these enterprises is beyond the capacity of the school alone, yet not beyond the personnel and material capability of the school. The suggestions are all predicated on the assumption that school and community share common goals. As you think about the aforementioned suggestions, develop some of your own. Consider the following questions: What would the effect on school motivation be if teenagers were paid to tutor elementary school children? If mothers had day care from early morning until evening for their young children, what effect would it have on school attendance and community morale? If teenagers received school credit for out of school work, and pay as well, would it increase the likelihood that the minority student would attain a high school diploma?

Should the School Modify Group Values?

Society expects the school to socialize the young so that they may lead successful, effective lives. *Acculturation* is the process by which young children learn the cultural patterns of their society. *Culture* can be defined as the way in which we characteristically respond to life. It is our patterned ways of behaving, which include our "way of life," our language, dress, outlook; both our ways of enjoying life and the means by which we satisfy our needs.

As children develop new associations and become members of a classroom group, they accept new ways of behaving. Both the adult representatives at school and the peer group enforce new standards and values. Motivated by peer pressure, each child soon desires to belong and to be "accepted." During the acculturation process, the child learns to "value." To value signifies "choosing." The individual chooses to eat beans instead of potatoes presumably because he enjoys doing so. The president of the company arrives promptly at 9 A.M. every day because he "values" punctuality. The college student proofreads papers before submitting them because she would feel embarrassed if there were structural or spelling errors. The school develops these kinds of values as it socializes the student.

The socializing role of the teacher has stirred a great deal of controversy in the urban school. Suppose you overheard a father speaking to his oldest son in the following way:

Pedro, remember, it is your job to take care of your sisters and brothers. You must wait and walk them to school and you must wait at the school and bring them home with you. You are a man, a baron, my son. You must be strong and not cry. I depend upon you. A man does not cry, ever. You must be quiet in school and listen. Be silent and you will learn. Do not disturb the teacher. Do not answer back to your teacher. The teacher has many students.

The following values are inherent in this passage: family solidarity, family ties and responsibility, masculinity, machismo (manliness), respectfulness, obedience. As you review the formal and the informal structure of the American school, is it possible that there will be a conflict of values as the teacher pursues the socialization process? Let's listen in as one teacher talks about Pedro:

Yesterday, Pedro was late to class again. When I asked him about it, he would not reply nor would he even look at me. No matter how I scold, he does not even blink an eye. I am baffled. And in class, he will barely answer. He seems displeased if I call upon him and he never asks for assistance although I know he doesn't understand.

As we analyze the value conflict in this situation, we need to reflect on the goals of education in our country.

What happened?	*How was it interpreted?*
Pedro "waited" at home for his brothers and sisters. He delivered each child to the appropriate classroom, thereby making himself late.	Pedro is late—as usual. He does not value punctuality.
The teacher scolded Pedro. Pedro did not "talk back."	Pedro is unresponsive, sullen, impudent.
Pedro, although still young, did not cry or show any hurt or remorse.	Pedro is unrepenting and disrespectful.
Pedro is quiet in class; feels it is an imposition to bother the teacher with questions or answers which may be unworthy of her time.	Pedro is disinterested in learning. He acts bored and disenchanted with school.

Looking at Pedro's actions in this way, we can "see" that he demonstrated all the values his father taught him. Yet, both he and his teacher have completely misunderstood each other. Neither actions nor motivations were interpreted accurately by the teacher. Although Pedro has sat in the same classroom for almost a whole semester, he and his teacher are virtually strangers.

Acculturation vs. enculturation

Minority groups are experiencing a new-found pride in their cultural heritage. Cultural pride is usually expressed through language, dress, foods, and values. Traditionally, the school has represented majority America, and most teachers have been members of the lower middle socioeconomic class. And the teacher, as society's socializing agent, expressed and demanded in the classroom the values of the majority culture. Since 1956, when Martin Luther King, Jr. led his first successful boycott in Montgomery, Alabama, minority groups have searched for and demanded an end to the myth of the great American "melting pot." Perhaps historically America needed the melting pot theory in order to build a "nation of nations,"[7] for without it an amalgamation of diverse populations would have been impossible. But as the country developed, the pride of diversity from city to city also materialized.

The concept of *enculturation* has special significance as the role of the teacher in the socialization process is considered. Enculturation is accepting that ethnic groups need cultural identity. Instead of the melting pot theory of assimilation, enculturation is a movement to preserve diverse cultural patterns; it is a movement to enhance instead of to reject cultural identity. Barbara Sizemore described enculturation in this way:

> Recently, a great awakening occurred. It has been described as a
> new-found pride in blackness and the African heritage. This awakening
> has spurred a search for a new set of values and a lost identity and has
> produced drives for enculturation instead of acculturation, for
> liberation rather than integration, and for ethnic preservation not
> ethnic assimilation.[8]

The urban student is bicultured. He is urban cultured as well as black or Puerto Rican or Chicano cultured. He does *not* lack culture. Whereas acculturation is the process of adapting and conforming to the majority concept of culture, enculturation is the process of developing self-identity.

Most texts concerned with the teaching of minority populations stress specific minority values. Yet, most experts would agree that it is literally impossible to provide a list of values which all members of an ethnic or interest group would accept. For instance, high school Chicano activists would certainly not choose to assimilate as their less active parents might. The teenage follower of Stokely Carmichael who believed in the philosophy that blacks should TCB (take care of their own business) will not accept the philosophy that the individual must seek his own niche of achievement in society. Values are dynamic; overt behavior changes from generation to generation, and even among groups within the same generation and within the same ethnicity. Yet, the consequence of urban life in the ghetto or barrio does produce some common cultural patterns.

Few would argue that the school has some responsibility in the inculcation of values. But since all communities and groups do not accept the same values, the school cannot possibly go about the task of placing the stamp of approval on some values and attitudes while rejecting others. Traditionally, the school has emphasized the following kinds of values: cleanliness, punctuality, materialism, ambition, "proper" dress, achievement, future satisfaction of goals. Whether or not these values are worthy or desirable is irrelevant, because in point of fact the urban school failed to inculcate them. The school also failed to accept the fact that to espouse one set of values or goals as preferable was tantamount to pronouncing judgment on all other group and minority values. The result of such a conflict has been the alienation of minorities and groups low on the socioeconomic scale.

Success in the United States is based on social, academic, and vocational achievement. To the extent that low socioeconomic groups have been disadvantaged, that disadvantage has been reflected in these three areas. Therefore, this text proposes sets of behaviors to induce school success.

SCHOOL SUCCESS-ORIENTED BEHAVIORS

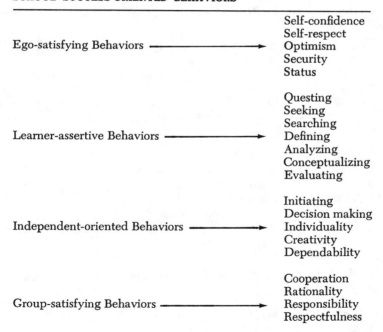

Ego-satisfying Behaviors ⟶	Self-confidence Self-respect Optimism Security Status
Learner-assertive Behaviors ⟶	Questing Seeking Searching Defining Analyzing Conceptualizing Evaluating
Independent-oriented Behaviors ⟶	Initiating Decision making Individuality Creativity Dependability
Group-satisfying Behaviors ⟶	Cooperation Rationality Responsibility Respectfulness

These behaviors differ from "typical" school values because they can be developed through appropriate teaching strategies.

The problem facing the urban teacher is that of developing values that will facilitate student learning, success, and achievement in the school while at the same time not damaging or detracting from the cultural backgrounds of the students. If school success behaviors are examined as prerequisites for learning and they are looked at as if they were on a continuum, then desirable learning attitudes and behaviors can be designated. The classroom teacher working toward these defined values and goals for urban teaching will neither step on cultural toes nor meet the hostility of a minority parent. As the effective urban teacher plans the content of lessons, he or she utilizes these values as an integral part of teaching strategy. The following classroom episode will illustrate:

In a fifth-grade classroom, the students were studying the westward expansion of the United States. The teacher's objectives included:

1. Using a variety of maps of the United States, the learner will formulate decisions about a way of life which results from a historical time period and a geographic location.
2. Working in small groups as students develop location skills and become involved in value decisions, they will share responsibility, work cooperatively, behave respectfully toward each other.

The students were given the following information and a historical map of the United States:

It is Spring in the year 1825. You and your family of five have just arrived in the community. There are about twenty other families living in the community. You are faced with many decisions to make in order to provide a good life for your family. Some of these decisions include the following:

1. What is your occupation?
2. How will you provide food for your family?
3. What kinds of food will you eat?
4. What will your house look like?
5. What games will your children play?
6. What other decisions will you make which will affect your way of life?

Look at the map and choose the community where you and your family are to live.

1. Galveston, Texas
2. San Diego, California
3. Tucson, Arizona

Remember that in the year 1825, these communities were not states but territories. They did not belong politically or legally to the United States.

Student behaviors

The students assisted each other to read the handout and to observe the historical map. They located each community on the map, then discussed and finally compromised before deciding on their choice of a community. They questioned each other and exchanged information about what they knew of the climate, word meanings, and topography. Slowly they began to ask pointed questions. They selected materials, collected data, and compiled them. They began to make decisions about their way of life in terms of the available data. To locate information, they used the index of one book, a dictionary, the contents of another book, and an atlas. They also studied filmstrips about life in the southwestern part of the United States.

Each group contained students with reading problems. They were assisted by other students. Sometimes opinions and data would conflict. The students would often debate their own point of view and finally compromise, utilizing group opinion and the data that supported majority thought. The teacher in this incident planned a teaching strategy to develop basic skills along with group-satisfying behaviors. Chapters 2 and 5 will provide additional examples of this type of teaching strategy. The students became intensely involved in and excited about a learning activity that had many interpretations and dilemmas. Committee work proved to be both ego-supportive and group satisfying for the students. Teacher and students felt successful.

Does (Can) the School Provide Equal Educational Opportunity for All Children?

Equal educational opportunity implies equal access to the "fruit" of education. This signifies:

- Opportunity to interact with the best teachers
- Opportunity to use the best facilities, including equipment and materials
- Opportunity to share the wealth of school support
- Opportunity to interact with other students
- Opportunity to study all subjects
- Opportunity to prepare for all vocations

Teachers described in this textbook as urban specialists, are embarrassed by illiteracy statistics because teaching literacy skills is the major function of the school. Society expects that teachers are competent to teach the basic skill subjects (reading, writing, arithmetic, spelling). But both the high dropout rate of minority Americans and the scores of minority Americans on achievement tests clearly attest to the school's failure to develop literacy skills for all students. Urban specialist teachers are anxious to improve their track record. The "new" specialist teacher accepts responsibility for student failure; he or she is also committed to achieving succesfsul and efficient teaching and learning.

Support for the public schools is receiving new attention by state legislatures and the federal government. In a few states the courts have ruled that the property tax as a support base for the schools is illegal. In California, the Supreme Court ruled that education is of "fundamental concern" to society because it is essential to the maintenance of a "free enterprise democracy," that it is universally relevant, continues over a lengthy period of life, molds the personality of youth in society, and is so important that society has made it compulsory. The court ruled that the present system of school district support was dependent upon the pocketbook of the child's parents and that such a system was unconstitutional.[9]

In recent years the specification of teachers' and students' race, sex, and national origin has facilitated data gathering that could ultimately lead to the redistribution of teachers and students to achieve racial balance and "affirmative action" in higher education. The U.S. Department of Health, Education and Welfare, which enforces civil rights laws, has threatened to withhold federal monies in a number of school districts if racial integration is not initiated. However, the department is dependent on congressional support. If support is withdrawn or if the data gathering is banned, then HEW cannot make investigative decisions. These decisions will ultimately affect equal educational opportunity.

Role selection and designation

Doctor, lawyer, Indian chief, butcher, baker, garbage collector . . . who has the ultimate wisdom to assign a role for each child? Traditionally, the school has acted as though it had that wisdom. Utilizing IQ tests, achievement tests, teacher-made tests, and the teacher's subjective judgment, the school has separated, sorted, and siphoned students into various tracks to "accommodate their needs." Whereas some schools group students only to teach skill subjects (reading, spelling, arithmetic), other schools retain these groupings or labels throughout the entire school day. Although there is some justification for grouping students to teach similar content and to meet similar learning needs (homogeneous grouping), there is little justification for retaining these skill group labels throughout the school day in the teaching of physical education, music, art, science, and social studies. The student who is poor in reading may well be a whiz in science. Heterogeneous grouping (dissimilar grouping) allows students to develop unique competencies, leadership skills, and the opportunity to interact with a greater variety of individuals. Yet, most schools group to meet reading needs and the student may be stuck with the same label during his entire school career.

Both peer group and teachers influence the child's motivation and level of aspiration.

> . . . not only the immediate results of school work, but a whole series of influences, converge to consolidate different expectations which may be thought of as the children's "levels of aspiration." Generally some differentiation of friendship groups along this line occurs, though it is important that it is by no means complete, and that children are sensitive to the attitudes not only of their own friends, but of others.[10]

The practice of "tracking" a student as a low achiever or a scholar may influence the jobs he seeks, the reality of life that he accepts, and his own sense of power or powerlessness. Some students accustomed to being designated low achievers are unable to accept praise.

> Resigned to the "realities" of life, they had difficulty accepting praise. They had been taught that they were unworthy and to distrust anyone who thought they were not. Praise challenged their self-image. John B., for example, was a senior who planned to pump gas after he got out of the army. He also wrote poetry. He alternated between being proud of his work and telling me that it was "bullshit." He was threatened by his creativity. The school had "tracked" him into a "low achiever" class since grade one, and after 18 years he wasn't about to challenge that authoritative definition.[11]

Economic status in the United States often reflects the number of years the individual has "survived" in school. Black Americans, Mexican-Americans, Puerto-Rican Americans, and Indian Americans have an extremely high dropout rate (see Table 1.2). Fifty percent of the unemployed young people between the ages of 16 and 21 are illiterate.

Role selection. Can and should teachers sort their clients into the social roles that they will play for the rest of their lives? Can teachers perform the job efficiently and accurately? As yet the school does not possess the psychometric tools with which to test the young in order to develop an accurate profile of their interests and capabilities. Nor is the school financially able to employ trained personnel to carry out the task.

Resentment from minority communities focuses upon the teacher's early labeling of students as "retarded," "slow," "disinterested," "low achiever." Many students so labeled have later been found to have language or physical problems that went undiagnosed and untreated. Since economic status seems to relate to the number of years the student spends in school, the process by which role selection is performed will continue to exercise a profound influence upon the student's fu-

Table 1.2. High school graduates and school dropouts, 16 to 21 years old—employment status, by sex and race, 1965 to 1970[a]

Employment status, sex, and race	Graduates				Dropouts			
	1965	1968	1969	1970	1965	1968	1969	1970
Civilian noninstitutional population	4,898	5,418	5,339	5,823	2,986	2,734	2,683	2,757
Not in labor force	1,129	1,342	1,115	1,257	1,123	1,071	1,096	1,146
In labor force	3,769	4,076	4,223	4,566	1,863	1,663	1,588	1,611
Percent of population	76.9	75.2	79.1	78.4	62.4	60.8	59.2	58.4
Male	1,617	1,513	1,650	1,966	1,265	1,041	977	1,024
Female	2,152	2,563	2,573	2,600	598	622	611	587
White	3,375	3,598	3,742	4,065	1,469	1,315	1,223	1,243
Negro and other	394	478	481	501	394	348	365	368
Employed	3,451	3,700	3,897	4,038	1,585	1,415	1,358	1,264
Percent of labor force	91.6	92.2	92.3	88.4	85.1	85.1	85.5	78.5
Male	1,512	1,419	1,540	1,730	1,105	913	868	805
Female	1,939	2,341	2,357	2,308	480	502	490	459
White	3,116	3,344	3,490	3,636	1,266	1,153	1,058	1,011
Negro and other	335	416	406	402	319	262	301	253
Unemployed	318	316	326	528	278	248	230	347
Percent of labor force	8.4	7.8	7.7	11.6	14.9	14.9	14.5	21.5
Male	105	94	110	236	160	128	109	219
Female	213	222	216	292	118	120	121	128
White	259	254	250	429	203	162	165	232
Negro and other	59	62	76	99	75	86	65	115

[a] In thousands, except percent. As of October. Data for high school graduates relate to those not enrolled in college and include those who attended college prior to survey date; data for dropouts relate to persons not in regular school and not high school graduates. Based on samples and subject to sampling variability.

SOURCE: U.S. Department of Labor, Bureau of Labor Statistics; *Special Labor Force Report*, Nos. 66, 108, 121, and forthcoming report. *From Statistical Abstract of the United States 1971* (Washington, D.C.: U.S. Department of Commerce, Bureau of the Census), p. 112.

ture life. Herman Sillas, a Los Angeles attorney, commented that the system of tracking Mexican American students has done irreparable harm. A class action case before the courts, filed by the Los Angeles Model Cities Center for Law and Justice, focuses upon the problem:

> The suit questions the validity of all tests given to bicultural children in determining whether they will be placed in basic, general, academic or honors courses of study (or tracks). The suit contends that current techniques for grouping students by ability generally doom Mexican American children, in great and unfair disproportion, to the humdrum lower tracks and deny them the opportunity to get the kind of basic education they need to move on to college and into the professions.[12]

Equal educational opportunity does not imply educational uniformity. Instead, it signifies an education based upon a commonality of need and differentiated to accommodate variances in geographic locality, social class, aspiration, and cultural and ethnic diversity. Quite obviously there is a relationship between education and occupation, and to some extent occupation and income (see Table 1.3).

Since 1954, when the United States Supreme Court made its historic decision that racially separate schools were illegal (*Brown* v. *Topeka, Kansas, Board of Education*), plans have been proposed to remedy or alleviate unequal educational experiences. Three types of plans proposed in the main (1) to compensate segregated communities, (2) to desegregate the communities, and (3) to develop specific teacher education programs to prepare teachers for inner city teaching.

Compensatory education. These plans have attempted to correct educational deficiencies, to provide cultural enrichment, to develop early childhood programs for the preschooler, and to develop extracurricular programs. Remedial programs have focused on the teaching of reading and mathematics. Cultural enrichment programs have attempted to make up for experiential deficiencies through trips to beaches, mountains, theaters, and museums. Early childhood projects attempt to develop the preschooler's "readiness" skills for school. Extracurricular projects have been aimed at both students and parents to develop more positive attitudes toward school. Some of these projects sought to involve parents in school programs to develop cultural identity through ethnic studies classes. Some programs have employed parents as classroom aides.

Desegregation. These plans focus on the following types of strategies:

Site Selection. This strategy would suggest rectifying segregation through appropriate school planning so that new schools would be located so as to encourage racial balance.

Table 1.3. Major occupation group of employed persons, by sex, race, and years of school completed, 1959 and 1970[a]

Year, sex, and occupation group		White			Negro and other		
		Total	*Less than 4 years of high school*	*4 years of high school or more*	*Total*	*Less than 4 years of high school*	*4 years of high school or more*
1959							
Male, number	**1,000**	**37,766**	**18,740**	**19,026**	**3,745**	**2,928**	**816**
Percent, by occupation:							
White collar		39.7	20.3	58.8	12.6	5.3	38.8
Blue collar		45.5	58.9	32.3	59.3	65.4	37.3
Service, incl. private household workers		5.6	7.2	4.0	14.3	12.6	20.2
Farm		9.2	13.7	4.9	13.9	16.7	3.7
Female, number	**1,000**	**17,776**	**6,994**	**10,782**	**2,484**	**1,725**	**759**
Percent, by occupation:							
White collar		61.1	31.5	80.3	17.6	5.8	44.5
Blue collar		17.2	31.4	8.0	14.7	15.7	12.4
Service, incl. private household workers		18.5	31.6	10.0	64.3	73.8	42.6
Farm		3.2	5.5	1.6	3.4	4.7	0.5

1970

Male, number	**1,000**	**42,434**	**14,701**	**27,733**	**4,629**	**2,626**	**2,003**
Percent, by occupation:							
White collar		44.3	18.5	58.0	23.2	8.8	42.1
Blue collar		45.0	64.8	34.6	61.1	71.6	47.3
Service, incl. private household workers		5.6	7.5	4.6	11.1	12.6	9.2
Farm		5.0	9.1	2.9	4.6	7.0	1.4
Female, number	**1,000**	**25,040**	**6,926**	**18,114**	**3,551**	**1,656**	**1,895**
Percent, by occupation:							
White collar		64.7	30.3	77.9	35.1	10.3	56.8
Blue collar		16.3	35.6	9.0	18.4	21.5	15.8
Service, incl. private household workers		17.5	31.0	12.3	45.8	67.0	27.3
Farm		1.5	3.2	0.8	0.7	1.2	0.2

[a] Relates to civilian noninstitutional population 18 years old and over as of March of years indicated. Based on Current Population Survey; see text, p. 1.

SOURCE: U.S. Department of Labor, Bureau of Labor Statistics; *Special Labor Force Report*, No. 125. From *Statistical Abstract of the United States 1971* (Washington, D.C.: U.S. Department of Commerce, Bureau of the Census), p. 111.

Princeton Plan. This strategy has worked extremely well in small communities. The plan pairs three elementary schools in fairly close proximity. Students are distributed to the three schools based upon grade levels (K–2), (3–4), (5–6). Some districts have used a Middle School concept to distribute the students to develop a racial balance (K–2), (3–5), 6–8).

Boundary Lines. This strategy suggests that district or city boundary lines be redrawn to achieve racial balance. Many recent court cases have been based upon the claim by minority groups that school boundary lines have been manipulated to achieve segregation.

Open Enrollment Plans. Northern cities have attempted to encourage students to enroll in "open" schools out of their neighborhood in order to achieve racial balance. In the main this plan has been ineffective because the burden of decision as well as the cost of transportation has been left to parents.

Busing. This strategy directs school districts to bus students out of their neighborhood school to a school in a different neighborhood in order to relieve crowded school conditions and to achieve racial balance. The busing proposal has resulted in the greatest controversy of any of the desegregation plans. Parents fear long bus trips, envision problems when their children become ill during the school day, and social problems at the end of the school day. In large northern cities, school segregation corresponds to residential segregation. The busing remedy, according to James Coleman and his associates, has resulted in continuous loss of white students from central city schools.[13]

School Closing Plan. This strategy calls for the closing of inner city schools (which are the oldest schools in a city) and redistributing the students to other schools or implementing the site selection strategy. The plan has been successful in some of the smaller cities (Berkeley and Sacramento, California; Englewood Cliffs, New New Jersey).

Magnet School Plan. The magnet school plan has been used at the high school level. In Los Angeles a program designed jointly by the Los Angeles City Schools and the University of Southern California (Area Program for Enrichment Exchange) sought to interest high school students to attend a different high school for part of the school day in order to participate in a specialized program. Each participating high school developed a specialized program (and was designated as a "specialist" school) in the arts, science, commercial studies. The school district provided busing and the university provided specialist consultants to the designated high schools. The plan was and is successful as a voluntary program; however, it does not accomplish racial balance throughout the school day.

Educational Park Plan. Havighurst in the 1960s espoused an educational park concept in which 10,000 to 15,000 students would attend school from preschool through the high school years on a large campus site chosen so as to include all socioeconomic classes. Thus far the educational park concept has not been tested.[14]

The desegregation strategies have had varying success. In 20 years, the schools have not rectified society's errors. Perhaps it is unjust to expect one institution to accomplish what other institutions have been party to—and failed to alleviate.

Teacher education programs. Attempts to alleviate social injustice have also been made through teacher education. Utilizing federal funds and designing specialized programs of their own, teacher education institutions have provided programs focused upon inner city teaching. Programs such as Teacher Corps and Career Opportunities sought to hire minority people and provide them with an education directed toward teaching. These two programs paid the minority individual to work in the school as an aide or assistant and to attend the university in the afternoons.

Career Opportunities program was funded in 37 states (initiated in 1967), and in many cases the recipients had not attained a high school diploma before beginning the program. COP funds went directly to the local educational district. Program planning involved the local school district, a community college, and a university. In Compton, California, for example, students attended Compton Community College and then the University of Southern California, where they were awarded a bachelor's degree and teaching credential. Some students continued their education and earned master's degrees. Other programs sponsored by educational institutions, without federal funds, have focused on urban education semesters and urban teaching. Each of the programs has attempted to sensitize the preservice teacher to minority education. Statistics are unavailable to determine the adequacy of the teacher preparation programs or whether the graduates stay in the profession.

Summary

Urban teaching may be different from teaching in a rural or suburban school as a consequence of one or all of the following factors:

- The diversity of students' needs, interests, and abilities, which may affect the quality of interaction among students, teachers, and environment

- The size and migratory and temporal condition of the school population of students, teachers, and administrators
- A teaching-learning environment desiccated by age

The structure of all schools is much the same, with variances often due to specific school needs and the viewpoint of teachers and administrators. Learning environments are dependent upon the creative instincts of the teacher, his own needs and educational goals. The urban specialist teacher, as we shall see in successive chapters, should provide an enriched environment to encourage student involvement and learning.

All schools function to provide an environment where the individual is nurtured, where capacities may be developed to the fullest. The school as a societal institution is responsible for transmitting and conserving culture as well as creating a better society. The school cannot rectify all of society's ills; neither can it ignore them.

Controversies in this chapter have focused upon the role of the school in responding to, initiating, and implementing change:

In the urban environment, through accommodation and adaptation of school facilities and school services; through citizen access, participation, and involvement in goal setting; through interaction of school, community, and other institutions

In values, through the development of strategies for school success; through meeting the needs of enculturation while providing access to acculturation

In providing equal educational opportunity, through an honest appraisal of teacher effectiveness; an examination of school support; an analysis of role selection and designation; desegregation plans and teacher education programs

In this introduction to the urban school environment, some of the problems and unique situations that confront the urban teacher were delineated. Since all the problems have societal implications, their resolution will be dependent upon all people and all institutions; however, there are decisions and urban teaching priorities which can alleviate problems that have practical teaching solutions and for which urban educators are held accountable. These will be discussed in Chapters 2 and 5.

Notes

1. JOHN DEWEY, *Intelligence in the Modern World: John Dewey's Philosophy,* ed. Joseph Ratner (New York: Modern Library, Random House, 1939), p. 403.
2. Student teacher (anonymous), Los Angeles, California, 1974.

3. CASEY BANAS, *Chicago Tribune,* November 26, 1974.

4. DANIEL LEVINE and ROBERT HAVIGHURST cite fourteen social institutions which are interdependent and service urban communities. "Social Systems of a Metropolitan Area," in *Metropolitanism: Its Challenge to Education,* ed. Robert J. Havighurst (Chicago: University of Chicago Press, 1968), pp. 52–53.

5. ROBIN WILLIAMS, *American Society* (New York: Knopf, 1951), p. 456.

6. Educational Policies Commission, *The Purposes of Education in American Democracy* (Washington, D.C.: National Education Association, 1938).

7. LOUIS ADAMIC, *A Nation of Nations* (New York: Harper & Row, 1944).

8. BARBARA SIZEMORE, "Social Science and Education for a Black Identity," in *Black Self-Concept,* by James A. Banks and Jean D. Grambs (New York: McGraw-Hill, 1972), pp. 141–142.

9. *Serrano* v. *Priest,* 487 Pac. 2nd 1241, 5 California 3rd. 584, L.A. 29820, Supreme Court of California, August 30, 1971 (modified October 21, 1971).

10. TALCOTT PARSONS, "The School Class as a Social System: Some of Its Functions in American Society," in *Culture and School,* ed. Ronald Shinn (Scranton: Intext, 1972), pp. 349–350.

11. PATRICIA MICHAELS, "Teaching and Rebellion at Union Springs," in *Myth and Reality,* ed. Glenn Smith and Charles R. Kniker (Boston: Allyn and Bacon, 1972), p. 39.

12. HERMAN SILLAS, "Chicanos vs. the Education Establishment," *Los Angeles Times,* 1974.

13. JAMES COLEMAN. "Racial Segregation in the Schools: New Research with New Policy Implications," *Phi Delta Kappan,* October 1975.

14. ROBERT J. HAVIGHURST and BERNICE L. NEUGARTEN, *Society and Education* (Boston: Allyn and Bacon, 1967).

Workshop I

In education a workshop is a course designed to serve several purposes: Exchange of ideas by individuals involved in a similar endeavor, practical application of skills, and development of curriculum materials. The workshop sections of this text should serve similar purposes. Each chapter workshop will focus on the concepts, issues, and problems discussed in the chapter. This will be accomplished through suggested readings, exercises, and activities. For instance, Workshop I asks readers to read to gain knowledge, to investigate school facilities and classroom environments for another institutional setting; to describe student interest; to participate and interact, and to evaluate their personal values.

Teachers need to learn observation, interpretation, and decision-making skills related to teaching behaviors and curriculum design. Each of the workshop sections will have a variety of exercises to enable the reader to practice, to interpret, and to create. The exercises will require the reader to observe children at work and play tasks in schools or in other institutional settings. Appropriate settings include children's hospital wards and schools, youth centers, scouting activities, YMCA, YWCA, probation camps and schools, church activities, park and recreation sites, vocational rehabilitation centers, Big Brothers centers, Braille Institute schools, Catholic Welfare Bureau, Crippled Children's Services.

The reader objective(s) for a workshop lesson will be stated at the beginning of each exercise. Sometimes possible solutions to the problems or exercises will be included; in most cases, however, the range of possible responses is so diverse that "answers" would be impractical.

The Melting Pot—Enculturation

OBJECTIVE: Read to gain knowledge about a multicultural society.

Discuss the concept of the "melting pot" in American history. Debate myth and validity of the concept.

Read:

Adamic, Louis: *A Nation of Nations* (New York: Harper & Row, 1944).

Fuchs, Estelle: "American Indian Education: Time to Redeem an Old Promise," in *Teaching Multi-Cultural Populations*, ed. James C. Stone and Donald P. DeNevi (New York: Van Nostrand Reinhold, 1971).

Litsinger, Dolores: *The Challenge of Teaching Mexican-American Students* (New York: American Book, 1973), chap. 1.

Sizemore, Barbara A.: "Social Science and Education for a Black Identity," in *Black Self-Concept*, by James A. Banks and Jean D. Grambs (New York: McGraw-Hill, 1972), pp. 141–142.

Tyack, David B.: "Becoming an American: The Education of the Immigrant," in *Challenges to Education*, ed. Emanuel Hurwitz, Jr., and Charles A. Tesconi, Jr. (New York: Dodd, Mead, 1972), pp. 332–339.

Does the School Teach Values?

OBJECTIVE: Read to gain knowledge about school values, teachers, and value change. Contrast the following author's opinions:

Hook, Sidney: "The Teaching of Values," in *Radical School Reform* (Boston: Little, Brown, 1973), pp. 190–196.

Farber, Jerry, *The Student As Nigger* (North Hollywood, Calif.: Contact Books, 1969).

Postman, Neil, and Charles Weingartner: *Teaching as a Subversive Activity* (New York: Delacorte Press, 1969), chap. II.

Pounds, Ralph L., and James R. Bryner: "Contrasting Viewpoints as to the School's Role," in *Challenges to Education*, ed. Emanuel Hurwitz, Jr., and Charles A. Tesconi, Jr. (New York, Mead, 1972), pp. 9–27.

Multicultural Education

OBJECTIVE: To identify appropriate goals for multicultural education.

Which of the following would be appropriate goals for multicultural education?

1. Knowledge of diverse cultures and languages
2. Knowledge of the concept of Manifest Destiny
3. Knowledge of black contributions to America
4. The relationship between self-concept and enculturation
5. The impact of racism
6. Reverence for American history
7. Knowledge about intelligence testing
8. Obliteration of cultural differences
9. Options for minority groups
10. Historical and current dissatisfactions of minority groups
11. Knowledge about dialects in the United States
12. The contribution of American Indians on reservations and in the cities

All are relevant goals for multicultural education except 2, 6, 8.

Answer

The Social Composition of the School
and Classroom Achievement

OBJECTIVE: Read to gain knowledge about the effect of the social composition of the school and classroom achievement.

James S. Coleman's 1966 report is often cited by the courts to justify desegregation orders. How does the 1966 Coleman Report differ from Coleman's new research concerning racial segregation in the schools?

Read and compare:
Coleman, James: *Equality of Educational Opportunity* (Washington, D.C.: U.S. Department of Health, Education and Welfare, 1966).
Coleman, James S., Sara D. Kelly, and John Moore: *Trends in School Segregation, 1968–1973* (Washington, D.C.: Urban Institute, 1975).

Social Service Institutions

OBJECTIVE: Read to gain knowledge about social institutions in urban communities; develop a community profile for your community.

Read one of the following:

"Social Systems of a Metropolitan Area," in *Metropolitanism: Its Challenge to Education*, ed. Robert J. Havighurst (Chicago: University of Chicago Press, 1968), pp. 52–53.
Williams, Robin: *American Society* (New York: Knopf, 1951).

Develop a community profile listing social agencies that offer assistance to urban dwellers and teachers in urban schools. Consider the following needs: consumer aid, health services, family planning, mental health, legal aid, babysitting, volunteer services, recreation.

School Facilities and Environment

OBJECTIVE: Identify school facilities; evaluate use of facilities.

Do school facilities meet the needs of students? Consider space, furniture, equipment.

	Yes	*No*	*Explain*
Auditorium			
Cafeteria			
Lunch areas			
Lavatories			
Play areas			
Gymnasiums			
Library			
Classrooms			
Laboratories			
_____			
_____			

Given a substantial amount of funds, cite five environmental areas on the school grounds you would choose to revitalize.

Present problem	*Desired change*

Formal and Informal School Structure

OBJECTIVE: Identify and describe formal organizational structure in schools or other institutional settings.

Formal structure may be defined as the *expected* organizational pattern for actions and human relationships.

Informal structure may be defined as the behaviors that often accompany and result from the formal structure. (Reread text)

Examples of formal structure	*Examples of informal structure*
6-period day	Sanctions, rewards
Roll call	Paying attention
Bell ringing at end of period	Selection of content
Textbooks	Valuing, loving

Classes were in session. Ms. Brown was teaching, standing near her classroom door. She and her students heard the sound of running feet and she opened the classroom door. A lone boy was running down the hall. Ms. Brown was about to command the boy to stop, but instead she shrugged her shoulders and smiled. Explain Ms. Brown's behavior in terms of the formal and informal structure of the school. (Why was she about to command the boy to stop? Why did she not do so?)

Describe the formal structure in another institutional setting (hospital, camp, YMCA). Identify behavior which communicated to you that the individuals involved were "aware" of the structure.

(Continued on Page 30)

Presumably there was a school rule governing "running in the halls," otherwise Ms. Brown and her students would not have paid any attention. The rule would represent the *formal* structure of the school. Informally Ms. Brown shrugged and smiled. One can only surmise

Possible Answers

(*Possible Answers continued from Page 29*)

Ms. Brown's perception: The boy was late; nobody except the boy was in the hall, therefore no one would be injured if he ran; he ran because he felt like it; what difference did it make? Beyond surmise, we know that Ms. Brown did not command the boy to stop; therefore, she did not enact the formal rule and behaved informally. We do not know whether or not this decision was "typical" of Ms. Brown and therefore an integral component of her behavioral structure, but her students would be aware of her pattern of imposing sanctions or rewards or ambivalence.

Learning Centers

OBJECTIVE: Identify classroom environmental stimuli used for motivation, support, and reinforcement purposes.

Learning centers enrich the classroom environment. They function to motivate, support, and reinforce learning. There are many different types of centers in use in elementary and secondary classrooms.

A *listening* center is one type of learning center and may have the following equipment: tape recorder or phonograph, speaker, earphones (headsets) for five to eight students, follow-up (reinforcement) materials. The major purpose of the center is to develop auditory discrimination skills. Additional purposes include development of critical thinking skills, development of independent study skills, development of student experiential background.

1. If the children in a second-grade classroom were listening to a story, what could the teacher assign that would be indicative of their development of comprehension skills?
2. If students in an eighth-grade history class were listening to the Battle of Lexington, what could the teacher assign them to do that would be indicative of their development of comprehension skills?

Possible Answers

1. Using pictures related to the story, students could arrange them sequentially. Students could list details of the story. Drawing their own pictures and numbering them, students could identify what happened first, second, third, etc. Students could fill in sentence completion information about the story. Students could match statements about the story with the characters who made it happen. Additional activities are possible.
2. Students could identify the cause and effect of the battle. Students could draw or describe the events of the battle. Students could role-play the opposing claims about the battle.

Learning Centers

OBJECTIVE: Create a student learning center for motivation, support, or reinforcement of a skill.

List three learning centers you would like to use in your classroom.

Describe each center in terms of equipment.

Identify the purpose(s) of each center.

Describe a student activity and a reinforcement activity for each center.

Rate Student Interest and Participation

OBJECTIVE: Describe student affective behavior; self-evaluate objective/subjective judgment.

Use a (lesson) (club program) (other) that you are teaching, leading, or in which you are a participant or an observer.

1. a. Identify the student interest level:
      ( ) High   ( ) Average   ( ) Low
   b. Identify your basis for judgment:
      Students' responses   ( )
      Students' attention   ( )
      Students' activities   ( )
      _____   ( )

2. a. Identify student participation level:
      ( ) High   ( ) Average   ( ) Low
   b. Identify your basis for judgment:
      Students' activities   ( )
      Students' responses   ( )
      Students' questions   ( )
      Students' research behavior   ( )
      Students' interactive behavior
         with other students   ( )
      _____   ( )

3. State the *purpose* of the (lesson) (club program) (other).

Rate Interaction—Teacher-Students

OBJECTIVE: Describe behavior; identify motivation of teacher/leader.

Interaction may be described as human behavior that results in cooperation, conflict, or competition between individuals and among groups.

Use a classroom lesson or out of school activity. Tape record a ten- to fifteen-minute segment, then listen to it.

1. Identify the purpose of the activity.

2. Identify teacher/leader responses to students:
   Questioning   (   )
   Reassuring   (   )
   Justifying   (   )
   Routine   (   )
   Empathetic   (   )
   Disciplining   (   )
   _____   (   )

3. Identify students' responses to teacher/leader:
   Questioning   (   )
   Responding   (   )
   Evaluating   (   )
   _____   (   )

Interaction Among Students

OBJECTIVE: Describe behavior.

Describe an incident you would characterize as *cooperative*.
Describe an incident you would characterize as *competitive*.
Describe an incident you would characterize as *conflict*.

Classroom Interaction Exercise 1

OBJECTIVE: Describe behavior; analyze alternatives; infer options.

DIRECTIONS: Teachers' classroom behavior causes students to react in certain ways. Fill in the following chart listing the possible teacher/leader behavior (verbal or nonverbal) that caused the student reactive behavior. Then suggest some possible alternate teacher behaviors and the alternate student reactive behavior it would elicit.

Teacher behavior ⟶	Student reactive behavior ⟶	Alternate teacher behavior ⟶	Alternate student reactive behavior
	Anger		
	Embarrassment		
	Withdrawal		
	Submission		
	Aggressiveness		
	Confusion		
	Boastfulness		
	Violence		

Bridgeport Unified School District

OBJECTIVE: Self-evaluate personal values.

BOARD RULE #5301—CERTIFICATED PERSONNEL

Effective with the 1977–78 school year all certificated personnel are to be rotated every three years regardless of position or status.

June 22, 1975: Executive Meeting of Bridgeport Teachers' Association Re: Board Rule #5301

Speakers: Executive secretary, Bridgeport Teachers' Association, two teacher representatives, principal representative, superintendent of Bridgeport schools, representative of the United States Office of Education.

The following is a transcript of that meeting:

Executive Secretary: Board Rule #5301 impinges upon teachers' personal freedom. If this rule is put into effect, the school district can assign teachers wherever whim decrees. Some teachers may be driving as many as 70 miles per day. No employee should be required to make such an unreasonable sacrifice. This rule will hinder teacher recruitment as well as retention.

Supt. of Schools: Recent rulings by the Department of HEW and the State Board of Education require that a school district make every effort to reduce inequality in the schools. Board Rule #5301 is the result of an effort to equalize our school faculties. As you are all aware, we have attempted busing programs in the school district as well as a policy of open enrollment at our schools to encourage racial balance of pupils. The busing program has been highly successful for our bussed pupils, albeit unpopular with the white population of our city. The open enrollment policy actually aids very few of our students. It is time for the teachers of Bridgeport to make an effort to give the pupils of this city a balanced educational experience.

Teacher Representative: The teachers do not desire to impede social progress. We favor integrated schools and have gone on record many times indicating our desire for racially balanced schools. We do not view Board Rule #5301 in a similar vein. Nowhere in the Education Code or the Administrative Code does it state that it is a teacher's duty to take a job anywhere the school district desires. Unless the school board rescinds this rule, Bridgeport teachers may be forced to strike.

Principal Representative: It is virtually impossible to make a school function, effectively, carrying out planned goals and serving the pupils of the community unless a principal has the right to choose his own personnel. It would be exceedingly difficult to plan and implement objectives unless one could be reasonably confident of a loyal and secure staff with the assurance that you as an administrator would be retained at a school.

Representative, U.S. Office of Education: Inner city schools contend with dilapidated equipment and buildings and overcrowded classrooms. They also contend with faculty assignments made on the basis of race and seniority. Some of Bridgeport's schools have had a 60% turnover of personnel each school year. Primarily these schools have been located in the inner city. The result of a turnover of such dimension means that inner city schools receive the newest teacher, the youngest teacher, the least experienced—in other words, the teacher without seniority or tenure. Unless this is rectified, Bridgeport will not receive federal funds.

Teacher Representative: It has been customary in our state for teachers to choose where they desire to work. We do not believe that this is unusual for school teachers or any other public employee. State law does not give the school board the right to arbitrarily transfer teachers from one school to another. Recognizing that our city has a ghettoized pattern of housing, naturally our schools will likewise be segregated. Teachers, like the rest of the city's population, tend to live in segregated communities; our faculties are segregated, therefore, through neither fault nor design. The teachers of Bridgeport fail to see why they should be penalized for a system of housing that has persisted through the ages.

The notes of the Bridgeport Teachers' Association Executive Meeting were mailed to the district's 25,000 teachers. The following evaluation was requested by the Bridgeport Teachers' Association:

1. Do you favor integrated school faculties achieved by means of Board assignment?
2. Do you favor integrated school faculties achieved by means of voluntary teacher transfers?
3. Do you favor a teacher strike if Board Rule #5301 is put into effect?

If you were a Bridgeport teacher, how would you vote?
Should Bridgeport reject the federal funds? why?

The urban specialist teacher: role, decisions, tactics

Ted Dixon was late to class. As he entered the classroom, he could see that one group of students was reading with the teacher at the front of the classroom, the rest of the students were working either at desks or at different "centers." He proceeded to scuff his shoes as he walked, slammed his books down on his desk, and then he sat looking expectantly at the teacher.

His teacher nodded at him, raised her voice slightly, as she continued her reading lesson with the children in front of her. As the other children in the classroom looked at the teacher and then at Ted, they realized that their teacher did not feel badgered, nor was she lured to interrupt the classroom routine. When it was time for the groups to "change places," the teacher walked over to where Ted was sitting. She pulled out the chair next to Ted and sat down. Very quietly, so that other children could not hear, she talked to Ted.

"Did you have breakfast this morning, Ted?"
"No. Nobody got up."
"Is that why you were late?"
"Yes."
"What about your sister, did she go to school?"
"I woke her. She came."
"Do you have any money for a snack today?"
"I got a dime."
"It will be recess soon. Buy yourself a hot drink or a roll."

The teacher then went on with her teaching and after a bit Ted began to work.

This urban specialist teacher had developed attitudinal propensities and specific decision-making competencies that led to success in the urban classroom. These competencies affect the teaching/learning process, the classroom environment, and the interactions that normally occur. Ted Dixon's teacher could have refused to allow him to stay in the classroom. She might have demanded an immediate explanation. She could have separated Ted from the rest of the class or she could have kept him after school. But she did none of these things. Let us find out why. To analyze this incident, it is necessary to list "what happened and why"; it is also necessary to decide "what did not happen and why."

What happened?	*Why did it happen?*
Ted was late to class.	He was not awakened. He did not wake up "on time."
Ted scuffed his feet, slammed his books, did not work.	He was angry (he had not been awakened); he was embarrassed (he was late); he was hungry (no breakfast).
The other children momentarily stopped work, looked at the teacher, then continued to work.	The teacher nodded to Ted to let him and the other children know that she had "heard" him.
	She raised her voice slightly so that all the children would know she intended to continue the lessons.
During a teaching break, the teacher talked quietly to Ted.	Ted had purposefully interrupted the class; he was *asking* to be talked to.

What did not happen?	*Why did it not happen?*
The teacher did not scream at Ted.	To scream would have meant total destruction of the teaching-learning mood.
	Ted would have accomplished wrecking the morning for the class just as his own morning had been spoiled.
The class did not cease work.	By nodding and raising her voice, the teacher let everyone know that she was "aware" of Ted, but refused to allow any interruption to spoil the class endeavor.
The teacher did not make an "example" of Ted. Nor did she make him a hero.	Talking quietly to Ted allowed everyone to forget and forgive him.

This teacher demonstrated many subtle techniques that are clues to personal characteristics and to effectiveness in the urban classroom. (1) The teacher failed to be "ruffled" by an interruption. (2) By nodding and raising her voice slightly, she maintained the structure of the lesson, yet acknowledged a new situation. (3) The way in which the teacher questioned the boy indicated insight into his personal history. (The question as to whether or not he had eaten breakfast; the question about his sister.) (4) The teacher exhibited warmth and concern but did not pry. (The teacher asked about his breakfast, whether or not he had money for a snack, then suggested that he buy something at recess time. The teacher avoided questions about "other" family members and responsibilities.)

To develop greater insight about the urban teacher, this chapter is divided into three parts. The first section deals with the teacher's concept of role and its effect upon his/her actions in the classroom. The second section considers the teacher's decision-making tasks and the range of options available to the urban teacher. The third section describes some specific skills and techniques through which the urban teacher specialist accomplishes desirable goals.

Teacher Role

Attitudes about self and role and teaching philosophy affect professional judgment. To achieve understanding about *who* he is to teach, the teacher must first be capable of appraising himself. A teacher's concept of role may result from how he feels about himself, how he thinks others feel about him, what he thinks society expects of him as a teacher, his concept of how he is to teach, and his feelings about who he is to teach.

Wallen and Travers[1] correlated teachers' classroom methods with personality needs. They noted that teaching methods differ most in the way in which teachers handle classroom control. They reasoned that teachers meet their own need structure by being either highly permissive or exercising tight classroom control. Lippitt and White[2] related teachers' leadership style, teachers' classroom behavior, and the consequent student behavior. Their research efforts identified three leadership styles (authoritarian, democratic, and *laissez faire*) and the resultant response to each leadership role. The Lippitt and White experiment concluded that there was highest classroom morale with a democratic leader and more sustained work when the democratic leader was absent, but it was the authoritarian leader who achieved the highest productivity. An example of differential teacher behavior in terms of leadership style is illustrated by two urban high school teachers.

Mr. Jordan's classroom was arranged in a manner similar to most high school classrooms with the chairs attached to each other and facing forward toward the teacher's desk. Mr. Jordan's 11th grade United States History class members were accustomed to being met at the classroom door by their teacher. As Mr. Jordan greeted each student he would hand him a sheet of paper. For the first seven minutes of class the students would answer questions written on the board. As they wrote, the room was punctuated with the usual kinds of comments:

"Gee, Man. How we 'spozed to know that?"

"What'sa matter, Jed, didn't you do yer readin?"

Mr. Jordan observed his students and then began to talk. The students quieted and set to work taking lecture notes. After about thirty minutes the students were told to turn their paper over and see if they could improve upon their original responses to the questions written on the board. As the bell rang, each student put his paper in a box specially prepared for that purpose, and then left the classroom.

In the same high school but in a different classroom, the students entered a room furnished with tables and chairs arranged in small clusters. As they entered their classroom, also an 11th grade history class, the teacher, Mr. Roxbury, walked around to each group of students and talked informally.

When all were seated the teacher stated: "Today we are going to pretend to be Kansas farmers." As he talked he passed out "role" cards to each group of students. He quickly called on different groups to read their role card to the class. After all the groups had recited, he continued with his explanation.

"This is the game of farming and the year is 1880."[3]

The students were drawn into the game quickly. As they "played" the groups talked and questioned each other. Often the teacher would be summoned by a group for an explanation.

Toward the end of the period, the teacher began the debriefing stage. Each group was asked to assess its farming accomplishments and financial well-being. The students laughed and noisily contributed the information. With the assistance of Mr. Roxbury, the students identified events and the consequences of their first year as Kansas farmers.

As the bell rang, the students were assured that they would have another opportunity to become better farmers.

Mr. Roxbury and Mr. Jordan were experienced urban teachers. How did their leadership roles affect their teaching style and behavior? How did it affect their students?

A large body of historical research in teacher education has focused upon teacher characteristics and teacher behavior. Early researchers described the affective environment of the classroom. Anderson[4] described teachers' classroom behavior using a category system which defined dominative and integrative teacher behaviors. Withall[5] classified teacher statements to students in terms of the inferred intent. The statements were either learner-centered or teacher-centered. Flanders[6] developed a system of interaction analysis that distinguished between teacher acts which were restrictive vs. those teacher acts which increased student freedom.

Later research was concerned with the kinds of meanings transmitted between teachers and learners. Ryans[7] studied the identification, analysis, and description of teachers' classroom behavior patterns, educational viewpoints, attitudes, and intellectual and emotional qualities. The study isolated the various dimensions of teacher behavior into scales to evaluate and predict teacher characteristics. The

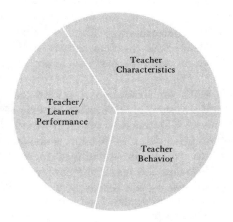

relationship between the teacher's attitude and expectations about *who* he teaches and the effect upon student performance has been tested by a number of recent studies. Kranz, Weber, and Fishell[8] and Jones[9] revealed that teachers at both elementary and secondary levels tended to ask more questions and bestow more praise upon high-achieving students than upon low-achieving students.

A study of first-grade teachers by Brophy and Good reported that teachers were more likely to praise high-achieving students (12 percent of the time) than low-achieving students (6 percent of the time):

> An additional finding of interest was that when high-achieving students made no response, said they didn't know, or answered incorrectly, teachers were more likely to stay with the students (that is, repeat the question, provide a clue, or ask a new question). In contrast, teachers were more likely to "give up" (that is, to give the answer or call on another student) under similar circumstances with low-achieving students. The teachers were twice as likely to stay with high-achievers as they were to stay with low achievers.[10]

Similar studies relating differential teacher behavior to high- and low-status children have revealed fewer contact hours between teachers and low-status children as compared to the contact hours between teachers and high-status children. The alienation of children perceived by teachers as low achievers prevented the students from achieving their learning potential and from receiving cooperative learning from peers.[11]

There seems to be little doubt that teachers' expectations can act as a self-fulfilling prophecy, if in fact teachers perform in the classroom in ways which result in differential treatment for those students perceived to have potential vs. those perceived to have little potential. The research of Rosenthal and Jacobson[12] resulted in a great deal of controversy when other researchers were unable to replicate their study. However, many researchers do support the basic premise that teachers' expectations affect student performance. The Rosenthal and Jacobson study withheld information about the true nature of IQ and achievement scores from teachers in order to test the hypothesis of the self-fulfilling prophecy.

In an elementary school in south San Francisco, a random sample of low socioeconomic status children were chosen as an experimental group and designated as "bloomers." The teachers were informed that these children would make substantial gains in IQ and achievement scores. The teachers were told to expect these children to make a dramatic "spurt" in achievement during the coming school year. Another group of children was identified by the researchers and designated as a control group. The children designated as a control group were not identified to the teachers. Rosenthal and Jacobson were primarily concerned with whether or not it was possible that a designated group of children for whom intellectual growth was expected would indeed achieve greater growth (favorable change) during the course of one school year as compared to another group of children not identified as "spurters" to their teachers. Questions subordinate to the primary concern were the following:

1. Would older or younger children be more likely to be affected by a favorable teacher expectancy?
2. Would boys or girls be more likely to be affected by the favorable teacher expectancy?
3. Since the children were ability grouped in a fast, medium, or slow track, which group would more likely be affected by a favorable teacher expectancy?
4. Would those children with a greater degree of "Mexican-ness" as exhibited by facial appearance be more likely to be affected by a favorable teacher expectancy?

The results of the experiment indicated that the teacher's expectancy served as a *self-fulfilling prophecy.* Younger children achieved more favorable gains than did older children. Although girls showed a slightly greater spurt than did the boys, each sex profited in the area of functioning in which they were already advantaged. None of the ability tracks did better than any other; all groups profited. Mexican boys with a greater degree of "Mexicanness" achieved greater gains and profited more by the favorable teacher expectancy.

To fully appreciate the implications of this experiment, it is important to consider the following possibilities:

Children's age. Some research seems to indicate that younger children are more susceptible to change than older children. Other research suggests that younger children are more sensitive to adult attitudes. There is also the possibility that teachers would not have as high an "expectancy" for an older child whom they "knew." Research on teacher effectiveness also indicates the possibility that lower grade teachers are more competent than teachers in the higher grades.

Minority appearance. Research indicates that teachers tend to expect more of girls in the lower grades than boys. Is it possible that boys with a greater degree of "Mexicanness" were at the bottom of the heap until identified as "bloomers" and as a result had that much more to gain with the change in teacher expectancy?

Psychological effects. Peter and Carol Gumpert, in reviewing the Rosenthal and Jacobson research, made the following comments:

> . . . a person is more likely to perceive a barely perceptible stimulus if he expects it than if he does not.
> . . . we are likely to see what we expect to see, and we tend to interpret ambiguous events in such a way as to confirm our own predictions.[13]

Teacher attitude and expectation appear to affect student motivation and achievement. Competent urban teachers *expect* their students to learn. Ms. Angus is a typical example:

> Ms. Angus had been identified as an urban specialist teacher. She taught at the Colby Elementary School. The ethnic survey for the school revealed a student population that was composed of the following: 0.1% American Indian, 10.9% black, 0.5% Oriental, 42% Spanish surname, 23.5% Filipino and other minorities, 23% white (other than Spanish surname). When Ms. Angus discussed her students with other teachers, she never referred to a child as "black" or "Mexican." Instead, each child was characterized as an individual with particular characteristics. For instance, Conrad was the boy who developed a headache every day at mathematics time; Susan had the bubbly nature, sparkling eyes and a hot temper; Ramsey was outstanding as a team captain, but terrible when he had to sit still.

Ms. Angus could recite a list of distinctive characteristics about each of her students. When she talked about them, her eyes lit up (very much like Susan's eyes) and she expressed the sentiment that *her* children were smart. She cared and worried about each of them. Sometimes she cried for them, often she laughed about them.

Although Ms. Angus had a keen sense of humor, she rejected "ethnic" jokes. She also had an acute dislike for colleagues or others who described an individual using ethnicity as a part of the description. Her colleagues found her outspoken and uncompromising about the practice of attributing cultural or ethnic stereotyped behavior to students or the community.

Ms. Angus's beliefs clearly rejected stereotyped thinking. *Stereotyping* can be defined as categorizing according to a fixed concept or idea based upon a favorable or unfavorable belief. Individuals who persist in stereotyping have a need to defend, justify, or rationalize their own conduct in relation to their categorical thinking. The practice of stereotyping limits or screens out individuals ability to perceive others accurately. It is crucial for teachers to be able to perceive individual differences. It is especially critical in the urban school.

Teachers' interpretations of their own classroom roles affect performance, and sometimes teaching priorities. The following study is illustrative: Interviews with 50 urban teachers in elementary and secondary schools revealed personal concerns that could be related to the individual's concept of "role." The teachers were asked: "What do you consider to be your most important function?" The responses, in order of majority concern, were as follows:

1. Setting an example
2. Providing discipline
3. Teaching the basic skills
4. Teaching students to be independent
5. Motivating the students

Additional responses considered by the researcher to be subsumed in the preceding categories included relating to the students, motivating students to want to participate, teaching reading, and keeping students in school.

The teachers interviewed were considered "effective" in their teaching situation. Their comments provided many insights into urban teaching. The conversations are condensed and paraphrased as follows:

SETTING AN EXAMPLE

My students are young and impressionable. Most of them have been in day-care centers for as long as they can remember and most of them still go to the centers after school. They barely see their mothers. The most important thing I do is show them how a responsible adult acts and to help them act responsibly. I want to be friendly and to listen to their problems; I give them lots of opportunities to talk to me.

I moonlight. I have to in order to support my family. Most of my students are aware that I sell insurance after school. I don't hide it because I think it is important that high school students realize that you're not a phony. Sometimes I'm not as prepared as I would like to be, but I think most of the time I really teach and the students are really learning in my room. I try to make my government class relevant to the students. During an election I bring in the ballots and candidates' statements. I express my concerns and get the students to express theirs.

A student can't learn if he has problems which so consume him that he can't think of anything else. I try to let the students talk about their concerns and see if they can help each other. I let them know that people are supposed to cooperate and work together to solve problems. Sometimes our problem-sharing time seems to usurp other teaching, but I consider that giving up that time is like setting an example.

PROVIDING DISCIPLINE

When I first started teaching here the kids were hard to control. But I pretty soon made it clear that in my classroom there would have to be order. If there isn't order you cannot teach. I think I would be derelict if I didn't enforce some standards. The parents in this neighborhood know me and what I expect. And I think that the parents expect a teacher to provide discipline.

You can't get to be a teacher or anything else that is important in our society unless you are disciplined. I don't want to be a dictator in my classroom, but I'm not going to have the students walk all over me. I work on discipline first: bringing books and notebooks to class, paying attention, being polite.

Discipline has a lot to do with respect. If you respect others then you are polite to them. I try to be polite to my students and demonstrate respect for their feelings and ideas. I expect them to do the same for me. It works!

TEACHING THE BASIC SKILLS

I teach fourth grade. I expect that before my students leave me they will do perfect cursive handwriting, know their multiplication tables, and progress in reading. If they don't learn, I'm not teaching. I'm paid to teach. The parents in this community expect me to teach their children and by golly I'm going to do it.

I really don't believe that there are kids that can't learn. If a teacher makes subjects interesting and is really concerned about teaching, then his children will learn at least the basic skills. I think it is wrong to pass children into the junior high school if they haven't achieved the basic skills. However, I don't think that teaching the basic skills should stop with elementary teachers.

When I teach math I talk about cars, contracts, bank statements, checkbooks, budgeting, grocery bills, etc. If a teacher teaches his subject and really levels with the kids so that the subject corresponds to what is real, not only do the students like it, but they learn.

TEACHING STUDENTS TO BE INDEPENDENT

I want my students to learn how to solve their own problems. I try to give them practice in practical kinds of problems such as, if your lights suddenly go off, what do you look for? How do you fix a fuse? Who would you call if it were not the fuse that was the source of the problem? I give lots of "what should you do" sort of problems and then I try to praise the students with the most imagination or the most practical solution.

I try to teach "problem approach" procedures. Through the years I have found that my students are afraid to try to solve a problem. The first thing I do is set up a "model" with specific instructions for solving the model problem. Then I proceed to give the students a number of similar problems until they become adept at using the model procedures. Next I begin to throw some curves—just slight ones at first so that I don't destroy confidence. By the end of the semester, my students are independent learners.

MOTIVATING STUDENTS

I never start a lesson by saying, "turn to page blankety blank." Nothing could be less motivating than that. I start with a story, a picture, a problem, sometimes I bring in some props. One day I began a history lesson by playing some "pop" music. I passed out a written copy of the words and asked the students to sing. Then we analyzed the words and their significance to us today. We began studying history by focusing on what's happening right now in our country and all over the world.

I never considered going to school a punishment. I began to think about it and realized it was partly because my folks were always so interested in what I was doing. Perhaps some of my students do not get that same interest at home, but I try to make up for it by making each day so exciting that the students will feel that they just can't wait to come back. When my students are absent for no reason, the first thing I do is examine what and how I taught. I consider: How can I make it more interesting and appealing to the kid who was absent?

Teachers perceive themselves in different ways: some behave as models, moral leaders, guidance counselors; others as disciplinarians and taskmasters; still others want to be remembered by their students as scholars and subject matter specialists. Teachers' self-perceptions affect their classroom performance and competence with students. Teachers perceive students as they perceive themselves; teachers whose self-image is positive and self-confident accept others and seem to relate positively to students in the classroom. Teaching characteristics affect teaching behavior, which in turn affects students' self-concepts and achievements.

In the next section the decisions teachers make in order to bring about the teaching/learning process will be considered. Each teaching decision should be based upon "who you teach," and "what you expect to accomplish." The urban teacher will make these decisions as he meets the challenge of teaching in the urban school.

Teaching Decisions

Teaching in an urban, rural, or suburban school involves a number of interrelated tasks:

- Diagnosing needs, interests, and abilities
- Defining instructional objectives
- Selecting appropriate content
- Choosing a teaching strategy
- Creating a learning environment
- Selecting or designing instructional materials
- Developing evaluation procedures.

Each teacher decision is based on qualitative factors that impose implementation constraints. Teaching objectives are derived from the goals of society, and from the needs and interests of children and subject matter specialists. The goals of society are those of American society in general as well as the specific goals of the community. Objectives derived from past, present, or future needs and interests of society comprise the social foundations of education. The child, as a source of teaching objectives, contributes his uniqueness as an individual, and these objectives comprise the psychological dimensions of education. Academicians contribute knowledge of the disciplines. The teacher derives information from these three sources to plan meaningful curriculum experiences (see Figure 2.1).

As the "practitioners," teachers choose the means to achieve curriculum goals. Defining objectives and selecting content will be based upon teachers' knowledge of students' needs, interests, and abilities.

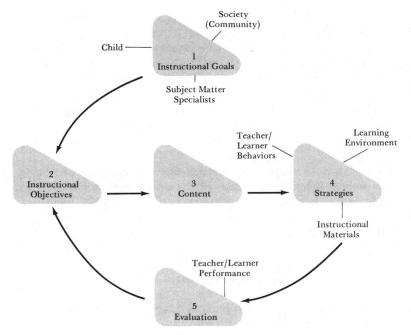

Figure 2.1   Teaching Decisions

Teachers choose strategies for teaching that may be based on students' learning styles, students' learning needs, subject matter goals, personal teaching philosophy, and the teacher's personal commitment and style. The chosen teaching strategy then imposes constraints that limit the range of possible options relating to teacher behavior, learner behavior, the learning environment, instructional materials, and evaluative procedures. Teachers use a variety of approaches (strategies) to achieve their goals. Joyce and Weil, in a publication that discussed approaches to teaching, commented that ". . . there are many kinds of *good* teaching, and that the concept *good*, when applied to teaching, is better stated, 'good for what?' and 'good for whom?' "[14]

In this section we will consider some of the teaching decisions that are made by urban specialist teachers. By examining these decisions, some insight relating to the urban teacher's role, perception, and tactics should be apparent. Since Chapter 5 is concerned with strategies for teaching, this chapter will give examples of teachers at work but will not dwell upon procedural methods.

Understanding students' needs, interests, and abilities

Even experienced teachers often comment that their first encounter with a new class can be somewhat of a fright. Whether the teacher works in an urban school or a rural school, his or her first responsibility is to get acquainted with the students. In what ways are these students unique? In what ways are they similar to all other students? Affecting the individual teacher's classroom performance will be knowledge about the school community, knowledge of child growth and development, his or her self-perceptions, perception of students and their parents, and understanding of subject matter goals.

Teachers in the urban school may not live in the community; therefore, their knowledge about the life style of their students may not be the result of first hand experience. Many successful, competent urban teachers do not live in the community where they teach; however, *no* urban teacher is effective if he or she lacks depth of understanding about the social conditions of the community and the cultural background of the students.

To develop knowledge about the school community, new teachers, accompanied by other teachers or administrators who are well acquainted with people in the community, often tour the neighborhood. During these tours, teachers take note of the following: residential patterns, businesses, services, opportunities for work, recreation facilities, opportunities for field trips, resource people in the community, cultural sites, neighborhood problems, and relationship of government and institutions to the community. Attending neighborhood functions and advisory council meetings at the school will also assist the teacher new to the school to develop understanding and a personal relationship with community members.

Contributing to teachers' conceptualizations of students' needs and interests will be knowledge of the educational implications of culture and social class upon the teaching/learning process. For instance, are the students recent immigrants? Are they first-generation, second-generation or third-generation Americans? Recent immigrants could be expected to exhibit a greater degree of "Mexicanness," "Irishness," and so on. Where is the school community located? What is its economic and geographic relationship to other urban, suburban, business, or industrial centers?

The majority of students in urban schools are from low socioeconomic families and/or minorities. Their unique needs and adjustments are no longer shrouded from either public or professional view. Some urban students are recent arrivals from the rural South, Appalachia, rural communities in Mexico or Puerto Rico, or rural areas of Europe. Many urban students speak languages other than standard English in the home either because the student's native language is other than English or because of ghettoized experiences that restrict the use of standard English. Still other urban students are from working class families. Each group of students is different and defies one set of criteria.

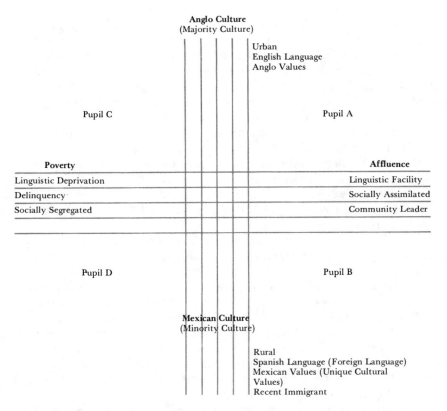

Figure 2.2   Cultural Diversity, Economics, and Acculturation (From Dolores E. Litsinger, *The Challenge of Teaching Mexican American Students* (New York: American Book Co., 1973), p. 46.)

Teachers need knowledge about the influence of culture, language, and socioeconomic status in order to develop a perspective about students. There is the danger of overgeneralization if an attempt is made to classify each student using a predetermined set of hypotheses. Each student must be considered as an individual. Litsinger,[15] in discussing the cultural background of Mexican-American students, provided an illustrative grid that related cultural diversity to economics and acculturation (see Figure 2.2). A similar grid for other minority Americans would also yield evidence of great cultural diversity.

Urban teachers review sociocultural factors and influences as they observe students in order to determine interest and motivation for learning. The following social factors can be expected to affect students:

High-density housing
Noise
The exodus of socially upward bound families to the suburbs
Migration and emigration of neighbors
Crime
Unemployment
Lack of employment opportunities
Problems related to poverty
The possibility of family instability related to unemployment
Preoccupation and "busyness" of the adults in the home
The absence of adult models in the home
Financial inability to acquire school-related environmental stimuli
Language other than standard English spoken in the home

All these factors to a greater or lesser degree will affect students' interest and self-concept in the school. Different sets of social and/or cultural influences, as well as many of the same, could be identified for students in suburban or rural schools.

Teachers use many devices to become acquainted with their students. Urban teachers utilize a number of subjective (nontest) techniques to facilitate their understanding of students' diversity. Some of the techniques that have proved effective are as follows:

1. Teachers ask students to stand in two circles and close their eyes. The teacher then pairs students. Each pair sits down and with their eyes closed they take turns describing themselves to their partner. (Who am I? What do I look like? Who is my family? What do I like? What am I afraid of?) After six minutes, each individual introduces his partner to the teacher and the whole class.

2. Primary children (grades K–3) enjoy outlining each other on large sheets of butcher paper. Each child then draws on his own picture his "insides" (feelings, thoughts). Finally, the children display their self-portraits on the bulletin board. Each child stands by his picture to describe personal feelings and thoughts. Some teachers prefer story writing about the feelings and thoughts. Sometimes the children "dictate" their stories to classroom aides.

3. Teachers ask students to draw their classroom as they would like it to be. Drawings are displayed and explained.

4. Older students may be asked to pretend that they are attending a new school with no friends with whom they are acquainted. Students write about what it is like to be lonely, their fears, and their hopes.

5. During tense moments, some teachers find it effective to ask students to write about what makes them angry, anxious, embarrassed or aggressive.

6. Students are asked to work in small groups (note the student council game, Chapter 5). Groups are to identify rules they consider useful and appropriate to their school and classroom and rules they feel are harmful.

7. Storywriting, pictures, sociograms are all effective means to have students identify who they admire, desire to work with, perceive as bigger (more powerful).

8. Some teachers like to show students pictures of other people and have them answer the questions: "How do you think the people feel?" "What do you think the people will do?"

9. Students in grades 4 through the high school years may identify their "life cycle." Students relate important happenings in the past or expected in the future, such as birth, schooling, siblings, profession, occupation, marriage. Students outline these as if on a time line, and may list in addition their problems or expectations. Students may also list qualifications for success and barriers to overcome.

10. Students may be asked to identify their expectations about their teacher in terms of teacher personality and responsibilities.

11. Students may draw or write how they would like to be different, if they could. Afterward they share it.

12. "Take a student to lunch technique"—some teachers ask students to sign up for a bag lunch with the teacher, alone. Teacher and student then become acquainted apart from the rest of the class; however, this technique takes about seven weeks with the ordinary classroom of students.

13. Students are divided into groups. Each student has a turn to teach his group a specific skill. The teacher (child) may not discipline or act negatively to his group. The teacher rotates around the room, observing.

14. Students write stories around a theme such as "If I were the leader. . . ."

15. Primary teachers give students puppet families and ask them to "act out" a family problem, celebration, or future expectation.

16. Older students may draw cartoon strips using themselves as the hero or heroine.

17. Teachers write conflict situations in order to observe students' decision-making and language skills, using questions such as: "What's for Breakfast, Lunch and Dinner?" or "What Do You Do When You Need Help?" (Note strategies in Chapter 5.)

18. High school teachers may also hand out a written conflict situation and ask students to identify differing value positions, relevant information, and decisions made. These should identify students' ability to perceive beliefs, data, propaganda, rationality, and so on.

19. Role plays provide many insights about student language,

self-concept, and decision-making skills. Students may role play conflict situations in the newspapers or social and classroom problems.

20. Provide two telephones as props. (The telephone company is always happy to oblige. Sometimes the phones will even be connected so that they will ring!) Students are asked to make a date to "play," "cruise," or do homework together.

The purpose of these kinds of tactics is to provide teachers with interactive means to gain knowledge about students' conceptual levels, skills, and attitudes. If a teacher needed to find out where a student was in terms of ball-throwing skills, he would not give the student a paper and pencil test; yet, too often urban students who are deficient in language skills are given achievement tests that only prove that the student lacks reading, language, or an experiential base in order to compare favorably with nationally standardized norms.

Urban teachers suspect the predictive value of group IQ tests. Too many of these tests have not been validated with specific minority groups, such as Mexicans, Indians, blacks, or Puerto Ricans, in the test sample. Indeed, some tests may be normed in the West or North and have little predictive value in the East or South. Psychologists and psychometrists have the ability to use individual IQ tests (Stanford-Binet and the WISC IQ test) to detect patterns of intellectual abilities. In some urban schools these trained specialists provide assistance to the classroom teacher by suggesting specific improvement techniques.

Urban teachers use diagnostic tools with care. They choose testing instruments validated to the population they are testing that measure what they need to learn. Diagnostic tests exist to assist the teacher choose appropriate objectives in basic skills to meet developmental needs. Many teachers become highly skilled in designing their own simple paper and pencil tests to diagnose students' levels in arithmetic and spelling. Some developmental reading tests are printed in Spanish.

Much of the diagnostic process occurs as a natural outcome of teaching and as an integrated unit with lesson evaluation. Diagnosis and evaluation occur as continuous operations to facilitate the teacher's strategic decision making (see Figure 2.3). Teaching/learning activities are often designed to measure students' growth through process accomplishments: ability to classify, compare, contrast, generalize. Some evaluation occurs through the assessment of an actual product: dramatization, graph, report, debate. Specific signs of student success that may be considered as approach patterns will be identified at the beginning of Chapter 5.

The following incident is an example of the ongoing nature of diagnosis and evaluation in social studies. In a fifth-grade classroom

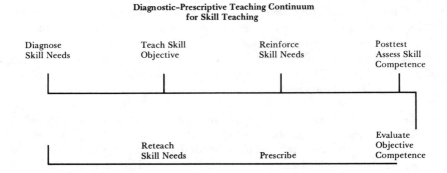

Figure 2.3   Diagnostic-Prescriptive Teaching Continuum for Skill Teaching

the students were studying about culture. The students during previous lessons had compared the food, music, and art preferences of different cultural groups. The teacher was anxious to evaluate student growth and developed the following creative activities for individual work:

1. Pretend that you were to live with a Mexican/Italian/Indian/ Chinese family. How might your evening meal be different from what it is now?
2. Using magazine pictures or your own drawings, arrange a living area that will identify your cultural background.
3. Plan a trip to the supermarket. In what ways would the items in your shopping cart be different for each of the cultural groups? In what ways might they be similar?
4. Thinking about each cultural group, which one would you care to join for a weekend? why?

The students were given a choice of these activities and two days to complete the assignment. Each student had an opportunity to share his work. Prior to the students' choice, the teacher had explained to the students that this was an assignment which would assist the teacher to decide what they knew and what they still needed to learn.

Defining instructional objectives

Once teachers have specified their instructional goals based upon an understanding of their students, knowledge about the community, and knowledge of appropriate subject matter, then they are ready to begin the specification of instructional objectives. The purpose of teaching is to affect change. Instructional objectives are designed with that purpose in mind. There are different kinds of change: behavioral, social, environmental, emotional, developmental, and so on. It is at this point in the decision-making process that teachers need to know what it is they want to teach and how they can recognize whether or not they have taught it.

Purposeful teaching is extremely complex. As teachers consider instructional objectives, they must also decide which procedures and instructional materials will elicit the desired change. A desired teaching strategy may have one or multiple objectives. Each objective is specifically stated in terms of the desired learner behavior. Since the objective may be stated as a very narrow construct, the desired change can be directed toward "how to think" competencies, skill development, or decision making. The following episode is an example of the "back stage" planning teachers must do in order to define appropriate instructional objectives.

Mr. Blakely taught 37 sixth graders in Detroit, Michigan. Many of the students' families were unemployed. Many were unskilled laborers. Mr. Blakely stated that his teaching *goal* was as follows: Working cooperatively in small groups, students will generalize about the similarity of economic problems related to urban living confronting urban populations in the United States. His *performance objective* was this: The learner will identify at least three problems affecting the economic status of urban residents.

Mr. Blakely analyzed his teaching problem in order to identify learner behaviors; he realized that his teaching goal subsumed different kinds of learning in terms of knowledge, thinking, skills, and attitudes. To accomplish the goal, Mr. Blakely's students would need to achieve the following tasks:

Analyze the work status of inner city residents by identifying the percentage of the population available for work.

Research the percentage of unemployment in poverty areas.

Identify the occupational structure in the inner city.

Identify the composition of the work force in an urban area as it relates to skilled, semiskilled, or unskilled labor.

Research the opportunities for employment in the inner city as well as employment opportunities beyond the inner city.

Mr. Blakely also recognized the need for additional learning experiences before the students would be ready to accomplish those tasks. The learning prerequisites in objective terms included these items:

1. Students would need to define the following concepts: economy, labor, work force, industry, occupation, capital, technology, skills, urban vs. suburban, poverty.

2. Students would need to read graphs related to the labor force, such as unemployment in urban neighborhoods.
3. Students would be required to read maps in order to identify urban centers and poverty areas in the United States.
4. Students would need to acquire background information about their own urban neighborhood in order to compare it with other urban centers. Students would be required to identify the assets and liabilities related to their neighborhood work force and the opportunities for employment.
5. Students would need to study transportation, health, and other related problems, such as population density.

Mr. Blakely then made a chart (Figure 2.4) of the learning requirements in terms of knowledge, skills, thinking, and attitudes. He used his chart to design specific teaching objectives and a teaching strategy related to each of the students' cognitive and affective needs as identified on his chart. His teaching goal required multiple objectives and interrelated teaching strategies in order to achieve the learning outcome.

Achieving goals, another perspective

Success in the urban classroom occurs progressively. Each success is not an isolated happening. The student volunteers an appropriate response because the teacher encouraged him to do so. The encouragement that the child received also encouraged all the other students within hearing range. The consequence of the teacher's response or action will ensure positive conditions for future success.

Mager suggested a list of positive practices to ensure student success and self-esteem. As you read the following list, adapted from Mager, compare his practices with the tactics you use or the tactics you observe.

Acknowledging students' responses, whether correct or incorrect, as attempts to learn, and following them with accepting rather than rejecting comments

Reinforcing or rewarding subject approach responses

Providing instruction in increments that will allow success most of the time

Eliciting learning responses in private rather than in public

Providing students with statements of your instructional objectives that they can understand when they first see them

Providing enough signposts so that students always know where they are and where they are expected to go

Detecting what students already know and dropping that from the curriculum

Figure 2.4. Mr. Blakely's chart of learning prerequisites

Knowledge	Thinking	Skills	Attitudes
Concept definitions:	Observing, compiling, and analyzing information related to neighborhood, businesses, opportunities, transportation, number of residents, labor force	Reading employment graphs and poverty figures	Identification of individual and societal responsibility for education, health, welfare, transportation for the nation's people
economy			
labor			
work force		Reading population density maps and identifying population centers	
industry	Comparing data for major urban centers		Identification of the consequences of poverty
occupation		Reading census reports	
capital	Summarizing information, interpreting information in terms of similarities and differences		Identification of personal goals related to anticipated or desired future life style
technology		Graphing	
skills			
urban	Relating the interdependence of geography, industry, and life style	Outlining maps	
suburban			
poverty		Summarizing information	

Providing feedback that is immediate and specific to the students' responses

Giving students some choice in selecting and sequencing subject matter, thus making positive involvement possible

Providing students with some control over the length of the instructional session

Relating new information to old, within the experience of the students

Treating students as people rather than as numbers in a faceless mass

Using active rather than passive words during presentations

Making use of those variables known to be successful in attracting and
holding human attention, such as motion, color, contrast, variety,
and personal reference

Making sure that the student can perform with ease, not just barely, so
that confidence can be developed

Expressing genuine delight at seeing the student succeed

Providing instructional tasks relevant to your objectives

Using only those test items relevant to your objectives

Allowing students to move about as freely as their physiology and
their curiosity demand[16]

All teachers need to decide which goals have the greatest value
for their students. Urban teachers identify goals of independence,
social participation, self-confidence and self-respect, motivation to
seek and to challenge. The goals that urban teachers choose focus
upon the student in the urban school. The goals are, in essence, behavioral and emphasize the "behavioral" learning problems of the
urban student rather than focusing upon curriculum per se. The urban
teacher examines the goals in order to decide the specific teacher and
learner tasks to ensure success. If it is important for students to learn
cooperative behaviors and social participation skills, then it is the
teacher's responsibility to provide learning experiences that will necessitate cooperative behaviors. The teacher interprets his own behaviors (tasks) to include the development of group projects such as
research tasks, conflict situations, science experiments, role plays,
creative projects. Next, the teacher analyzes the learning behaviors
involved in each project to ensure the achievement of the desired goal.
Here is an example.

Mr. Blakely had two major components in his teaching goal: cooperative group work and research. After identifying the tasks involved in the learning experience and selecting the appropriate
instructional materials, he proceeded to divide the students into
heterogeneous groups. When the students were seated in groups,
he commented: "On my way to school this morning I noticed a
number of men and women standing on the corner near Wood-
ward Ave. Why do you think they were standing there?" The stu-

dents responded: "They're out of work." "Need jobs." "If you stand there, everybody will know that you are looking for work." "People who need workers, come by there and pick you up." "You only stand there in the morning time."

Then the teacher said: "Many people are out of work in our city. Do you think there is a similar problem in other cities?" The students responded: "I heard there's a street corner in Chicago where people go and stand when they're out of work." "My mother said that there's unemployment all across the country." "My dad said there just aren't any jobs anywhere." The teacher then said: "How could we find out if people in other cities are having similar problems?"

Mr. Blakely had motivated the students and interested them in a common experience and problem. He proceeded to give the students an opportunity to suggest ways "to find out." He suggested that each group choose a group leader and a group recorder and that each member of the group consider himself an investigator (a "detective"). The project consumed five class hours during which, at different times, Mr. Blakely would do some short "on the spot" directed teaching, such as facilitating the definition of "work force" and "capital."

Several of the groups decided to concentrate on a specific large city, and in the evaluation they furnished information relating to that city's problems. Each group had the opportunity to present its group research while the other groups listened. Mr. Blakely achieved group-satisfying behaviors as well as knowledge, thinking, skills, and attitudinal goals. His strategy involved three distinct phases:

Phase I. *Motivation and Initiatory Experience.* This first step is crucial to total success. During phase I the urban teacher relates the teaching goal to the students' experience base. He begins with what is relevant to the students (the "here and now" approach) and makes it as concrete as possible.

Phase II. *Developmental Period.* The teacher facilitates active participation in the learning process and begins to reward thinking and reflection vs. impulsive answers or hurried product responses. The teacher assists students to choose resources and illustrates relationships.

Phase III. *Conclusion or Evaluation Period.* During this phase students share accomplishments. Teacher is attentive and responsive. Concluding experiences are sometimes production-type lessons in and of themselves. (Note the culture activities conceived by the fifth-grade teacher). The teacher again seeks to facilitate the application of knowledge extending what the students have learned to new situations and new areas of study.

Table 2.1 illustrates behaviors, behavioral goals, and the means to

Table 2.1. School success-oriented behaviors

		Means to achieve	
Emergent behaviors	Behavioral goals	Teacher behavior	Learner behavior
Ego-satisfying behaviors	Self-confidence Self-respect Optimism Security Status	Define class organization, structure, requirements, constraints. Provide motivation, acceptance, clarification, reinforcement. Provide appropriate learning tasks and responsibilities.	With knowledge of class organization, structure, requirements, and constraints, develops personal goals for work, companionship, leisure. Chooses activities for work, play, and leisure. Chooses both independent and group activities. Acts as a leader and a participant.
Learner-assertive behaviors	Questing Seeking Searching Defining Analyzing Conceptualizing Evaluating	Develop challenging tasks for independent and group inquiry. Develop problem-solving skills and social conscience skills utilizing conflict situations.	Utilizes vocational, research, value clarification skills in large group, small group, and independent tasks. Participates in buzz groups, dramatics, construction, exhibits, debates, interviews, panels, reporting.
Independent-oriented behaviors	Initiation Decision making Individuality Creativity Dependability	Provide time, space, materials for independent projects; environmental, creative, skill oriented.	Defines goal, decides means, develops project or specific task. Participates in cartooning, crossword puzzles, cooking, modeling, sewing, reading, picture-making, hobbies.
Group-satisfying behaviors	Cooperation Rationality Responsibility Respectfulness	Develop group projects and tasks: research, conflict problems, art projects, music making, science experiments, group roles in simulations.	Participates as both a leader and group member in small group projects, discussions, games, simulations, art and music works, experiments, choral speaking, listening activities, puppeteering, plays, service projects.

achieve the goals. Each of the emergent behaviors is related to priorities in the urban school: Ego-satisfying behaviors lead to development of self-concept, pride, and identity; learner-assertive behaviors lead to development of process-oriented behaviors—thinking, reflecting; independent-assertive behaviors lead to development of decision-making skills; group-satisfying behaviors lead to development of communication skills, social participation skills. These are the kinds of goals that urban teachers consider vital to school success.

Selecting appropriate content

Teaching experiences for children are always more effective when they focus initially on the "here and now." This is as true for the children of suburbia as it is for the multicultural child in the urban school. This does not preclude other studies about other peoples and other times, but it does signify where to begin. The challenges of urban life present vast possibilities for relevant curriculum.

Ochoa and Allen suggested a list of concepts representative of urban life and from which teachers could build important knowledge and attitudes about city life.[17]

alienation	congestion
anonymity	de facto segregation
city	ghetto
civil rights	integration
class mobility	megalopolis
community control	metropolitan area
rural	standards of living
segregation	subculture
slum housing	suburban
slum landlord	unemployment
social activist	urban
social class	urban renewal
pollution	race
power	racial strife
prejudice	welfare
protest	

The list, as its authors suggest, is not exhaustive and is totally dependent upon the learning environment and the teaching strategy.

All children like to read about themselves. Too often in the past the urban child was deprived of self-identity because the books and media were about people, places, and things unrelated to growing up in the city. Materials (books, media) must contain content support if conceptual learning is to take place. Teachers in the urban school suggest that content should be selected for its integrative potential. For instance, Mr. Blakely's teaching goal provided content "mileage." He integrated social studies, mathematics, reading, and language and had the opportunity to teach spelling and handwriting.

The urban environment presents many content springboards:

The need for personal identity

The need for social participation

The need for social planning (health insurance, social security, unemployment, child care agencies, protection, medical-dental facilities, recreation)

The need for city planning (housing, industry, renewal)

The need to solve city problems (crime, air and water and waste pollution, noise, density, mass transit)

Each of these areas can be expanded to focus on the derivation of the problem, other peoples, other cities and civilizations, the role of law and government, and the role of individuals and groups, as well as planning for the future.

Planning for creativity is an important content component. Urban specialists often choose the subject areas of music, art, and literature to provide opportunity for students to develop personal statements of creativity; however, all subject fields can contain creativity modules. The following teaching episode is an example:

> Ms. Williams' fourth graders were studying about magnets. After group investigation, the students had discovered that magnets attract things made of iron and steel and repel things made of paper, wood, or glass. The students also found out that magnets pull strongest at their poles and that the force of magnetic strength depends upon the strength of the magnet and the size of the object.
>
> Ms. Williams then asked the students if they knew anything about early communication across great distances of the United States. Reading out of their science book, the children learned about telegraphic communication. Next Ms. Williams provided the students with copper wire, nails, scissors, sandpaper, and dry cells and allowed time for them to experiment. It was not long before the students began to construct electromagnets. Students were soon able to generalize about the uses of electric currents as the current moves along a circuit.
>
> The next day Mrs. Williams provided wood, nails, wire, sandpaper, scissors, and pieces of tin. Using their science books as a bibliographic resource and their previous experiences with magnets and electromagnets, the children began constructing telegraph keys and sounders.
>
> Some of Mrs. Williams' students became deeply involved in the study of electricity and went on to build simple motors. Two of the children who lived in the same apartment building developed a telegraphic communication system between their apartments and designed their own code.

Content selected for urban students should include understandings related to the child's own world; understandings related to the contributions of men and women in all kinds of roles; understandings related to the contributions of *all* Americans to the total development of our society; understandings related to the contribution of labor and the entrepreneur to the total development of our society; understandings related to our role in the environment; understandings related to the effect on human beings of drugs and alcohol. Content selections should be made on the basis of facilitating the following teaching opportunities:

Opportunity for integrativeness (mileage). Content should be chosen so that subject fields and disciplines can be combined to enhance applicability and reinforcement possibilities.

Opportunity for in-depth study and saturation type learning. Students (and adults) enjoy pursuing a study until satisfied that the end has been reached.

Opportunity for creative study. This may include laboratory experiences or the creative aspects of any discipline. Too often urban students are deprived of these kinds of experiences and instead provided with remediation-type learning.

Opportunity for multiple experiences to conform to a variety of learning styles. It should be possible to present information in different ways so that students do not "screen out" the presentations. The use of a variety of approaches also ensures needed repetitions.

Opportunity for sequencing and continuing study. Wide applicability and extended study will motivate the urban student. Content should be appropriate to teach in small programmatic modules. Teachers need to illustrate relationships and assist students to detect relationships.

Opportunity for active student involvement and participation. Urban students learn best through active involvement. Content should provide experiences for students to "do" instead of watch, listen, or read about.

Opportunity for individualization and differentiation of instruction. Content should consider the diversity of the urban classroom in terms of abilities, interests, and learning styles so that it is possible to provide individual, small-group, and large-group instruction.

Opportunity to integrate vocational and technical skills. Content should provide opportunity for students to appreciate technology, to learn about skills and the total complex of roles and needs in our society.

Opportunity to offer students "choices" for concentration. Active involvement in the learning process requires the learner to take a first step—to commit himself. When students are provoked to choose, they become involved in and committed to the learning enterprise.

Opportunity for successful achievement. This is what it is all about.

All the other opportunities will facilitate the accomplishment of success. Content must be meaningful *to students*. Content must be chosen with regard for time and space, materials, and human resources for accomplishment. Students need feedback to tell them they are achieving. Content progression along with conferences and verbal and written comments from the teacher will provide student assurance of achievement.

Choosing strategies for success

Our urban teachers have conceptualized goals, objectives, and content. Now they are ready to decide "how to make it hapnen." The decision they make will define not only their own behavior in the teaching process but the learner's behavior as well. Their decision will encompass the organization and management of their classrooms, the learning environment in the classroom, and the instructional resources needed by teacher and students. The teachers' decisions will also, in a sense, "give them away"; the teaching decision will be a reflection of their personal philosophies, the way in which they interpret their roles as teachers.

The teaching strategy is a planned maneuver organized to accomplish a specific objective. Some strategies are designed to accomplish "input" goals; others are designed for "output" purposes. Input goals focus upon information-giving activities. Learners consume information or knowledge as they participate in an input activity. During input activities students are collecting, using their senses to assist them. The teacher assists, directs, or guides instruction by arranging and making information available. Output goals focus upon process-type activities. Students use the knowledge they gained, their experiential backgrounds and skills to produce and ultimately to develop new meanings. Illustrative examples follow:

Experiences leading to input goals	*Experiences leading to output goals*
Textbook reading	Student creativeness
Lecture	Student experimentation
Films, slides, filmstrips	Listing, grouping, classifying
Video, "listening" activities	information
Field trips	Role playing, dramatizing
	Analyzing, synthesizing data
	Characterizing, evaluating and
	decision making

Sometimes a strategy is named according to the activity or learning experience or process it induces. Thus, some strategies are called role-playing strategies or information processing or concept attainment, inquiry, socratic, and so on. Input strategy using a lecture is universally understood and requires no introduction or set of rules for teacher and learner behaviors. Strategies are planned to enable teacher and learner to manage the teaching/learning process. The teacher's organizational plan structures the learning process so that students work individually, paired with another student, in a small group, or in a large group. All teaching strategies facilitate instruction in one or more of these grouping procedures.

Teachers choose to group or to individualize instruction depending upon the teaching purpose and the teaching strategy. The *individualization* of instruction facilitates recognition of student individuality in terms of ability, interests, and emotional and physical growth. Achievement is enhanced because the child is not competing with others for teacher attention. The student works at his own rate of growth and develops the capability for organizing and directing himself. He develops understanding about his personal concerns, develops self-respect and independence. He develops his personal creative competencies as he works alone and generates alternatives. Teacher-student rapport and cooperation is strengthened through tutor, guide, and "model" relationships.

A *small-group* organizational strategy may be used to teach any subject of the curriculum. The strategy is inherently flexible and is welcomed by both the shy student desiring anonymity and the aggressive learner. Groups are usually heterogeneous, but may also be ability-grouped for teaching specific skills. Heterogeneous grouping has specific advantages:

> Students' diversity of interest and strengths provide opportunity for leadership and participation roles to vary from day to day during the different activities.
>
> Students learn to perform and accept "cooperative" teaching responsibilities. They develop their own competence as they assist others to learn.
>
> Students develop higher morale as they accept team responsibilities.
>
> Students never feel "tracked."
>
> Teachers assume more of a guidance and learning facilitating role. They are free to observe, diagnose needs, and prescribe appropriate actions.

Groups may be formed by student choice or teacher designation. The optimal size for the group is five to seven members. Group members need physical space for work. They must be able to face one another in order to share information, debate a point of view, or carry out a group task. Any classroom where the desks are not bolted to the floor is appropriate (see Figure 2.5). Teachers use the small group strategy for a variety of purposes:

To facilitate student interaction

To provide opportunity for languaging

To motivate affective involvement

To facilitate team learning, cooperation, and production

To provide opportunity for decision making

To provide practice in leadership and modeling behaviors

The small-group strategy is extremely popular in the urban classroom since it develops social participation through an analysis of group processes and builds communication skills.

Large-group instruction is used by many teachers throughout the school day. It seems to be the simplest grouping plan in terms of seating arrangements; yet its disadvantages for teaching often outweigh the advantages.

Advantages	*Disadvantages*
Input activities for large groups of children: films, lectures, guest speakers, choral speaking, singing, drama	Individual needs subordinate to group needs
	Impeded supervision and guidance of differentiated assignments
Sense of belonging, morale	Prohibits teaching to the quick and slow students
Facilitates teaching of new skill to all simultaneously	Increases disciplinary and control problems; tempts teacher to make "an example" of disruptive student; tempts student to become an instant hero
	Increases the impersonality of the teaching/learning process
	Inhibits self-direction
	Vision and hearing problems increase
	Inhibits student leadership
	Difficult to locate instructional materials appropriate to all students
	Inhibits social participation

Large-group instruction does not appear to be the most effective organizational plan for the urban classroom considering the multiplicity of students' abilities and interests. The teaching purpose should determine the size and organization of the group. Since most teachers remember large-group instruction from their own school days, it often appears to be the most natural organizational plan. However, teachers who vary the size and composition of the instructional group during the school day often find that it provides a spark to the entire school program.

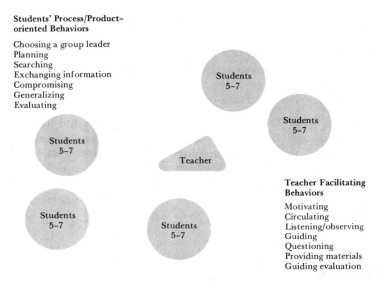

Students' Process/Product-
oriented Behaviors

Choosing a group leader
Planning
Searching
Exchanging information
Compromising
Generalizing
Evaluating

Teacher Facilitating
Behaviors

Motivating
Circulating
Listening/observing
Guiding
Questioning
Providing materials
Guiding evaluation

Figure 2.5 Classroom Schema of Small-Group Strategy with Teacher and Student Behaviors

Strategy options. Teaching strategies transform content into interrelated experiences so that students can learn. Strategies should be both varied and balanced between input and output. Role playing all day would cause bedlam; reading all day induces boredom. Output strategies result from previous input lessons. Whether teaching a subject field by itself or integrated with other subject fields, teachers have many options for making subject matter interesting. An example of sequencing and varying the teaching strategy is provided by a first-grade reading teacher whose instructional objective was to develop semantic skills. The students will identify colors with names, match colors with names, choose colors using names.

Strategy 1. Students name colors in the classroom: on themselves, on the walls and bulletin boards. Students look out of the window and name colors provided by nature.
Strategy 2. Teacher introduces a chart that shows a red car, a green tree, blue sky, black cat, orange pumpkin, yellow banana, brown chocolate bar; under each item appears the word written in script. Students orally read the color below each item.
Strategy 3. Teacher displays only the written word for each color. Students are chosen to match the word with the appropriate word on the chart.
Strategy 4. A new chart is displayed with just colors. Students use the word cards from the previous activity to place under the appropriate color. Students lead these activities and choose each other. The teacher observes.

Strategy 5. The following assignment appears on the board: Draw 4 red apples. Draw 5 green balloons. Draw 2 yellow houses. Draw 1 black car. Draw 3 brown bears. Draw 6 orange boats. Draw 4 blue balls. (The colors are written in script; the objects are identified with pictures.)

Strategy 6. The teacher reads a story about colors to the students.

The teacher varied the students' learning experiences and his own role by using directed discussion with oral participation, supervised directed reading, the game of matching, reinforcement with a written assignment that integrated mathematics, and a listening activity.

The following diagram illustrates a partial listing of strategy options appropriate in the classroom. The teacher's role changes as the strategies move from left to right on the continuum.

Expository teaching	*Directed discussions*	*Role plays, simulations*	*Discovery, inquiry*
Lecture	Socratic questioning Analysis	Gaming Dramatizations	Inductive thinking Group investigation Reflective thinking

On the far left the teacher provides all the information to the students, and older students may be taking notes for eventual memorization. Moving to the right is a strategy that utilizes directed discussion and allows the teacher to assess student thinking. The teacher questions to elicit specific types of thinking. Utilization of the discussion strategy allows the teacher to guide the students and facilitate analysis, synthesis, inference, and evaluation. As the strategy moves still farther to the right, the teacher provides fewer cues to the students. Role playing and gaming (simulations) provide greater student involvement and decision making; the teacher provides motivation and situational structuring. At the extreme right the teacher encourages creative, independent, and group investigations. Students are encouraged to reflect and utilize their personal resources. Both hypothesis formation and the proof process belong to the students as the teacher serves as a guide and resource person.

Each strategy leads to different goals; each strategy defines both the teacher's and the learner's behaviors. Research has not determined the "best" teaching strategy; however, there are indications that teachers should exercise strategic flexibility to enhance motivation and to develop the full spectrum of learner behaviors. Students exposed to flexible teaching that provides self- and group-instruction, self- and group discovery and small- and large-group discussions will develop a wide range of alternative learning approaches.

Learning environments. Similar to the strategies they support, learning environments are designed to serve specific purposes. A learning environment may be defined to encompass the human relationships (roles, responsibilities, behaviors) of teacher and students and the supportive instructional materials (books, media, realia). The range of teaching and learning behaviors is either facilitated or constrained by the classroom learning environment. The classroom that is designed with desks bolted to the floor in rigid rows and with bookcases containing only textbooks will certainly limit the range of possible teaching roles and student learning alternatives. However, the classroom that is designed with flexible seating arrangements, learning centers, and print and nonprint instructional materials will facilitate a wide range of teaching and learning options. The learning environment of the classroom is another way in which the teacher expresses his or her teaching philosophy.

The classrooms of the two urban high school teachers, Mr. Jordan and Mr. Roxbury, exhibited different learning environments. Utilizing a lecture style, Mr. Jordan created a more structured environment than did Mr. Roxbury, who played the game of farming with his students. There has been a great deal of controversy about whether or not urban students *need* a more structured environment than suburban or rural students. There are effective urban teachers who use a variety of styles; some are structured, some are not. If there are common characteristics among these teachers, it has been my experience that it is a commonality of flexibility, openness, and acceptance of all students. Specific suggestions relating to organization, management, and discipline will be considered at the end of this chapter.

Considering again the diagram of strategy options, we can see that it is possible to discriminate among the environments necessitated by the chosen strategy.

Strategy	*Learning environment*
Lecture Film "Teacher input"	Controlled environment, high structure important
Directed discussions, questioning, analysis	Controlled environment, moderate to high structure
Role-playing, simulations, gaming, dramatizations	Open environment, moderate structure
Discovery, problem solving, group investigations	Open environment, low structure

In terms of teaching tasks, each environment is characterized by a slightly different style.

Environment	Teacher behavior
Controlled environment, high structure	Teacher controls the dialog; teacher sets the stage and controls student responses. Limited instructional materials needed.
Controlled environment, moderate to high structure	Teacher initiates discussions and programs questions to elicit desired responses. Teacher controls student interaction to fit discussion. Some supportive instructional materials needed.
Open environment, moderate structure	Teacher initiates problem or conflict situation. Teacher often guides the problem resolution as it moves from stage to stage. A great deal of student interaction is encouraged. Students are expected to accept responsibility for problem solving. Variety of instructional materials needed.
Open environment low structure	Teacher facilitates democratic processes. Students define problems and initiate methods for solving them. Teacher provides many resources and encourages students to use resources out of the confines of the classroom.

Choosing instructional materials. During the 1960s it was common to hear directors of educational projects comment that "the textbook is dead." During the 1970s we know that the textbook is alive and well, but it has been joined by a number of other print and nonprint materials that enhance the learning alternatives in the classroom. The term *instructional materials* refers to both print and nonprint items—textbooks, tests, systems, and materials such as manipulative devices, pictures, tapes, records, and multimedia.

Teachers choose instructional materials to provide students with a type of second-hand reality. If students were able to have first-hand experiences in their subject fields, they would have less need for instructional materials. But the school, to some extent, has always been removed from data sources; therefore, material resources are selected to provide knowledge (data) and understanding (meaning). It is the teacher's responsibility to choose materials that meet the educational purposes, the teaching methodology, and the diversity of students' needs. Specific guidelines for choosing materials include the following:

Instructional materials should accurately portray the range of human roles, human attributes, and human potential.

Instructional materials should accurately represent American society, including the contributions of all cultural and racial groups.

Instructional materials should accurately represent the effects on the individual and on society of narcotics, alcohol, tobacco, crime.

Instructional materials should portray our role in, and responsibility for, the protection of our environment.

Instructional materials should represent the range of beliefs on controversial issues as well as methods for analysis of controversial issues.

Instructional materials should be chosen to facilitate student thinking and decision making.

Instructional materials should be accurate, objective, and relevant and provide authentic data to the students who will use them.

Instructional materials should accommodate differences in learning styles, interest, and ability.

Instructional materials should be attractive, motivating, and current.

Elementary teachers should also consider these problems when they choose science, health, social studies (and sometimes mathematics) textbooks: The *readability* of a textbook has to do with the student's ability to decode and to comprehend; many research studies indicate that textbooks are designated at least one grade above the average student's reading ability. *Concept load* has to do with the generalizations and big ideas that are considered fundamental to understanding the structure of a discipline; many textbooks present these concepts too fast and the concept load may be too intensive unless the teacher provides other experiences to bridge the gap between student and textbook. *Indefinite terms* dealing with time, space, and quantity are confusing to young children. They can read them, but they are unable to relate them to their own life cycle. Some of these terms are "little while," "few," "many," "later," "good old days," "several," "mile," "century ago," "historically." The *reading skills* involved in the use of many textbooks or material systems have not been taught during "reading" time, and should be taught within the context of the subject where the book or system is used. These skills include location and reference skills and specific comprehension skills related to the subject field.[18]

Many urban students in the past have been extremely sensitive to the use of textbooks; too often they were the source of boredom and frustration. However, the current use of newspapers, magazines, paperbacks, and instructional material packages has proved quite motivating and successful.

Choosing evaluative methods

Diagnosis and evaluation are two sides of the same coin. Evaluation should be a continuous process in order to provide teachers and students with insight concerning actual progress in relation to expected progress. Evaluation of teacher and learner performance can be used to improve both the teaching and learning process. Determination of "where we are" should provide direction in terms of "where we want to be." The teacher's decisions are related to the scope (depth of cognizance) and sequence (in what order?) of learning tasks. In the past, teachers often relied on textbooks to determine the scope and sequence of learning, but the textbook has not proved to be a reliable source. It is the responsibility of teachers and students to determine proper and needed learning tasks.

Evaluation of the basic skill subjects can readily be accomplished if teachers learn to recognize developmental characteristics. For instance, skills in oral language communication precede written skills. This is true in all languages; thus, the child who speaks a language other than standard English should *not* be held responsible for reading skills in standard English *until* he has mastered oral language skills. The development of oral language is dependent on tangible experiences from which vocabulary and concepts are built. The learner expands his oral language as he learns to express himself cognitively and affectively, but he cannot do this unless he is also expanding his experiential base.

Language specialists DeStefano and Fox presented common speaking patterns that could be identified by the classroom teacher in order to evaluate progress and choose sequential learning skills:

Subject + Verb + Direct Object (transitive)
    The cat likes hot milk.
    He hit Billy.
Subject + Linking Verb + Predicate Nominative
    The cat is black.
    He is silly.
Subject + Verb (intransitive)
    The cat sat on the mat.
    The birds are flying.

However, DeStefano and Fox warned that the speech of different cultural groups sometimes varied slightly; teachers should be alert for frequencies and patterns that were different from those reported.[19]

Testing student knowledge of facts has not been a difficult process, but testing students' effectiveness in applying knowledge is considerably more significant and should be the purpose of evaluation. The following will provide an example:

In a junior high school classroom the teacher had his students number off: one, two, one, two, etc. All of the number ones were to debate a specific value position; all of the number twos were to debate the opposing viewpoint. Each pair of students sat by themselves for their debate. After five minutes the teacher suggested that each student reverse his position and debate the opposing viewpoint.

The teacher observed and listened to his students. The following lists illustrate what teacher and students learned:

What the teacher learned	*What the students learned*
The teacher identified:	The students recognized:
1. Which of the students were flexible enough to reverse value roles.	1. Opposing viewpoints exist in every value question.
2. Which of the students could define the problem and identify the relevant values.	2. It is difficult to "change gears" and reverse your role or belief.
3. The extent of understanding of the value problem by students.	3. It is impossible to debate, rationally, without a factual base.
4. Which of the students could apply knowledge of the problem and relate it to opposing viewpoints.	4. To debate effectively, it is necessary to anticipate the opposing viewpoint.

There is no magic formula for the evaluation of students' decision-making skills nor even their oral language skills; however, the observant teacher can recognize developmental levels and characteristics, thus enabling teacher and students to plan purposeful learning goals. The relationship between teaching strategy and evaluative method is illustrated in the following situation:

> The second-grade class had been talking about the need for rules in the classroom and at home. The teacher wanted to "test" the extent of internationalization of the concept of rules. He proceeded to direct four teams of students to play two games of sockball. While the students played, the teacher observed.
>
> The students hollered, yelped, and disagreed with each other. After about seven minutes, and after listening to the complaints of several children, the teacher stopped the two games. Teacher and students squatted on the playground and the teacher commented: "In both of your games I noticed that you were having a great deal of difficulty. What was the matter?" The students immediately responded that many of the students did not know the rules of the game and so were unable to play fairly.

The teacher in this incident accomplished "teaching" and "evaluation"; he did it by design.

> A high school teacher tested his students' ability to interpret data. He gave his students a newspaper article and asked them to list all the statements they considered to be *facts* and all the statements they considered to be *opinions*. The teacher then directed a discussion in which the students demonstrated their ability to differentiate between relevant information and propaganda.

Using this strategy, the teacher was able to "test" his students' ability to use interpretive reading skills. There are tests that would have accomplished this same task, but sometimes the tests are not appropriate to, or motivating for, a specific group of students. It is particularly important for the urban teacher in a multicultured classroom to be alert and sensitive to students' developmental levels and the many ways in which to teach and test to discover these levels.

Urban Teaching Specializations

Like other professionals, teachers have developed a number of specializations. In the urban school, specialist teachers direct programs in language, reading, mathematics, early childhood, and act as special resource teachers. Each of these programs will be considered as they pertain to the urban school.

Language as an urban specialty

National recognition of the problems of students whose primary language is other than English did not occur until 1968 when Congress passed the Bilingual Education Act, Title VII.[20] A recent Supreme Court decision will have an effect upon language instruction in the public schools. A unanimous decision by the Court ordered, in a case affecting Chinese pupils, the San Francisco Unified School District to provide instruction in Chinese for students who do not speak enough English to participate effectively in school. The implication is that school districts across the nation will have to provide language training to students whose primary language is other than English.[21]

Several types of programs have been developed to assist non-English-speaking students. Some programs are known as English as a Second Language (ESL), some as ESD (English as a Second Dialect), others as Bilingual-Bicultural programs. Some programs provide Spanish for Spanish speakers (SSS), others include Spanish language arts (SLA). There are major differences among these programs, and it is important to discriminate the various components found in each type in order to assess a program and its value for students.

A language program suggested by Herschel T. Manuel develops both English and Spanish:

> Provide a full year of education for children five years of age, with a gradual transition from speaking Spanish to speaking English and an emphasis on preparation for reading English. This pre-first grade experience may be expected to prepare the children for more nearly normal progress with other children and thus diminish the retardation which in later years is a major cause of dropping out of school.

Begin instruction in reading English when the children have reached an adequate state of readiness [Manuel means oral language readiness].

Begin instruction in reading Spanish when the children have mastered the basic techniques of reading English, and give instruction in Spanish as a language through the elementary grades to all who qualify. The "mastery" of basic reading techniques may be tentatively defined as the average-and-above level of achievement reached by children in general at the end of grade 3. If English-speaking children are enrolled in the same school, they may be given instruction in oral Spanish beginning in grade 1, in preparation for beginning to read Spanish when their achievement in English has reached the same level.

Encourage the more able pupils to continue the study of Spanish beyond the elementary level.[22]

The Spanish-speaking youngster who also speaks a little bit of English encounters many language problems as a consequence of Spanish linguistic patterns that may interfere with the student's speech in English. The urban teacher needs to be alert to these problems. Brussell, paraphrasing Chavez, described the problem:

. . . the short *i* in miss may be pronounced by the Spanish-speaker as the *ee* in meet, since *i* carries the sound of *ee* in Spanish. Similarly, the *sh* of the English word show may be pronounced by the native Spanish-speaker as the *ch* in the English word church. In addition, a difference in concepts between the two languages may cause the listener to note a difference even when no accent is present. In Spanish, some words are plural, but their English counterparts are singular, such as the word nose. In speaking English, the Spanish-speaker may say, "I hit them against the door."[23]

Just as the cacophony of the urban school may sound strange to the school visitor, the urban student may have a similar problem. In order to learn a new language or standard speech, the ear must be trained to hear the sounds of the language. The student may "sort out" those sounds and rhythm patterns with which he is unfamiliar. For this reason, most language specialist teachers insist upon a long period of oral and aural presentation.

Some bilingual teachers utilize the *oral-aural* or the *audiolingual* method for teaching a second language. These teachers stress speaking and listening skills. The child must be proficient in these two components of language arts before the teacher attempts to develop the communication skills of reading and writing. The teacher presents words in meaningful sentences, stories, and music instead of compelling the student to study meaningless patterns or word lists. The teacher serves as a language model and the student practices by imitating the teacher. As the children imitate the teacher, they learn correct language patterns; grammar is not taught separately out of context. Sometimes the teacher uses mechanical devices such as tape recorders and language masters to create "speech centers" that assist the student with language drills. A major teaching goal is to facilitate the process of internalizing the English language through repeated practice. The language specialist teacher speaks at a normal rate of speed so that the student learns to hear and speak utilizing proper intonation, rhythm, and stress. To assist the student to respond in a socially accurate manner, a study of contemporary culture sometimes accompanies the language program. The language teacher directing this type of program must study contrastive linguistics in order to prepare for possible areas of interference.

Students who speak other dialects instead of standard English also need special language assistance. Again, the most important aspects of this type of program are the facilitation of a positive student attitude, delineation of areas of *important* difference between the spoken dialect and standard English, and opportunity for repeated practice in an accepting environment. Mildred Donoghue[24] suggests that language teachers self-evaluate using the following questions:

> Is what I am teaching about the language the most important matter that my pupils can study at this time?
>
> Is my language teaching completely unbigoted?
>
> Am I honoring my obligation as a language teacher to provide the most useful alternatives or options for my pupils' self-fulfillment?
>
> Is my language teaching utilizing the most timely and dynamic principles and data for undertaking the system of language?
>
> Am I taking every advantage of the opportunities in my class to develop healthy attitudes toward brotherhood, social justice, and human rights?

Most federally funded bilingual programs include a component called *bicultural*. There are some important differences between ESL programs and bilingual-bicultural programs. Often the bilingual-bicultural program develops the student's primary language first. Since the student begins school with appropriate concepts and experiences developed in his primary language, many language specialists believe that an immediate change to a foreign tongue has a stunting effect upon the student's language development. Readiness activities as well as initial reading lessons are taught in the child's primary language. Both skills and content subjects are presented to the child in his primary language. As the child progresses in his primary language, foreign language teaching is initiated. To build confidence and self-identity, the bicultural element of the program teaches the student about his native background, personal history, and culture. This component of the program proceeds along with the development of communication skills.

Bilingual-bicultural programs vary from school to school. Some language teachers teach both the primary language and English *concurrently*. First the student receives directions and concepts in his primary language, then the teacher introduces the foreign language (English), again teaching content and providing directions in the second language. The advantage to the student is that he already understands the content and the directions before he hears them in the foreign language; thus he is able to associate the meanings in the appropriate context.

Some recent studies by college students in the Los Angeles area seem to indicate that students who are taught English within a content field, such as social studies or science, derive greater syntactical achievement than when the language experiences are taught through "modeling" exercises.

A new program designed to assist Asian American children who have limited ability to speak English is the KEYS project (Knowledge of English Yields Success).[25] The objectives for the Los Angeles City School District's KEYS projects include:

Understanding and expressing ideas orally in English.

Responding successfully in oral English, in prereading activities, and in reading

Developing an understanding of the culture of the English-speaking school community

Expanding the knowledge of their own and other Asian cultures within the community

The projects also provide in-service training for teachers and teacher aides in techniques and methods of English as a second language (ESL) and aspects of bilingual education. Staff development emphasis is placed upon background information relating to the Asian languages and cultures, building awareness of linguistic and cultural interferences that children must overcome, and the development and maintenance of a positive self-image for children.

Another component of the KEYS project relates to the selection, adaptation, and development of materials. Both the professional staff and the community in each project school are involved in the location of appropriate materials and the adaptation and development of new materials. Ethnic communities involved in this task include Chinese, Japanese, Korean, Samoan, and Tagalog.

Urban language teachers are confronted with a number of controversies as they make decisions that affect students:

If the child's primary language is other than English, and the school teaches the child English, how will the child relate to his parents at home? Will the child lose respect for his parents?

Will the child's values relating to his primary culture change? Will there be a value conflict at home?

Should the school teach the child about his primary culture (bicultural education) to build the child's self-concept or should the school concentrate on the majority culture?

If the teaching of a secondary language (English) is initiated with a very young child in kindergarten or first grade, will it "set him back" in terms of developmental conceptualizations?

Can the elementary student handle two languages concurrently?

Does foreign language teaching stifle creativity and higher-level conceptualizations?

Should language teaching occur only in the basic skill subjects? Will this bore the students?

Should the student be taught to read in his primary language so that his development will proceed in a typical fashion? Will this impede development of English language skills?

Why does society value the bilingual and multilingual individual but look down upon any group that speaks a foreign tongue?

Since many Mexican-American students actually speak a combination Spanish-English, which language is dominant and in which language should teaching begin?

If the teacher decides to develop the primary language first, when should he change and begin instruction in English?

Why do many children try to hide their knowledge and ability to speak a foreign language?

If bilingualism is an asset, should all children in the urban school receive foreign language instruction? Should this instruction occur in the typical classroom or only in a "language" teacher's classroom?

When teaching speakers of other dialects, the language teacher is confronted with stylistic variations. Are informal structures to be considered "wrong," "bad" or "improper"?

Should the language teacher consider himself to be a "guardian" of the language?

Should mastery of standard English be enforced? If it is, will the student be able to communicate effectively in his "native" dialect?

If the child is encouraged to learn and to use standard English instead of his native dialect, will he lose respect for "home" values and culture? Will his self-concept be affected?

Language teachers respond to these challenges and controversies in individual ways. Sometimes decisions are made jointly by language teachers, administrators, and community representatives, as in the KEYS program. Sometimes the teacher specialist must educate his or her professional colleagues so that each is alert to the problems of the foreign-speaking and nonstandard English-speaking student. Although a great deal of research exists relating to each of these controversies, no single formula for success will eliminate all problems. Still, many bilingual and language specialist teachers are discovering individual systems for success.

Reading as an urban specialty

The International Reading Association has identified roles and responsibilities for reading specialists. In the urban school there is often a special reading teacher, a reading clinician, or a reading consultant. According to the IRA, the roles and responsibilities are as follows:

Special teacher of reading. Major responsibility is for remedial and corrective and/or developmental reading instruction. The teacher should identify students needing diagnosis and/or remediation; plan a program of remediation from data gathered through diagnosis; implement such a program of remediation; evaluate student progress in remediation; interpret student needs and progress in remediation to the classroom teacher and the parents; plan and implement a developmental or advanced program, as necessary.

Reading clinician. Major responsibility is to provide diagnosis, remediation, or the planning of remediation for the more complex and severe reading disability cases. The clinician should demonstrate all the skills expected of the special reading teacher and, by virtue of additional training and experience, diagnose and treat the more complex and severe reading disability cases; demonstrate proficiency in providing internship training for prospective clinicians and/or special teachers of reading.

Reading consultant. Major responsibility is to work directly with teachers, administrators, and other professionals within a school to develop and implement the reading program under the direction of a supervisor with special training in reading. The consultant should survey and evaluate the ongoing program and make suggestions for needed changes; translate the district philosophy of reading with the help of the principal of each school into a working program consistent with the needs of the students, the teachers, and the community; work with classroom teachers and others in improving the developmental and corrective aspects of the reading program.[26]

A question that is often asked is this: If all teachers should consider themselves teachers of reading, why is it that there are "reading" specialists in the school? Teachers, even in the elementary schools, often develop specialties or areas of competence which their colleagues recognize. All teachers *do* teach reading, yet particularly in the urban school, there is a need for additional teachers to work with students and to act as resources for other teachers. (Although the IRA has defined specific roles and responsibilities for reading specialists, the implementation of these roles varies from school to school.)

Some reading specialists work only with those students identified by their classroom teacher as in need of additional or specialized help in reading skills. Other reading specialists believe in working with all students for 20 to 40 minutes per week; these teachers pursue what is sometimes called a "preventive" teaching philosophy. Many reading specialist resource teachers in the urban school are funded through federal funds for compensatory education, Title I of the National Elementary and Secondary Education Act, 1965. Others are supported through state or district funds. The federally funded teachers are required to work with students in all elementary grades. State-designated specialists may work with students at specifically defined levels as in California, where the Miller-Unruh specialists work only with students in the first three grades.

The reading specialist teacher works both individually and with small groups of students. The specialists emphasize when working with other teachers and with students that it is much easier to prevent poor reading habits than to correct them after they have developed. The specialists use diagnostic-prescriptive teaching techniques and materials. The reading laboratory is often filled with many different types of media to accommodate variance in learning styles. Reading specialist teachers develop new materials of their own and assist classroom teachers to develop new materials to meet special student needs. The reading teacher must also respond to professional, community, and societal pressures.

Reading teachers direct themselves to the following tasks:

Assessment of student reading skills using a sequenced skill test to evaluate student strengths and weaknesses

Placement of students at specific skill levels

Grouping of students with similar learning needs for efficient instruction

Collecting supportive instructional materials: games, worksheets, books, tapes, etc.

Providing instruction in small groups and individually according to needs

Providing reinforcement and enrichment activities

Posttesting to evaluate objective attainment

Reteaching where needed

Some urban reading teachers proceed through the first four tasks and then direct the classroom teacher to provide the instruction and reinforcement activities, reserving the testing, evaluation, and placement tasks for themselves.

Mathematics as an urban specialty

Mathematics specialists are relatively new in the urban school. Similar to the reading and language specialist, the mathematics teacher often builds a laboratory in which to work. Advocates of "new math," the specialists take their cues from Piaget and incorporate many manipulative devices to facilitate diagnosis and instruction. The laboratory may be equipped with commercial or teacher-made aids: geoblocks, rods, centicubes, ice cream sticks, beads, fraction bars, multisensory and visual aids, scales, polyhedra dice, rulers, meter sticks, place-value charts, abacus, peg games, and so on. The math laboratory often looks like a giant playroom and children seem to respond to it immediately. The laboratory may be complex, with computers, overhead projectors and calculators, or extremely simple. Its purpose in the urban school is to transform mathematics concepts from abstractions into concrete situations so that students can understand and apply mathematics in their lives.

The specialist mathematics teacher relates mathematics to the children's social experiences:

> If tacos cost 25¢ each or five for a dollar, could you save money by buying five for a dollar?

> If gasoline costs 56¢ per gallon or 53¢ per gallon if you pump it yourself, and if you need ten gallons of gasoline, how much could you save if you bought gas at the self-service gas station?

The specialist mathematics teacher also teaches children about indefinite quantitative terms (few, many, long ago) and relates these terms to other subject areas. The children learn to read and make time lines, thermometers, maps, graphs, weather records. The teacher often uses the community as a resource and invites post office workers, clerks, and others into the classroom.

In most schools all children have the opportunity to attend the laboratory instead of only those with "math problems." The teacher directs attention to diagnosing students' readiness for instruction. The teacher uses both developmental tests and manipulative devices to test and to observe students as they solve problems, count, group, discriminate. The teacher organizes materials for instruction and sequences them, thus creating a mathematics "program" for the students. Often the mathematics program can be self-scored so that students receive immediate feedback and reassurance. The classroom teacher shares in the instruction responsibilities and may share in the evaluation. The specialist teacher often designs the program and assists the classroom teacher to organize the materials for instruction.

Early childhood as a teaching specialization

The success of Head Start programs[27] gave rise to the early childhood movement as a teaching specialty in the urban school. Although the Head Start program was conceived as a preschool strategy, the early childhood programs in the elementary school often combine kindergarten, first, and second grades, and sometimes third grade. Early childhood education programs often use multi-age grouping, which places children of kindergarten, first, and second grades together in a self-contained classroom. Some schools develop an early childhood team with several teachers, parent aides, and college students utilizing a "team" approach to planning and instruction.

The early childhood specialist tries to identify learning problems before they happen. Utilizing the team, the specialist creates learning experiences to differentiate instruction for each student. The early childhood classroom stresses verbal skills, social skills, and readiness activities. Children learn to work together and tutor each other. Student leadership skills are stressed. The children share in preparing snacks for nutrition and sometimes the noon meal is prepared in the classroom. When the kindergarten children leave at noontime, the older children receive additional assistance in basic skill subjects.

Resource teachers

Many schools are finding it advantageous to release one teacher per grade level to serve as a resource teacher for the other teachers at that grade level. The resource teacher performs many of the same chores as the department chairperson in the junior and senior high schools. The resource teacher has the responsibility to identify new techniques, new strategies, and new instructional materials. The resource teacher guides the instructional planning for the grade level and may share instructional tasks, teaching one or more subjects in each of the classrooms. The resource teacher may also identify teacher in-service needs and establish a program for teachers in specific areas of need. Sometimes the school district uses the resource teacher to attend special meetings and classes and then to disseminate the information to others at the school.

Resource specialist teacher is a term also used to describe a teacher who has completed advanced preparation in special education. The resource specialist may have specialized knowledge of teaching learning handicapped, physically handicapped, communicatively handicapped, or severely handicapped students. This individual will often perform generalized achievement testing to prescribe specialized programs, methods, and approaches to be used in the teaching of exceptional children. Chapter 6 provides additional information about teaching exceptional children.

The urban school often has more specialists than the suburban or rural school because greater learning needs exist and because funds are available to the urban school for remedial and compensatory education, and cultural enrichment programs. Each school and its community is responsible for defining its own needs and program. An example of school-community decision making is provided by the program conceived at the Denker School in Gardena, California. A Community Advisory Council was established in 1973 to set school goals and to organize committees to establish a unique community-oriented school program. The following three figures (Figures 2.6, 2.7, 2.8) identify the groups involved in educational decision making at the Denker School, the team approach to provide differentiated staffing, and the team of supportive services that contributes to the child's success at the school.[28]

In this section of the chapter we have examined the decisions and some of the specialized functions of urban teachers. Along with the decisions of when to teach, what to teach, and how much to teach are other practical procedural considerations that "make" or "break" the

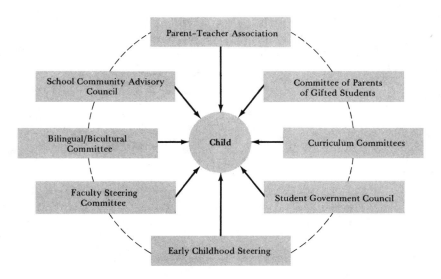

Figure 2.6 Advisory and Decision-Making Groups (From Meno Phillips and Marshall Sisca, *Denker Avenue Community Elementary School: An Educational Statement* (Gardena, Calif., 1973).)

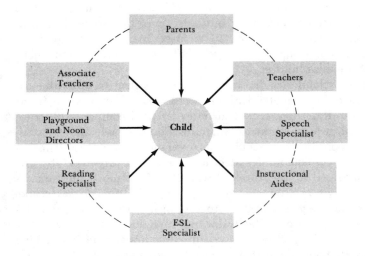

Figure 2.7. A Team of Learning Facilitators (From Meno Phillips and Marshall Sisca, *Denker Avenue Community Elementary School: An Educational Statement* (Gardena, Calif., 1973).)

Figure 2.8. A Team of Supportive Services (From Meno Phillips and Marshall Sisca: *Denker Avenue Community Elementary School: An Educational Statement* (Gardena, Calif., 1973).)

practitioner. The last section of the chapter will review the special skills and tactics that have proved effective for the urban teacher.

Instructional Tactics

Teachers new to the urban schools often anticipate classroom problems such as motivation, discipline, and student failure to listen. These kinds of problems are not necessarily unique to the urban school. They are usually attributable to teacher inadequacy: inadequate preparation of the classroom environment, inefficient use of teacher time, ineffective teaching. Classroom problems relate not only to the teacher's methodological skills but to managerial and organizational skills as well.

Motivation

Motivation is one of the most talked-about problems in urban schools. It is the point of view of this text that urban students can be motivated just as other students are motivated, as long as the teacher plans motivating experiences, offers students meaningful choices, recognizes signs of student growth, and encourages students by listening to them and offering accepting types of comments. All individuals are motivated in one or all of the following ways: social motivation, ego-integrative motivation, cognitive motivation. Social motivation has to do with the learner's relationship with others in the classroom, school and community; ego motivation refers to the learner's own self needs and desire to achieve; cognitive motivation refers to the motivating circumstances of the learning task itself.

The competent urban teacher expects students to learn, but is aware of students' special needs and interests. Maslow's actualization theory may be relevant to the urban student's motivational readiness to *seek* learning. Maslow developed a hierarchy of behavioral needs that he believed energized and directed human behavior. In order of importance, the needs were: (1) physiological needs, (2) safety needs, (3) love and belonging needs, (4) esteem needs, (5) self-actualization needs, (6) the desires to know and understand. According to the theory, needs must be satisfied sequentially.[29]

Since the desire to know and to understand is last, cognitive motivation (the learning task, of and for itself) may not be particularly effective in an inner city classroom. Social and ego types of motivation often provide better beginnings. Since children are primarily self-centered, motivation that applies to themselves and to their life style is much more interesting. The effective teacher chooses experiences that are relevant to students. Mr. Blakely planned his teaching strategy with a reference to the group of men and women waiting on a street corner to be employed. His students had intimate acquaintanceship with the problems of unemployment and the circumstance of waiting and hoping for a job. The motivation was *relevant* because it *connected* the student's reality with the classroom lesson.

It is not true that the urban student must be cajoled into learning; learning should be fun and the teacher can make it so. Most students learn more efficiently when activities are paced, active-passive sequenced. Urban students respond positively to action-oriented lessons. They respond to options in the class-room environment that allow them to assert themselves and choose an activity of self-interest. They respond to activities that provide feedback; thus self-scoring activities have potential in the development of self-concept.

The urban teacher who uses a "centers" approach to reading reinforcement provides choices and is infinitely more motivating to the urban student than the teacher who hands the student a worksheet to practice skills. Reading centers could include these centers:

A library center	The children read and practice a skill in the library area.
A listening center	The children listen to a story and then are directed to a follow-up exercise.
A viewing center	Students watch a filmstrip and are directed to record their observations.
A phonics center	This center may have a language-master machine and students may model sounds.
A read-along center	Students may read to each other.
A reinforcement game center	Students "play" reading games to practice a skill.
A writing and dictation center	An aide provides dictation for students to practice listening and writing skills.

In a reading centers classroom, the students choose the center where they want to work. Each day they choose a different center. Reading becomes something to look forward to and social motivation begins to develop into cognitive motivation.

In a sixth-grade classroom I visited, the teacher motivated by using "props." The teacher came to class with a suitcase filled with summer clothes and several prescriptions. The children asked the teacher whether he was planning to leave town. The teacher said, "Yes, would you like to guess where?" The teacher then opened his suitcase and began to unpack. The students were fascinated. At first the room was dead quiet as the students thought; then they began to question the teacher. "How come you got summer clothes?" (It was winter.) "Why you taking bottles of medicine, Mr. Dawson? Can't you get them where you are going?" After many questions and after the teacher pulled down a classroom map and provided a globe for some students to examine, they began to consider climactic conditions and remote areas of the United States, Mexico, and South America. As the students began to develop their theories, it suddenly dawned upon them: "Mr. Dawson, we're havin' social studies aren't we? You been teasing us."

Organization and management skills

Mr. Dawson preplanned his motivation and he organized his classroom for the kinds of activities he believed would ensure student achievement. The teacher's skill in organizing a classroom for instruction will be readily apparent to children and visitors. Classroom organization has to do with the way the room looks—the bulletin boards, chalkboard, independent centers, equipment, storage of instructional materials, retrieval of materials, bookcases, and so on.

Management in the classroom refers to the teacher's procedural skills. Are students grouped appropriately for instruction? If instructional materials are needed, are they reachable or will the teacher need to leave the teaching area in order to obtain the materials? If there is to be a reinforcement exercise, is it ready? If equipment is to be used, is it available and in working order? Can children find their own materials? If a classroom discussion is to be used to evaluate learning, has a system been developed whereby students arrange their chairs so that they can see and hear one another?

Students should assist in the development of classroom procedures and in the organization of their classroom. Some bulletin boards can be the responsibility of students. Classroom jobs can be distributed: windows, bookcases, monitor, game cupboard, audiovisual equipment, and so on. A record of classroom responsibilities should be available to remind students of their personal contribution to classroom organization and decorum. A classroom that is neat, attractive, and interesting motivates students to attend school and also develops group pride. Changing interest centers frequently is also important to maintain interest and motivation.

Discipline. Problems often develop in the classroom because the teacher has failed to establish needed routines, failed to organize the classroom for instruction, failed to motivate the students for learning, or failed to anticipate learning problems. Teacher and students each have expectations concerning proper classroom behavior. These expectations must be communicated in order to set up realistic standards and conditions for success. Teacher-student relationships should be based upon mutual honesty and respect. Teacher instructions and/or standards, if they are to be imposed upon students, ought to be direct and explicit. If students are expected to conform to a teacher-set standard of performance (neatness, promptness), then the expectation must be communicated directly to them:

> All lunches are to be stored in the closet.
>
> *vs.*
>
> Lunches are not supposed to be kept in desks.
>
> Do not sit on the tables.
>
> *vs.*
>
> Tables aren't for sitting on.
>
> Bill's group may line up at the door now to be excused.
>
> *vs.*
>
> Let's go to lunch, now. (And then the teacher ducks angrily as the whole class races for the door.)

Classroom standards are necessary to clarify instructional and routine items. What should students do if they fail to understand an assignment? How may they obtain assistance or communicate their problem to the teacher? A system for communication should be established. Routines need to be established for the following typical situations: sharpening a pencil, obtaining a drink, going to the lavatory, obtaining money to replace lost money, going to the lost and found, receiving first aid, leaving the classroom for any reason. Students dislike being surprised by either a new teacher or new regulations; they respond to definite and consistent standards.

Some behavioral problems, such as fighting, arrogance, profanity, or withdrawal, are best dealt with by providing students with a system for "blowing off steam." Acceptance of students' off-days, familiarity with their personal problems, or merely saying to the misbehaving student "OK, sometimes we all feel that way" or, "Would it help if you took a walk by yourself until you feel ready to come back and work?" are all effective. Sometimes a run around the track will release a student's hostility and allow him to face the rest of the day. Perhaps the most important point is that the teacher must not *assume* a personal affront is intended by the student's behavior. Classroom misbehavior may be a result of a teacher response or action, but it may also occur as a result of home, peer, or playground problems. Behavior is contagious in the classroom; therefore, the teacher should be circumspect in dealing with misbehavior. Talking quietly and without expressing undue emotion with the misbehaving student will often accomplish a great deal more in terms of mutual understanding and respect than if the teacher magnified the issue in front of the whole class.

Modeling. This technique can be used to influence behavior. The teacher dealing with the misbehaving student exhibits respect for the student (even though he does not accept the misbehavior). The purpose of modeling is to provide students with an example (a mirror) of appropriate behavior. Modeling differs from reinforcement because reinforcement is dependent upon student manifestation of the desired behavior; reinforcement assumes that the teacher will always be "right there" at the appropriate moment *and* that the teacher will recognize the appropriate behavior when it is displayed. Modeling *induces* appropriate behavior, and it is not dependent upon a one-to-one relationship of teacher to child.

A major consideration of the social psychologists who have studied the imitative behavior of young children is that quite often the child pantomimes, imitates, or models others' behavior even when no reward or inducement is given. Thus, it is apparent that the need for reinforcement to encourage behavior is not always a necessity. It is this consideration that has led urban teachers to consider the significance of modeling in the classroom.

> . . . (a) model can influence the child's behavior in two ways: first, by doing something which the child has never experienced before, thus inducing him to engage in new patterns of behavior; second, by doing something already in the child's repertoire, thus inducing him to engage in this particular behavior rather than in some other activity.[30]

To utilize modeling as an instructional technique, the urban teacher analyzes behavior in order to discover:

Is the desired behavior within the behavioral repertoire of the learner? (Has the student had the experience to reproduce the behavior?)

Is the learner physically able to perform the desired behavior? (If the teacher desires to elicit a specific sound from the student, does he hear it accurately?)

If the answers to both questions were "yes," then the teacher could consider the use of modeling as a technique to motivate the desired behavior. Waller and Gaa identified three conditions that affect modeling: the characteristics of the student, the characteristics of the desired behavior, and the characteristics of the model.[31]

The first condition (the characteristics of the student) is related to the student's psychological development. Does he have the capacity to perform the desired behavior and is he motivated to perform? The second condition (the characteristics of the desired behavior) is related to the act itself. If the act is complex, then it is desirable to break it down into simpler components of behavior. Each must be identified by the model and taught as a separate act. The relationship of one component to the next is important and must be identified in a sequential manner. Again, the relationship to foreign language teaching is illustrative. The foreign language student needs to be taught simple (present tense) constructs first, before he is taught to transform sentences or is expected to enlarge his vocabulary.

The third condition of the modeling process is related to the effectiveness of the model. Bronfenbrenner related seven characteristics of the model that influenced the effectiveness of the modeling process:

1. If the student perceives the model as possessing a high degree of competence, status, and control over resources within the learning situation, then the model will have greater influence.
2. If the model is perceived by the student as someone who is *important to him,* then the power of the model will increase.
3. Those individuals who play major roles in the student's life (parents, teachers, close friends, peers, siblings) because they offer support and control of his environment will in all likelihood be the most influential models.
4. To the extent that the student perceives the model as being "like himself," the power of the model will increase correspondingly. It is for this reason that teachers born and bred in the ghetto or the barrio have greater potential as models.
5. If the desired behavior is demonstrated by several "influential" models, it will have greater force than if exhibited by one model. It is for this reason that multi-aged teaching has great potential in the urban school.
6. Since the student desires to conform to his family and his peer group, influence of the model will increase if he exhibits a behavior conspicuous to the student's aspired group. Again, the importance of the student's own peer group cannot be underestimated.
7. To the extent that the student perceives the desired behavior as contributing (being consequential) to the model's pleasurable outcomes, then the student will be more likely to perform the desired behavior. (If the model were punished for the performance of the behavior, it would inhibit the performance of the behavior by the student.)[32]

Some urban teachers combine reinforcement theory with modeling to design teaching strategies for language arts, social studies, and science. To maximize the effect of modeling and reinforcement, the teacher can utilize small-group teaching to facilitate learning. Small-group teaching strategies are particularly appropriate because the teacher can reinforce the student-subject's peer group, which then acts as the influential model. By rewarding the peer group for exhibiting the desired behavior, the teacher is increasing the frequency of that behavior in the student-subject.

Rod never spoke in class of his own volition. When asked a question by the teacher, he would answer in a monotone and with as few words as possible. Rod was the student-subject. The desired behavior was to develop communication skills and increase his class participation. The teacher divided the class into small groups. Rod was with four other students (his friends) who were considered moderate in their class participation and in their language skills.

Each group was given a small map of the city. Each map had a designated mark (library, hospital, park). The groups were told to plan the safest route from school to the designated place on their map. As the groups discussed their problem, the teacher circulated and offered praise. Sometimes the teacher would stop the whole class to allow a group to share where they were going and how they planned to travel. The teacher continually reinforced the contributor's presentation with remarks such as: "Good thinking; you remembered that the R bus travels down Raymond Street."

In this way the teacher rewarded the participatory behavior of Rod's peers. Since Rod was able to identify with his peers, particularly his own group, they served as appropriate models to induce Rod to communicate and to participate.

The teacher's modeling influence has also been studied by Yando and Kagan to investigate the effect of teacher tempo on student response time. Since a reflective response pattern facilitates reading progress, Yando and Kagan were interested in whether or not student response time could be modified. Their subjects were first-grade students and teachers. Both teachers and students were tested to identify reflective and impulsive responders.

The primary question [the researchers] asked of the data was whether changes in response time or errors over the 7–8 month period were related to membership in the classroom of an impulsive or a reflective female teacher.[33]

The results of the investigation revealed that "children who showed the largest increases in response time were in the classroom of highly experienced reflective teachers."[34] The researchers concluded that although error scores were not necessarily altered, response time was modifiable. They also concluded that the school rewards reflectivity more consistently than impulsivity, and that response time is mediated by both modeling effects and by direct reinforcement.

Implications of the research suggest the possibility of matching teachers to students to encourage a reflective disposition. The researchers suggested specific training in scanning strategies during reading.

Yando and Kagan noted that since boys have greater difficulties in reading than girls, it may be attributable to impulsiveness and that consideration should be given to placing boys in the classrooms of reflective teachers.

The conference. Meeting with students individually is another technique that successful teachers are using to provide assurance and a meaningful evaluative system for students. The conference system allows the teacher to relate to the student individually instead of directing the student's progress as a member of a group. In the final analysis the teacher must confront each student individually if he is to evaluate student progress, but in some classrooms students never get the opportunity to sit down with the teacher alone and find out what is and what ought to be. The teacher-student conference can yield information not only about learning achievement, but also about other "typical" problems: motivation, discipline, student self-concept. Using the conference technique, urban teachers are conveying encouragement and optimism to their students and thereby providing needed motivation.

Listening. By listening to students (and this differs from "hearing"), teachers are able to demonstrate respect, interest, honesty. The teacher who is a good listener recognizes how the student feels or how the student perceived the situation. She tries to convey to the student that she respects him, no matter what happened, and that she is empathetic and sensitive to the student's feelings. By being a good listener, she is motivating the student to become an intelligent listener, and she is reinforcing listening behavior. The teacher is saying, albeit nonverbally, "I have time to listen to you; you are important." By so doing, the teacher has found another means to produce ego-satisfying behaviors.

Some teacher comments, stated nonjudgmentally, that exhibit teacher listening behavior are of the following types:

"I think I understand."
"OK."
"What else happened?"
"How did you feel about that?"
"Tell me about it."
"I know just how you felt."
"That is one possible interpretation."
"You were feeling scared after that happened."

Opportunity to listen to students individually occurs often when students enter the room, sometimes between subjects or on the playground, and with the utilization of the conference technique. Mr. Jordan, in the beginning of this chapter, made it a practice to greet each student at the classroom door and speak individually to his students at that time; Mr. Roxbury toured his classroom and spoke to students as they put their books down and became "settled." Teachers in the elementary school can find many opportunities to listen in the course of the school day.

Questioning. Successful teachers develop a variety of questioning behaviors. Questioning skills include clarification tactics, refocusing tactics, redirecting, and the use of silence as a teaching technique.

There are three somewhat indistinct categories of clarification tactics: acceptance statements followed by a question, clarification of instructions, and value-focusing questions. *Clarification and offering acceptance:* "When you said that Joe was a thief, did you mean that you were not treated in an honest manner?" (The teacher is proving that he is listening and accepting what the student has said, but is asking the student to clarify his concept.) "I think I understand what you said, but could you explain what you mean by enslavement?" (Again, the teacher is accepting and using the student's own concept, but is asking for an expanded version of the story.) *Clarification of instructions:* This happens quite often in the classroom when students ask for additional explanation of directions or a restatement of a problem. The teacher may respond with, "What do you think is meant by the term agitator? Do you think that you may need to define that term before you get on with the problem?" In a sense the teacher is restructuring the lesson in order to clarify the meaning to the students. Or, the teacher might handle the problem in this way: "Are you telling us that we need to find out the causes of the war before we can investigate the consequences?" *Clarification through value-focusing questions:* Questions focus on students' feelings, perceptions of reality, concept of alternative actions: "Jim, you said that you were upset about the election. Did you mean that you were personally, physically, upset about the outcome of the election?" "May, you said that you had witnessed the fight on the playground. Would you tell me your version of how it began?"

Value questions are most effective when they focus upon the content and force students to express an opinion, to consider alternatives, or to make a decision. The following provides a content illustration of value questioning:

> Sojo, an Indian boy of twelve, was expected to hunt and kill rabbits for his tribe. But Sojo hid when his friends went on a hunting expedition. His friends discovered that he had purposely avoided the hunt. If you were Sojo, what explanation would you make to your friends? What do you think will happen when you want to play with your friends? How do you think Sojo's father will feel about Sojo's actions?

As urban specialist teachers work with small groups of students, they sometimes find that a group is going off in the wrong direction. It therefore becomes necessary to *refocus* their thinking so that they will be able to study the pertinent issue or problem. Knowledge of subject matter content and the processes by which it is to be learned are vital if the teacher is to use this technique.

> The students needed to identify the reasons why groups of people migrate from one area or country to another. The students had assumed that all immigrants from Mexico were poor, rural farmers. The teacher commented, "What do you know about Mexican political leadership during the years 1876–1911? What happened to those people who did not favor the political leadership?"

Redirection is a questioning technique that is very useful in the urban classroom to encourage student participation. Having asked a question, the teacher listens to one student's response and then questions, "What do you think about that, Bill?" "Uh, huh!" "And you?" The teacher continues to look around at different students, encouraging them to express an opinion. The teacher does not give away his own viewpoint, nor does he repeat a previous statement.

A student has just posed the solution to a problem or expressed a point of view. Instead of asking another question or accepting the student's statement, the teacher waits for others to offer additions, comments, or new solutions. The secure teacher "waits the students out" and uses *silence* to continue the reflective act. He feels no need to "fill" every silent period. The students soon realize that they are still responsible for the problem.

Positive, direct, yet flexible teacher behaviors ensure student motivation, achievement, and success. The urban teacher plans *ego-satisfying* activities and communicates to students that sometimes:

"It's OK to fail." Every individual learns through experimentation, trial and error.

"It's OK to *not* understand." The teacher clarifies instructions and restates them in a variety of ways. Alternate activities, concrete and direct experiences are provided.

It's even OK to ask: "Am I doing OK?" The urban student needs reassurance; the urban teacher offers only meaningful praise, positive comments and reinforcement.

"It's OK to show friends your success." Behavior is contagious and the urban teacher expects that all students will acquire successful behaviors.

The urban teacher plans activities that will provoke students to inquire and to solve problems through *learner-assertive* behaviors. The teacher may develop some one-lesson or short-term tasks for an individual or a small group of students. For instance, how many college basketball stars playing in the Pac Eight conference this year were drafted by a professional basketball team? The teacher also provides the appropriate resource materials. (The sports section during the "draft" period always prints the information.) The teacher permits students to go to the library to interview resource people. The student must have the opportunity to "imitate" or model appropriate research behavior. The tasks are designed to develop locational skills and valuing skills. The teacher provides "time" and "space" for students to achieve goals. If the wherewithal is not provided, the student will become frustrated and decide that the teacher is a phony. The teacher provides for an evaluation. "What was your problem task?" "How did you try to solve your problem? What did you do?" "Who helped you?" "What questions did you ask?" "What difficulties did you have?" "How can we help you?" "Who has an idea?" "Did you come to a decision (conclusion, solution)?" "What will you do next?"

By planning purposeful activities that are both skill-oriented and content-focused, the teacher provides opportunity for individual progress and *independent-oriented* behavior.

> Knowing that students are often in fear of their classmates ("I don't want to look dumb!"), the teacher provides activities that encourage individual growth and creativity.

> Students are invited to ask questions and to write their questions down. Students are taught to sequence their questions to yield the desired information. (Many students will not ask questions when the whole class works together due to embarrassment and/or fear of "dumbness.")

> Students are asked to define the limits of their task. "What do you expect to accomplish?" "What do you want to do?" "How far will you go today?" "Will you need help?" "Will you tell me when you need help?" "What materials will you need?" "Will you share your accomplishment, project, book when you have finished?"

Recognizing that students need opportunities to develop cooperative behaviors as well as the need to hear conflicting points of view, the teacher provides *group-satisfying* activities.

> Whenever possible, the teacher assigns students to groups based upon *heterogeneity*. The teacher ensures that each student will have opportunity to be both a leader and a participant.

> Tasks, problems, or projects are developed that provoke discussion, disagreement, the need to listen, and the need to express. Some problems are designed to force students to "search out" new information.

The group task is designed to induce compromising and rational decision making.

The teacher provides time for groups to listen to each other and to see the accomplishments of others. Students discover that each group may have a different orientation toward the task or problem.

Each group develops camaraderie in work activity and a sense of intimacy. Friendship and group spirit are developed.

Summary: A Consideration of Teacher/Parent Relations

In this chapter we have reviewed some of the research about teacher personality, attitude, and expectations and their concomitant effect on leadership and function in the classroom. The specificity of the research is such that both the lay public and the profession accept the probability that the confident, secure teacher generates confidence and self-esteem in students. A teacher's self-image affects all relationships: within the classroom, with colleagues, with the community. If the teacher is a true professional, then he subscribes to the concept that the student is his client. Relationships with parents are also client-oriented. Some parents in urban areas have never attended an American school; others have had minimal experiences; still others are fully "at home" in the school. The teacher's sensitivity and perception regarding the feelings of his clients as they come to him for assistance will be reflected by what he says, how he listens, and the ways in which he reacts to parents and students.

In a true professional-client relationship, all personal insights, conversations, diagnoses, and treatment are private. Sometimes in the school environment this type of relationship is breached, violated over the luncheon table or forgotten on a playground tour. But the urban specialist teacher is sensitive to and respectful of his clients' feelings; he is bound by the ethics of the professional relationship.

The new urban teacher professional sometimes seeks out his clients (parents) in order to develop better relationships and to combat problems of vandalism and truancy. The following examples are typical:

> Teachers in one Los Angeles inner city school put aside a Saturday to have a "dig-in." Many of the teachers, carrying shovels, hoes and other garden equipment, returned to school to dig around trees and shrubs and to do some planting. Soon members of the community wandered over to find out what was going on and before long both teachers and parents were digging and planting together.
>
> Later, over cups of coffee and beer, the talk turned from gar-

dening to vandalism. An agreement was reached among the community members present that this was "their school" and that they would be willing to watch and report acts involving entering the school grounds with an apparent intent of vandalism.

A high school administrator heard via the gossip underground that the Friday night football game would be host to a student riot. He picked up his phone and began to call parents, including the parents of students who were bused each day to the school. He directed his counselors and vice-principals to do the same.

All adults were admitted free to the football game that Friday night and every Friday night thereafter. There was no riot. The temptation to slug it out diminishes with parental observation and supervision.

In a junior high school, teachers and administrators began to wonder about the increasing absence factor for their "bused-in" students. Playing a hunch, they began to call parents to find out why the students were absent. The parents were shocked! In a majority of the cases, the students had left home each day to catch the bus but had in fact, to the parents' dismay, gone elsewhere to spend the day. Truancy decreased as a result of the teachers' and administrators' foresight.

Truancy in some urban areas is used by teachers as a "cop out" to absolve themselves from guilt for ineffective teaching. Because learning can be fun (and so is teaching), the really effective teacher makes decisions that will yield high success and achievement for his clients. Students encouraged by success want to come to school.

The teacher who is effective in the urban school is considered in this text a "specialist" in urban teaching, one who has developed specificity for teaching multicultured children and is cognizant of the range of strategic options through which teaching/learning goals can be accomplished.

The urban specialist may also develop a specialization within a subject field or for a specific age group or learning problem. A laboratory situation with a designed learning environment may be created to treat the problem or to develop what has become known as "preventive" teaching. Urban specialist teachers accept responsibility to develop their own potential through continuing education.

Urban teachers have developed tactical competencies and style in the classroom. They utilize flexible teaching methods for motivation and provide for alternative learning approaches. They are systematic in the arrangement of both details and the structuring of classroom routines. Teachers deal directly and specifically with classroom problems and express themselves explicitly to students. All relationships with students, parents, and colleagues are honest and respectful.

Notes

1. NORMAN E. WALLEN and ROBERT M. W. TRAVERS, "Analysis and Investigation of Teaching Methods," in *Handbook of Research on Teaching*, ed. N. L. Gage (Chicago: Rand McNally, 1963).

2. RONALD LIPPITT and RALPH K. WHITE, "The Social Climate of Children's Groups," in *Child Behavior and Development*, ed. Roger G. Barker, Jacob S. Kounin, and Herbert F. Wright (New York: McGraw-Hill, 1943).

3. High School Geography Project of the Association of American Geographers, *Geography in an Urban Age* (New York: Macmillan, 1966).

4. RICHARD C. ANDERSON, "Learning in Discussions: A Resume of the Authoritarian-Democratic Studies," in *Readings in the Social Psychology of Education*, ed. W. W. Charters, Jr., and N. L. Gage (Boston: Allyn and Bacon, 1963).

5. JOHN WITHALL, "The Development of a Technique for the Measurement of Social-Emotional Climate in Classrooms," *Journal of Experimental Education*, 17 (March 1949), 347–361.

6. NED A. FLANDERS, "Some Relationships Among Teacher Influence, Pupil Attitudes, and Achievement," in *Contemporary Research on Teacher Effectiveness*, ed. Bruce J. Biddle and William J. Elena (New York: Holt, Rinehart and Winston, 1963), pp. 196–231.

7. DAVID G. RYANS, *Characteristics of Teachers* (Washington, D.C.: American Council of Education, 1960).

8. P. KRANZ, W. WEBER, and K. FISHELL, "The Relationships Between Teacher Perception of Pupils and Teacher Behavior Towards Those Pupils." Paper delivered at the annual meeting of the American Educational Research Association, Minneapolis, 1970, as reported in *Psychological Concepts in the Classroom*, ed. Richard H. Coop and Kinnard White (New York: Harper & Row, 1974).

9. V. JONES, "The Influence of Teacher-Student Introversion, Achievement, and Similarity on Teacher-Student Dyadic Classroom Interactions." Unpublished doctoral dissertation, University of Texas at Austin, 1971, as reported by Thomas L. Good and Jere E. Brophy in *Psychological Concepts in the Classroom*, ed. Richard H. Coop and Kinnard White (New York: Harper & Row, 1974).

10. THOMAS L. GOOD and JERE E. BROPHY, "The Influence of Teachers' Attitudes and Expectations on Classroom Behavior," in *Psychological Concepts in the Classroom*, ed. Richard H. Coop and Kinnard White (New York: Harper & Row, 1974).

11. R. RIST, "Student Social Class and Teacher Expectations: The Self-fulfilling Prophecy in Ghetto Education," *Harvard Educational Review*, 40 (1970) 411–451.

12. ROBERT ROSENTHAL and LENORE JACOBSON, "Pygmalion in the Classroom," *Urban Review*, III (September 1968).

13. Peter and Carol Gumpert, "The Teacher as Pygmalion: Comments on the Psychology of Expectation," *Urban Review*, III (September 1968).

14. BRUCE JOYCE and MARSHA WEIL, *Models of Teaching* (Englewood Cliffs, N.J.: Prentice-Hall, 1972), p. 3.

15. DOLORES E. LITSINGER, *The Challenge of Teaching Mexican-American Students* (New York: American Book, 1973), p. 46.

16. ROBERT F. MAGER, *Developing Attitudes Toward Learning* (Palo Alto: Fearon Publishers, 1968), pp. 58–59.

17. ANNA S. OCHOA and RODNEY F. ALLEN, "Creative Teacher-Student Learning Experiences About the City," in *Teaching About Life in the City*, ed. Richard Wisniewski (Washington, D.C.: National Council for the Social Studies, 42nd Yearbook, 1972), p. 91.

18. ROGER E. JOHNSON, "The Relationship Between Social Studies and Reading," in *Social Studies Review*, fall 1973, pp. 24–29.

19. JOHANNA S. DESTEFANO and SHARON E. FOX, "Children's Oral Language Development: The Literature and Its Implications for Teachers," in *Language and the Language Arts*, ed. DeStefano and Fox (Boston: Little, Brown, 1974), p. 55.

20. Title VII is an amendment to the Elementary and Secondary Education Act of 1965.

21. "Supreme Court Orders Special Instruction for Chinese Pupils," *Los Angeles Times*, January 22, 1974.

22. HERSCHEL T. MANUEL, "Teaching a Second Language to Spanish-speaking Children of the Southwest," in *Teaching Multi-Cultural Populations*, ed. James C. Stone and Donald P. DeNevi (New York: Van Nostrand Reinhold, 1971), pp. 265–266.

23. CHARLES B. BRUSSELL, "Cognitive and Intellectual Functioning of Spanish-Speaking Children," paraphrasing Chavez, "Preserve Their Language Heritage," in *Childhood Education*, XXXIII (December 1956), pp. 165–186.

24. MILDRED R. DONOGHUE, *The Child and the English Language Arts* (Dubuque: Brown, 1971), pp. 423–424, and Roger W. Shay, "Bonnie and Clyde Tactics in English Teaching," *Florida FL Reporter*, VII (spring–summer 1969), 160–161.

25. *Knowledge of English Yields Success* is funded through the Elementary and Secondary Education Act, Title III, PL89–10 for Innovative and Exemplary Programs, rather than under the Bilingual Education Act, Title VII.

26. International Reading Association brochure, Newark, Delaware.

27. Head Start was initiated in 1965 for four-year-old children of poor socioeconomic background.

28. MENO PHILLIPS and MARSHALL SISCA, *Denker Avenue Community Elementary School: An Educational Statement* (Gardena, Calif., 1973).

29. ABRAHAM MASLOW, *Toward a Psychology of Being* (Princeton, N.J.: Van Nostrand, 1962).

30. URIE BRONFENBRENNER, *Two Worlds of Childhood: United States and U.S.S.R.* (New York: Russell Sage Foundation, 1970), p. 125.

31. PATRICIA WALLER and JOHN GAA, "Motivation in the Classroom," in *Psychological Concepts in the Classroom*, ed. Richard H. Coop and Kinnard White (New York: Harper & Row, 1974), pp. 151–191.

32. BRONFENBRENNER, *op. cit.*, pp. 130–139.

33. REGINA M. YANDO and JEROME KAGAN, "The Effect of Teacher Tempo on the Child," *Child Development*, 39 (1968), 30.

34. *Ibid.*, p. 33.

Workshop II

The workshop section focuses on the perceptions, decisions, and tactics of the classroom teacher. Each of the activities is designed to direct the reader to analyze what is happening in the classroom and why it is happening. Some of the activities have been developed to suggest self-evaluation and to encourage new directions for thinking and exploration.

If the reader does not have the opportunity to observe, participate, or teach in a classroom, many of these same activities may be accomplished while working (or observing others working) with young people in another setting, such as camping, scouting, Y activities, a neighborhood setting, or the after-school playground. If you are a classroom "participant," observer, or student teacher, you may find it advantageous to record a ten- or fifteen-minute teaching episode for evaluative purposes. As you listen to the teaching episode, evaluate the following:

Teacher talk (too little, just right, too much?)

Student talk (too little, just right, too much?)

Teacher's leadership role (democratic, authoritarian)

Teacher responses (judgmental, accepting, supportive)

Teaching purpose

Management skills

Since competence is developmental, practicing teaching or leadership behaviors (strategies, responses, organization) improves performance. Redoing an episode with a different group of children or even with the same children will develop and reinforce new behaviors.

Choosing School Success Behaviors for American Indian Students

OBJECTIVES: Develop understanding about Indian American students; choose appropriate behavioral goals; designate appropriate learner behavior.

DIRECTIONS: Read Louise Miller's ten behavioral tendencies of American Indian students, *but remember that the tendencies vary depending upon geographic location.*

Review the chart on school success-oriented behaviors (Figure 2.4).

Choose appropriate behavioral goals for each of the ten tendencies.

What learner activity (note Means to Achieve in Figure 2.4) would you choose to accomplish your goal(s)?

Louise Miller* identified ten behavioral tendencies about which teachers of American Indians should be knowledgeable; the tendencies may vary depending upon geographic location.

1. Understand that Indians and non-Indians have different referents and perceptions to humor. These are often antagonistic to each other. Indian humor may not be humorous to non-Indians. Indians' formalized joking relationships (teasing) and storytelling (make believe) are intrinsic to Indian culture. This perception of humor may be seen as troublesome and disruptive by non-Indians. The teacher should be aware that this is a possible source of cultural misinterpretation and conflict.

2. Understand that Indian students have respect for and respond to family authority; however, response by learners to school authorities tends to be fearful. Indians tend to withdraw when faced with school authority.

3. Understand that the Indian learner is taught at home to be independent and self-sufficient, generous, quiet, and dignified. The Indian child is taught to avoid boasting about achievements.

4. Understand that Indian students prefer to work at their own pace, and tend to resist group activities which are competitive in nature. Teachers must understand that the standard group instructional mode in schools produces predictable academic failure for Indian learners.

5. Understand that Indian children are taught to be quiet and dignified. They find it difficult to respond to the non-Indian because of built-up distrust. Status and position does not impress the Indian; each person is judged on personal merits.

6. Understand that Indian students are very sensitive to personal dignification requirements. Negative remarks about clothes, home, or anything pertaining to Indians produces withdrawal and negative feelings which become progressively more intense with age.

7. Understand that the Indian learner feels it is important to show what you are and what you can do, but not in a boastful way. Indians have special concerns with pride for being "an Indian." They have strong feelings about the superior culture of the Indian.

8. Understand that Indian pride is severely injured by the negative approach the school uses in dealing with the American Indian in history.

9. Understand the dislike of Indian learners for competition expected in group academic environments. They will resist and withdraw when pushed.

10. Understand why the Indian learner develops feelings of

* "A Need for Competency-Based Teacher Education for Native Americans," in *Multicultural Education*, ed. William A. Hunter (Washington, D.C.: American Association of Colleges for Teacher Education, 1974), pp. 235–236.

rejection starting in the lower grades, based on perceived rejection by non-Indian peers, by teachers, by authority figures, and by community.

Teaching Methods

OBJECTIVE: Read to gain information about flexible teaching approaches. Contrast methods suggested by the following works.

Ausubel, David P.: *The Psychology of Meaningful Verbal Learning* (New York: Grune & Stratton, 1963).

Bruner, Jerome S.: *The Process of Education* (New York: Vintage Books, 1960).

Massialas, Byron G., and C. Benjamin Cox: *Inquiry in Social Studies* (New York: McGraw-Hill, 1966), chap. V.

Postmand, Neil, and Charles Weingartner: *Teaching as a Subversive Activity* (New York: Delacorte Press, 1969), chap. III.

Sanders, Norris M.: "Changing Strategies of Instruction: Three Case Examples," in *Social Studies Curriculum Development . . . Prospects and Problems*, ed. Dorothy McClure Fraser, 39th Yearbook National Council Social Studies (Washington, D.C., 1969), pp. 167–170.

Community Profile: A Team Report

OBJECTIVE: To describe, compare, and analyze a school community in terms of cultural priorities, problems, interests, services available, and relationship to the larger community.

To develop understanding about the students you are to teach and to assist in the development of pertinent curriculum, prepare a community profile and culture report. Describe the school community. If possible, interview people who reside or work in the community. With at least two other team members, drive two miles in each direction around your school. To record your interviews, impressions, and observations, use a camera, taperecorder, personal drawings, and notes.

The following questions may serve as a guide to your observations. Be sure to add your own questions to this list. If you interview people in the community, record your questions.

1. Who lives in the community?
2. Describe the residential pattern.
3. Describe the natural and man-made environment of the community.
4. What businesses exist within the community?
5. What services are available to the residents of the community? (clinics, hospitals, recreation, transportation, police, fire department)

6. What businesses and services are noticeably absent?
7. In what ways are the businesses and/or services unique or appropriate for this particular community?
8. How are cultural preferences or priorities provided for in the community?
9. Identify any culturally oriented commemorative festivities that occur regularly in the community.
10. Identify businesses; public agencies; historical, recreational, and cultural sites; other facilities that would accommodate and be worthwhile for student field trips.
11. What kinds of work opportunities exist within the community?
12. Identify people in the community who could serve as resource persons in the classroom.
13. How does city government affect the community?
14. Identify problems within the community that relate to the larger community and/or government processes.
15. What special talents do you have that could be helpful to the community?

Student Evaluation

OBJECTIVE: To observe and evaluate student behavior.

Choose a specific subject and then rank the students in the classroom from high to low.

Describe three nontest means to become acquainted with students. Identify the students' grade level or subject field.

Student Evaluation

OBJECTIVE: Self-evaluate objectivity.

Choose the same subject field: Rank the students from high to low, but this time use objective evidence.

Student	Evidence

Teaching Style

OBJECTIVES: Identify leadership behavior; compare teaching styles; choose personal teaching style; self-evaluate.

Mr. Jordan and Mr. Roxbury demonstrated different strategies or models of teaching. Mr. Jordan used the lecture method to achieve his teaching objectives; Mr. Roxbury used group interaction and a simulation to achieve his goals. Both teachers were successful. As you review the two incidents, examine the classroom organization and management techniques used by the two teachers.

> How would you describe the leadership behavior of the two teachers?
>
> Is there any similarity in the way in which each teacher addressed his students?
>
> Do you think Mr. Jordan and Mr. Roxbury are self-confident individuals?
>
> Which strategy for teaching would you prefer to use?
>
> In what ways would your choice of teaching strategy reflect your personality characteristics?

The Teacher's Classroom Role

OBJECTIVE: Read to gain knowledge about the teacher's classroom role.

Contrast the skill needs of students experiencing expository teaching with the skill needs of students experiencing inquiry methodology. How does the role of the teacher change?

Amidon, Edmund, and Ned A. Flanders: *The Role of the Teacher in the Classroom*, rev. ed. (Minneapolis: Association for Productive Teaching 1967).

Elin, R. J.: "Listening: Neglected and Forgotten in the Classroom," *Elementary English* 49 (February 1972), 230.232.

Kohl, Herbert R.: *The Open Classroom: A Practical Guide to a New Way of Teaching* (New York: New York Review, 1970).

Massialas, Byron G., and Jack Zevin: *Creative Encounters in the Classroom* (New York: Wiley, 1967), pp. 23–26.

Mr. Blakely's Teaching Episode

OBJECTIVE: Identify interrelated subject fields; apply knowledge of curriculum to develop teaching objectives; self-evaluate objectives with others.

Mr. Blakely's primary goal related to the teaching of social studies. What other subjects were interrelated as Mr. Blakely identified the learning requirements? List the supportive instructional materials the students would need to accomplish the objective. How many additional objectives can you identify that are subsumed by Mr. Blakely's performance objective? Compare your list with that of a colleague or classmate.

Teachers' Questioning Skills

OBJECTIVE: Read to gain knowledge about the art of questioning. Why is it important to sequence questions?

Gall, Meredith D.: "The Use of Questions in Teaching," *Review of Educational Research*, 40 (December 1970), 707–721.
Sanders, Norris: *Classroom Questions: What Kinds?* (New York: Harper & Row, 1966).

Value Questioning

OBJECTIVES: Gain knowledge about effective questioning techniques; develop competence in forming value questions through practice.

Review the paragraph about Sojo and the value questions that follow it.

Assume that you are teaching high school students in an urban classroom. The following paragraph appeared in your local newspaper. What kinds of value questions could you ask to initiate a discussion about the news item?

> Juvenile delinquents commit 50 percent of all the city's crimes against property. Most of the juvenile delinquents live in the inner city. These young people believe that laws were made to protect the rich, not the poor. Many juvenile delinquents progress from minor crimes and misdemeanors to committing felonies because the juvenile court system does not punish them sufficiently.

Analysis of Specialized Programs

OBJECTIVES: Observe specialized programs in the school; observe and describe role of teacher specialist; analyze contributions and deficiencies of program.

1. Name the program or facility (ESL, math).
2. Identify the resource person or team. Describe duties.
3. Describe the learning environment. List equipment and instructional materials.
4. Who uses the environment, materials, equipment? (For whom was it designed?)
5. How does the program meet the specific needs for which it was designed?
6. How could you improve the program? List specific materials, resources, and techniques.

Strategy and Learning Environment Analysis

OBJECTIVES: Identify the objective of a teaching episode; describe teacher and student behaviors.

Identify the skill or subject being taught. *Describe* the teaching strategy, grouping pattern for students, and degree of teacher control of the learning environment. For assistance and review, refer to the chart identified strategy options and learning environments.

Teaching strategy	*Grouping pattern*	*Learning environment*

For the same lesson, identify the required teacher behaviors. Refer to the chart described environments and teacher behaviors for assistance.

Environment	*Teacher behavior*

Teaching Episode Evaluation

OBJECTIVES: Identify the objective of a teaching episode; describe teacher and student behaviors; describe instructional materials and classroom environment; evaluate effectiveness of episode in terms of the teaching objective; prescribe appropriate follow-up lesson.

Describe a teaching episode. Provide information relating to the following:

Identify the subject or skill being taught.

How were the students grouped for instruction?

List and describe the teacher behaviors during each of the three stages: motivation, development, evaluation.

List and describe the learner behaviors during each of the three stages.

How were the activities designed to accomplish ego-satisfying, learner-assertive, independent-oriented or group-satisfying behaviors?

State the teaching objective(s).

Describe the teaching strategy and the teacher's leadership role.

List and describe the instructional materials and equipment.

Rate the accomplishment of the objective(s).

What do you think should happen next in terms of a follow-up lesson?

School and Classroom Management Devices

OBJECTIVES: Develop personal observation skills of classroom management devices; evaluate devices in terms of classroom need and appropriateness.

Identify school and classroom management techniques utilized at the school where you are teaching or participating. The following questions may suggest areas of inquiry.

What happens when a student is late?

What happens when a student is absent and then returns to school? What is the process for readmission?

How do the students walk to and from their classroom(s)? in lines, in groups, talking, silent?

May students *choose* recreational activities during lunch and recess?

What happens if students forget homework, textbooks, or instructional materials?

What happens if a child feels ill during class?

Is there a dress code for students? Do you feel that it is realistic?

What happens when a student misbehaves on the playground or in the hall or classroom?

Are there clubs, school status groups, or athletic groups available? How do the students join these groups?

May parents visit in the classroom?

Do students ask questions of the teacher in the classroom? Do students direct questions to each other? Are questions and talk encouraged?

Do students work in groups or always alone?

Are students encouraged to compete with one another? how?

Are students encouraged to assist each other? how?

When students finish a work assignment, are they free to move about the classroom and choose another activity?

What is the process for allowing a student to go to the bathroom?

During a classroom discussion, do students speak freely?

If a student breaks a pencil, may he or she get up and sharpen it?

What happens if the student needs a new sheet of paper?

May a student obtain a drink of water if there is a fountain in the room?

Teacher-Parent Relations

OBJECTIVES: Describe teacher-parent interaction; identify means to facilitate cooperation and understanding.

How do teachers and parents become acquainted at your school?

What activities encourage parental involvement at school?

Describe three ways in which teachers could *initiate parental* cooperation and assistance.

Identify the ethnic/cultural population of your classroom.

Enumerate learning experiences that could incorporate cultural/ ethnic priorities.

Evaluate Instructional Materials

OBJECTIVES: Evaluate instructional materials in terms of cultural diversity, relevance to students, contribution to subject field and accuracy; develop ideas to improve instructional materials for classroom use.

Do the materials reflect cultural and racial diversity?

Do the materials reflect contemporary society as your students experience it?

Do the materials reflect the diversity of roles as fulfilled by minority peoples, both male and female?

Is the portrayal of "roles" restricted by tradition or reflective of modern society?

Is the portrayal of minority groups restricted to the root culture or representative of the mainstream and life style of the modern United States?

Is there a full range of vocational options represented?

If occupations and aspirations are discussed, are the choices and constraints realistic?

To what extent are technological achievements and developments described accurately?

Are the contributions of minority Americans discussed accurately and prominently?

Do the materials reflect the range of human emotions expressed by all people and both sexes?

If you were a textbook author, how would you improve the instructional materials?

Techniques for Ensuring Student Achievement

OBJECTIVE: **Self-evaluate understanding of text materials related to verbal teaching techniques.**

Refer to the text for assistance, then write an illustration of each of the following as you analyze the teaching episode.

1. An "accepting" teacher comment
2. A "clarifying" teacher question
3. A teacher comment that clarifies instructions
4. A value-focused question
5. A refocusing teacher comment
6. Redirection as a teaching technique

The students were studying about problems of cities. The teacher showed the students three pictures: a city street clogged by traffic, city buildings covered by a blanket of smog, a portion of the inner city littered with waste. The following discussion ensued:

Can you identify some problems of our cities? (1)*
SUSAN. Smog.
JEAN. Litter.
RED. Too much junk.
BILL. Pollution is ruining everything.

Bill, you said that pollution is ruining everything. Do you believe that pollution is spoiling our way of life? *(2)*
BILL. I think that pollution is wrecking our streets, our plants, and our parks. Pretty soon we won't even be able to enjoy a vacation.
MARY. I don't understand why pollution would wreck our vacations!

* Each teacher comment is numbered to enable you to check your answers.

Perhaps we need to define the term pollution. Who can explain it? (3)
JUAN. It means to spoil.

Any other ideas? Jill? (4)
JILL. Well, it means contamination.

Anyone else? (5)
TED. I guess it means unclean.

Let's go back to Bill's comment about vacations. What kinds of pollution are we exposed to and why would pollution spoil our recreation? (6)
SUSAN. Well there's air pollution.
MARIA. And water pollution.
JEAN. I suppose that picture about litter is another type of pollution.

Yes, that might be called waste pollution. (7)

After you have identified each of the six techniques by reading the teaching episode and referring to the text explanations, you may check each teacher comment by using the key.

Key to teacher comments

1. A "clarifying" teacher question
2. Clarification through a value-focused question
3. Clarification of instructions
4. Redirection
5. Redirection
6. Refocusing
7. Accepting

Accepting Teacher Comments

OBJECTIVE: Apply knowledge of verbal teaching techniques.

Write an accepting teacher comment (statement or value question) to respond to the following episodes.

1. (Tommy) "When I went home yesterday the Thugs gang beat me up. What should I do?"
2. As the teacher walked into the room, he saw a small group of students clustered together. They were conversing in loud voices. Suddenly one of the students noticed the teacher. All the students glanced up at the teacher; then, they closed the circle of their group and continued to talk in lowered voices.
3. The child was new to the class and glanced around hesitantly. He seemed fearful and stood just inside the classroom door. The teacher approached him and said:
4. Jim did not have his homework. It was the second time in three

days that he had failed to turn it in. The teacher felt angry and defeated, but did not show it as she said:

5. Yesterday Sheila failed her math test. Today she would not open the book to do her assignment. She never raised her hand to ask questions.

Interaction Exercise 2

OBJECTIVES: Self-evaluate understanding of text materials through classroom observation; describe a teacher's leadership style and teaching tactics, identifying evidence and effect on students.

What effect does the teacher's leadership style have on students? Cite the evidence.

Teacher's leadership style	Evidence	Effect on students

To what extent did the teacher use special techniques or tactics to facilitate instruction? Cite the evidence.

Teacher tactics	Evidence	Effect on students

Bill Green Incident

OBJECTIVE: Self-evaluate own perceptions and objectivity.

Bill Green, a skinny black boy of eleven, was in the fifth grade. It was the end of the school day. He gathered his books in front of him and with a slight smile on his face, glanced around at his classmates, then raced from the room. On the way home, he pushed a girl classmate, upsetting her books and making her fall. Two other classmates pursued him. He crossed the first street by dodging and darting between parked cars, ignoring the traffic light. In the second block, he upset an older woman who was carrying groceries. He did not stop to help her. He arrived home breathless and exhausted. There was no one at home to greet him.

DIRECTIONS: Write a brief description of Bill Green and his actions. Assign motives for Bill's actions. (Why did Bill behave as he did?) Predict what will happen the next day at school. (Pretend that you are the teacher. What will you do about the Bill Green incident?)

Check your perception and objectivity

1. Does a person's behavior have more than one explanation? What were some of the explanations for Bill's behavior? (Did your response to the second question offer a variety of explanations?)
2. How can you as the classroom teacher find out the cause of Bill's behavior? (Did your response to the prediction question offer different strategies for eliciting the information?)
3. Do you think Bill's behavior was intentional or accidental? (Did you differentiate between the two in your response to the first question?)
4. What are some possible events that might have caused Bill to react in the way that he did? (Did you consider these possibilities in your description?)
5. How will knowing the cause of Bill's behavior assist you?
6. What differences exist among observation of behavior, inference about behavior, and interpretation of behavior? (Did you differentiate in your description and consider those differences in your prediction about the following school day?)
7. What values might influence your observation, inferences, and interpretation of behavior in this story? (What bothers you about Bill's actions?
8. What nonverbal information did the incident give you? (Did you include the nonverbal information in your description?) *Key:* skin color, smile, age, grade, time, glance, sense of urgency, no person to greet Bill at home.

Transitional Neighborhood

OBJECTIVES: Recognize and identify stereotyped thinking; develop empathy and perspective about appropriate teaching behaviors.

A group of parents from the 77th Street School presented a list of demands to the board of education. Heading the list was the firing of one third-grade teacher. The 77th Street School serves an area described as "transitional." Caucasians are moving out and blacks are moving in. The school population is small, usually about 575 students. Seldom are there more than two classrooms to a grade level.

Teaching third grade at the 77th Street School is Ms. Jones, a two-year probationary teacher, and Mr. Blaise, a ten-year man. Both are Caucasian. In the parents' words, the problem is that "In Mr. Blaise's room the children aren't learning." They point to recently published reading scores, which indicate that for a five-month period Ms. Jones's class progressed from a 2.7 grade placement in reading comprehension to an average of 3.1, whereas Mr. Blaise's group deteriorated from 2.6 to 2.4.

The school board decided to interview the two teachers.

Mr. Blaise's case

1. His students had an average IQ of 88. He described the children as being culturally deprived. Their homes lacked books. They seldom heard their parents discuss anything. They had many psychological problems.
2. He believed that the children should be realistically prepared for the role they would take in society. They should not be frustrated by studies that demanded more than they were capable of achieving. "It was a teacher's duty to know his students' capacity."
3. He used forceful discipline in his classroom. "The children only respect you if you give them what they're used to." Children need to learn certain standards. Since they don't learn at home, the school should teach them to be neat and clean. They need to learn to obey, be punctual, and quiet in the classroom.

Ms. Jones's case

1. She was not really sure what the average IQ was in her classroom—"probably about 100, but IQ was really not so important." She knew that all the children in her room could learn.
2. She disliked rigid grouping and often used groups flexibly to teach reading and arithmetic. She wasn't concerned with ultimate goals in adulthood for the children, but thought that they should all learn to think and how to get along with each other.
3. She was worried that she didn't discipline the children as well as Mr. Blaise. "They are often noisy and excited." She thought that "It was a teacher's duty to like kids and get them to like you."

Why should Ms. Jones's class progress while Mr. Blaise's class deteriorated?

What should the school board do?

If you were a parent of a child in Mr. Blaise's class, what would you do?

The urban community

What can educators do? We can start by building just and equitable conditions in schools now. We can have respect and regard for students. We can develop programs designed to confront social ills. We can stop teaching students to conform. We can do more than just teach students to cope with the world as it is. We can teach them to question, to become skillful in bringing about political and social change. We can develop their (and our own) social consciences.[1]

Throughout the United States, parents are demanding quality education for all children. Teachers are confronted with challenges to differentiate instruction while meeting a commonality of needs, to develop self- and group-identity goals without limiting access to the majority society. Some Americans are protesting limited access to the opportunities of citizenship. Teachers must meet these challenges in urban and suburban schools, but the need is often greater and the problems more blatant in the urban environment. In this chapter the voices of the urban community, its goals, problems, and lack of unanimity, will be discussed.

Community and Culture

Sociologists sometimes define *community* as people who live in close proximity to one another and who share a likemindedness about common aspects of life, such as shared knowledge, goals, beliefs, and aspirations. But the urban community is many communities in terms of racial and cultural background and socioeconomic level. What urban students have in common is their bicultural way of life. For even though the urban student may be cultured in a typically "American" style, in an Indian tradition, a Mexican heritage, a black culture or Asian customs, he shares the urban culture. Therefore, only in a very limited sense can we discuss the urban student as a separate entity. *Culture* acts as a "blueprint for behavior."[2] It is the beliefs, attitudes, customs, rituals, language, and artifacts that represent the ways in which a people adjust to and deal with their environment and their society. Life in the city impresses upon and affects the ways of its residents, and in that way elicits some common cultural responses.

The urban school is more representative of the diversity of the American experience than any other institution. It is also more affected by the multicultural experience than any other institution. Historical perspective yields some information that seems to support the thesis that *the urban environment modifies sociocultural behavior*. Mumford[3] described a city as a magnet that attracted people from many different places. These people all had diverse interests and participated in diverse activities but shared in the work and the development of city institutions. As the people shared work activities, they also shared their own histories and in that way interacted and communicated. Just as the city attracted people from diverse places, so too did the city utilize people with diverse talents. As cities grew, work specializations and the division of labor also evolved.

The urbanization movement brought about some observable changes in the attitudes and behavior of the people involved. Church attendance among urban populations declined; activities considered "work" became separated from activities associated with the individual's personal life; relationships developed at work were considered separate and distinct from home relationships. With the separation of home and work came a preoccupation with anonymity. Urbanites seemed to protect themselves with a barrier or cloak of anonymity to preserve their personal selves and families from "other" contacts. Industrialization facilitated the growth of the modern city, but industrialization also resulted in a high concentration of populations, factories, slum housing, and lack of adequate municipal services. Problems related to urbanization include crime, housing, education, transportation, health, and employment.[4]

Many of the early immigrants to the city (1800–1920) were accustomed to city life, having lived in European cities. They migrated for political, economic, or religious reasons. These immigrants often had special talents that were needed in American cities. They had also enjoyed a stable family life and religious experience in their own society which they were able to transfer to their new environment. The early city immigrant was characterized as being purpose-oriented and deriving satisfaction from the attainment of specific goals. Many of these immigrants were members of the middle class society of Europe. In the rapidly expanding city environment, jobs were easily found, and the immigrant lived frugally and saved money. The wave of immigration characteristic of the early 1900s fed the cities with a continuous stream of human resources. The immigrants clustered together in the poorest sections of the city for protection, for housing, to preserve cultural identity, and to counteract the language barrier.

Through intense individual effort, the early immigrant achieved status. The expanding urban environment needed and developed talent. It facilitated *social mobility*. Through saving and purposefulness the newcomers were able to achieve the American dream and move up the social ladder. As early immigrants achieved status, they also fled from life in the city. American cities became characterized by urban sprawl as suburbs developed on the fringes of every large city.

But today's city immigrants have not migrated from large European cities. They are often a product of the slave experience. They may be agricultural workers or newly arrived from an impoverished experience in a totally different environment. Usually they do not have any of the specialized skills needed by an industrialized economy. Increased technology has severely limited the need for unskilled workers, and industry rarely offers training to the unskilled. An increase in the number of high school and college graduates has raised the educational requirements for many urban positions far beyond the experience of most minority applicants. Not only are the immigrants of the mid-twentieth century different from earlier immigrants, but the urban environment is not as hospitable to newcomers. Industrial changes since the late 1940s have affected the job market. The need for white collar workers now outpaces the need for skilled blue collar workers and service occupations normally demand more schooling in basic academic skills. Lacking work skills that are highly valued in the economic structure, the modern immigrant may be denied access to jobs, schooling, and housing.

Social Organization

Basic to the understanding of some of the problems in the urban community is the concept of social organization. Stratification of society refers to a classification system that ranks members of society either individually or by kinship groups. Sociologists studying society have developed systems for desribing social organization. Kahl identified seven dimensions sociologists measure to study American society:

Prestige. Some people in the community have more personal prestige than others, and are regarded by others with respect and deference.

Occupation. Some occupations are considered "higher" than others, partly because they are more important to the welfare of the community, partly because they require special talents, and partly because they pay high rewards.

Possessions, or wealth, or income.

Social interaction. In a large community, everyone cannot interact with everyone; patterns of differential contact arise; and people are most comfortable with "their own kind."

Class consciousness. The degree to which people at given levels are aware of themselves as distinctive social groupings. Americans are said to be less class conscious than Europeans; yet Americans, too, think of themselves as "working-class" or "middle-class"; and a large proportion identify "on the side of management" or "on the side of labor."

Value orientations. People differ about the things they consider good or important; and groups of people come to share a limited number of abstract values or value systems.

Power, or the ability to control the actions of other people. This dimension can be studied indirectly by delineating the cliques of important people in a community; or by studying the people who control the capital wealth of a community.[5]

To study the social structure of a large city, sociologists rely on information related to the individual's occupation, education, and income. There is general acceptance that society is stratified based upon socioeconomic criteria. Most social sociologists also accept that there are identifiable value, attitude, and belief differences among the various social classes. Hodges[6] identified a five-class structure for describing large cities: upper class, upper middle class, lower middle class, upper working class, and lower working class. More recent evidence by Harrington[7] and Riesman[8] and others would suggest that a five-class structure is an oversimplification of life in large metropolitan areas, where lower middle and working class groups affected by common problems and the mass media seem to be obliterating class differences; however, there is also evidence of a large poor class with distinct group characteristics.

Because social mobility (moving up the social ladder) is so crucial an issue in the urban community, it is important to distinguish among social stratification systems. Privileges in society are based upon the individual's standing in society or social class membership. If society's stratification system were based upon a *caste* system, then the individual's status would be *ascribed* (based upon birth). Within a caste system, there is no social mobility. If the system adhered to the form popular during European feudal times, classes would be based upon an *estate* system, in which mobility was limited but not altogether lacking. A third type of stratification is the *open-class* system. Theoretically, in the open-class system individuals compete for status.[9] Williams described the "ideal" open-class society:

1. This is a society of equality of opportunity and free, competitive placement. ("Anyone who has it in him can get ahead.")
2. Hence, success is solely a matter of individual merit.
3. Hence, those who are at the top deserve to be there, and those at the bottom are there because of lack of talent or effort: It is "their own fault."
4. Thus, the placement of individuals could not be otherwise without violating the value of individual achievement.[10]

The Americanization process normally meant discarding many of the immigrant's own customs, such as dress, diet, language, and health habits and the taking on of the American customs and values. Many of the early immigrants emigrating for political or religious reasons despised their native country and as a result welcomed the Americanization process as a means to wipe out their past histories. Other immigrants, clinging to bits and pieces of their native culture, often suffered a reaction as their children developed American ways of behavior and then began to instruct their parents. In many cases a conflict between generations developed as the children shrugged off traditional patterns of behavior.

Immigrant groups in the past have been classified as members of the lower class. Immigrants of the early twentieth century moved up the socioeconomic ladder as they developed working skills and became "Americanized." But many minority groups today protest that society is stratified not only along socioeconomic lines but also along ethnic, religious, and racial lines. There is evidence that when an individual is a member of a highly visible minority group, such as Puerto Rican, or Asian, it is more likely that ethnicity will determine social class membership and that the person will be affeted by prejudice. Today, many minority groups living in urban areas take exception to the "rags-to-riches," "melting pot" dream of the early American immigrant. Some, particularly young activists, believe that the stratification of society is so arranged that minority Americans have *ascribed* status, with limited access to material, intellectual, social, and political goals.

Educators have been interested in the study of social class structure beause in comparison to religion, race, or cultural background, the knowledge of students' social class allowed the teacher to anticipate some important group characteristics related to the (1) educational aspirations of students and their families, (2) parental achievement in education, (3) motivation for educational achievement, and (4) experiential background of students in terms of readiness for school. But if teachers are to deal honestly with their responsibilities, consideration must be given to those hypothetical questions posed by minority Americans and/or low income groups:

> If a *dual* stratification system is in operation, would social mobility be as motivating and satisfying to the minority individual as it is to the majority individual?

> If minority individuals are confined to a separate reward structure, does the stratification system serve as a trap for capable individuals?

> If the school represents middle class society, are those from the low socioeconomic group penalized, prohibited from voicing goals and aspirations, and denied access to majority satisfactions?

In past generations, the school took pride in being the "open door," the avenue for success for all Americans; of late, the school has been accused of denying access to opportunity and of distorting history.

Group characteristics are always suspect, and at best yield only generalizations. Statistics presented in Chapter 1 indicated that (1) minority Americans have a lower percentage of high school graduates and a higher percentage of dropouts; and (2) there is a relationship between education and occupation, and to some extent, between occupation and income. From these statistics one can assume the following statements to be valid:

> Minority Americans and/or low socioeconomic groups have not attained high levels of education.
>
> Parental achievement in school will affect the preparation and readiness of children for school.

One *cannot* assume these statements to be true:

> Minority Americans and low socioeconomic groups lack motivation for educational achievement.
>
> Minority Americans and low socioeconomic groups do not value *schooling*.

It is in terms of Kahl's seven dimensions for studying American society that minority individuals are sometimes stereotyped. Psychiatrist Coles stated: ". . . the ultimate reality is the reality of [economic] class. And it's around this issue of having and not having—and social and economic vulnerability versus social and economic power—that's where the real issue is."[11] The following study focused on the oft-repeated statement that low income groups do not value education. Cloward and Jones[12] identified three factors that affect school achievement among low income groups:

> Less instructional time in school resulting from teacher turnover, teacher inexperience, and geographic mobility of low income families.
>
> The promise of occupational rewards at a future date works adversely against low income groups since they cannot realistically anticipate rich, influential, or powerful relatives assisting them after graduation; racial barriers inhibit employment opportunities and contribute to pessimism of low income groups.
>
> "Our system of education places a strong stress upon doing rather than being, upon future orientation rather than an orientation toward the present or the past, upon the notion that man is superordinate to nature rather than in harmony with it or subjugated by it, upon the notion that man is flexible and plastic and capable of change rather than that he is essentially, and perhaps immutably, evil. A child who has not acquired these particular value orientations in his home and

community is not so likely to compete successfully with youngsters among whom these values are implicitly taken for granted."

In the Cloward and Jones study of Italians, Jews, blacks, East Europeans, Chinese, and Puerto Ricans living on New York's Lower East Side, the researchers identified three groups:

Lower class: Less than eighth-grade education, employed as unskilled worker, income less than minimum wage

Working class: Skilled worker, clerk, salesman, some high school education, average income for Lower East Side

Lower middle class: Professional or semiprofessional, some college education, income above national median

Among the questions asked by the researchers, the following are pertinent to the importance of education as perceived by the three identified groups:[13]

	Lower professional and semi- professional	*Working professional and semi- professional*	*Middle professional and semi- professional*
Percentage of respondents in each class who said that "getting ahead" meant obtaining or providing a good education, by level of occupational aspiration			
Percent saying good education	22%	24%	25%
Number of cases	248	243	131
Percentage of respondents in each class who said that education came to mind when they thought of a good life for the boys in the household			
Percent mentioning education	59%	67%	59%
Number of cases	157	123	41
Percentage of respondents in each class who said that education came to mind when they thought of a good life for the girls in the household			
Percent mentioning education	56%	65%	59%
Number of cases	148	105	37

SOURCE: Adapted from R. A. Cloward and J. A. Jones, "Social Class: Educational Attitudes and Participation," in Harry Passow, editor, *Education in Depressed Areas.* (New York: Teachers College Press, 1963).

The results of this study indicated that the importance of education for lower and working class groups (as characterized by these researchers) appears to be influenced by occupational aspirations. One could conclude that low income groups do not desire education for education's sake, but as a *goal orientation*.

> The point is *not* as has been so often suggested, that low income people fail to perceive the importance of education as a channel of mobility, but rather that their level of occupational aspiration influences their evaluation of education much more than is characteristic of the middle-class person.[14]

Cloward and Jones also measured the impact of educational involvement upon attitudes toward eduation and concluded that the lower class was especially influenced by educational participation. The researchers classified the respondents according to educational participation: NC, no contact with the schools; VO, visits only to the school; FP, formal participation.[15]

	Lower class			*Working class*			*Middle class*		
	NC	VO	FP	NC	VO	FP	NC	VO	FP
Percentage of respondents in each class who said that education came to mind when they thought of a good life for boys and girls in the household by extent of involvement in education									
Boys									
Percent of education	54%	61%	76%	69%	64%	65%	50%	53%	65%
Number of cases	54	74	21	29	47	37	4	17	17
Girls									
Percent of education	47%	56%	78%	70%	64%	61%	83%	40%	71%
Number of cases	47	70	23	23	39	36	6	15	14

SOURCE: From R. A. Cloward and J. A. Jones, "Social Class: Educational Attitudes and Participation," in A. Harry Passow, editor, *Education in Depressed Areas.* (New York: Teachers College Press, 1963).

Multicultural Groups in the City

Successful urban teachers urge their colleagues to develop sensitivity and understanding about the past histories of multicultural groups and the ways in which these groups have experienced prejudice in the American scene. A brief consideration will be given to four groups living in the urban environment: Mexican Americans, black Americans, American Indian, and Asian Americans. Suggested readings for deeper understanding appear at the end of the chapter.

Mexican Americans

The Mexican American population of the United States is primarily concentrated in the five southwestern states. As judged by socioeconomic criteria, Mexican Americans rank extremely low. Research indicates that to the extent that Mexican Americans move upward on the stratification hierarchy, they have achieved a greater degree of acculturation and in most cases have moved out of the barrio. Moore concluded that "middle-class Mexican Americans and Anglos respond almost identically to value questions relating to planning and contentment."[16] Housing patterns for Mexican Americans vary among the large cities of the Southwest. Since segregated housing patterns inhibit acculturation and assimilation, cultural ways of life are affected both by the cultural community in which the individual resides and by the pressures and penetration of the outside community. Mexicans living in Los Angeles, a city of rapid change, will be different from Mexicans living in Bexar County, Texas.

Mexican Americans have acculturated into the majority system less than other groups; consideration of their unique history is pertinent. As McWilliams so aptly pointed out, "Mexicans were annexed by conquest, along with the territory they occupied, and, in effect, their cultural autonomy was guaranteed by a treaty."[17] Therefore, the Mexican may live in the city as a recent immigrant or a native American. The process of acculturation for Mexicans cannot be related necessarily to number of years of residence in the United States. The Mexican population clustered in the Southwest lives close to Mexico and is therefore exposed to continual reinforcement of cultural patterns; similarly, the environment of the Southwest bears an unmistakable Mexican trace. Mexicans are proud of their people and their history and this pride is often reflected in the murals and pictures that adorn many public buildings and housing projects in the barrio.

The vast majority (over 80 percent) of Mexican Americans live and work in urban areas. Like other groups, they have been affected by changing family roles. Traditional value orientations included prizing of emotional relationships, which sometimes affected and negated desire for scholarly competitiveness; the recessiveness of the female, which affected sex roles; the primacy of the family, which resulted in both an extended family and the acceptance of family responsibility and loyalty. However, urban life is changing many of

Table 3.1. Spanish American population, 1969*

Characteristic	Total population	Total Spanish American	Mexican	Puerto Rican	Cuban	Central or South American	Other Spanish	Other origin
Total	198,214	9,230	5,073	1,454	565	556	1,582	188,983
Percent foreign-born	5.5%	20.7%	17.1%	0.5%	82.5%	63.7%	13.8%	4.7%
Spanish mother tongue	6,700	6,358	3,658	1,208	536	383	573	342
Percent of total	3.4%	68.9%	72.1%	83.1%	94.8%	68.9%	36.2%	0.2%
Spanish usually spoken	4,622	4,498	2,401	1,049	492	301	255	122
Percent of total	2.3%	48.7%	47.3%	72.1%	87.0%	54.2%	16.1%	0.1%

* Numbers in thousands. Excludes armed forces and inmates of institutions.

SOURCE: U.S. Department of Commerce, Bureau of the Census, *Current Population Reports*, Series 213.

these patterns. Changing sex roles affect family life in that the Mexican male is more apt to care for the children, consult his wife on family decisions, and interact in a more egalitarian behavioral pattern; and Mexican women are more apt to work and seek an education and less apt to be subservient to the male.

The traditional values ascribed to Mexican Americans are more apt to be related to the culture of poverty than to a rural folk culture. Cabrera reported:

> . . . those studies and reports currently available about the Spanish-speaking of America, or Mexican Americans, tend to emphasize the "culture of poverty" aspects of the socioeconomically poor of the Mexican American group. Emphases continue to be on traditional and stereotyped views of simple societal folkways and their anachronisms in an age of lunar orbiting. In other words, the literature and the common lecture about Mexican Americans are about the poor, the disadvantaged, and the quaint.[18]

By far the greatest deterrent to Mexican American assimilation can be related to language (see Table 3.1). Language facility is related to occupational achievement. Mexican people, according to Moore, are "loyal" to their language. Although the right to speak Spanish was not guaranteed in the Treaty of Guadalupe Hidalgo, Mexicans continued to speak Spanish in informal situations throughout the Southwest. Again the proximity to Mexico, the reinforcement of cultural surroundings, and the rights of a conquered people can be cited as attributing to this language loyalty. Perhaps also affecting, but failing to deter, the use of Spanish was the prohibition in most American schools to allow speaking or teaching in Spanish. With the imprint of Mexican culture visible in much of the Southwest, the prohibition of Spanish failed to affect its informal use among the Mexican population. Many Mexican American citizens have described the consequence of their dual language system. A student at the University of Southern California reported the following:

> To make it in the middle-class you've got to give up your language. You've got to consciously be Anglo in all of your ways. And if you do that, then your friends think you have abandoned them. They look down upon you and in a way you look down upon yourself. I remember in junior and senior high school really trying to forget any Spanish that I knew. But now I'm beginning to change my mind again. Maybe because times are changing, particularly in the schools. I think now I would be proud to really be bilingual.

The teacher seeking to understand Mexican students must also consider that many young Chicanos resent the concept of acculturation-assimilation. These young people do not want to surrender their bicultural-bilingual identity and heritage in order to gain entry or

success in the mainstream of American life. The concept of enculturation is profoundly affecting many new school practices. An interview
at the Huntington Drive School in Los Angeles is illustrative. Mrs.
Persidida Herrera, president of the school's Parents' Club, commented
through an interpreter:

> The feeling of all the parents is that this is a wonderful school because
> it understands our lack of English. It gives the children an opportunity
> to learn Spanish and English at the same time, and it expresses the
> ways of our culture.

The principal of the school, Harold Bertrand, who also speaks Spanish,
commented:

> Mexican American kids used to have a tremendous lack of success and
> often were treated as if they were dumb. We should adjust to the
> reality of a child's needs when he comes to school not speaking any
> English. It is the school which should make the adjustment, not the
> child.
>   The parents should not be misunderstood. They want their children
> to succeed, to be Americans, to be good citizens, to enjoy the benefits
> of this country. But they also want to be able to be proud of their
> heritage and to maintain a cultural identity.[19]

The Mexican American living in an urban area is more affected
by lower-class culture than by his ethnicity. Mexican-Americans are
extremely individualistic and are affected by geography, the dynamism
of their urban environment, generation, language, and culture. They
desire to be a part of the decision-making majority society. Language
and cultural differences will probably be apparent for generations,
but it is the viewpoint of many Mexican-American citizens (as well as
others) that it is the school's (and other institution's) responsibility
to adjust to the needs of the Mexican students, if society is to realize
the potential of this group of citizens.

Black Americans

Census figures provide evidence of the increasingly high concentration
of black Americans living in urban areas. (Note the population figures
for the Chicago city schools, Chapter 1.) A comparison of the black
population for the years 1963, 1966, and 1974 in Chicago indicated a
school enrollment change from 51 percent in 1963 to 56 percent in
1966 to 57.9 percent of the school population in 1974. The majority of
black Americans have migrated from smaller cities and southern rural
areas. They represent an unskilled group unable to avail themselves
of skilled job opportunities. In the main they are considered "poverty"
class; black Americans with semiskilled and skilled jobs primarily
are members of the working class.

Robinson, quoting Coles, compared class problems in the city of Boston to problems in other cities:

> That's the real struggle that's going on. And to talk about it only in terms of racism is to miss the point. It's working-class people who happen to be Black . . . poor people . . . both of whom are very hard pressed; neither of whom have got much leverage on anything. They are both competing for a very limited piece of pie, the limits of which are being set by the larger limits of class which allow them damn little if anything.[20]

Black Americans face problems no other immigrant group confronts. Segregation, discrimination, and prejudice have confined many black Americans to a ghettoized existence. The Cornell Studies in Intergroup Relations, reported by Williams, disclosed the following:

> Although the minority community bears a functional economic relationship to the majority community, the patterns of majority prejudice, discrimination, and employment of the language of prejudice (and the minority reactions to these phenomena) create a socially isolated subcommunity whose perceptions are bounded by the psychological limits of the minority community rather than those of the general community.
> Everywhere, the social isolation of the Negro subcommunities, stemming from a lack of complete integration into general community life, caused an identification with the national Negro community or with Negroes in other areas, as well as with the larger local community.
> In each community awareness of being Negro was high, the subject of intergroup relations was frequently discussed, and most Negroes tended to define situations involving interracial contact in racial terms. In each community the Negroes internalized the values and beliefs of the general community to the extent of feeling and expressing a certain amount of self-disparagement when viewing the Negro community as compared with the general community.[21]

Another consequence of an isolated community life has been that middle-class blacks enjoy a virtual monopoly in business and professional services within the black community. The vested interests of middle-class blacks in urban areas are often such that they do not welcome intrusion or competition. Many institutions in the black community have developed reactively in response to the social isolation of the community and as such represent a dual institutional system. These institutions, operated by middle-class blacks, perform a meaningful function within the black community, but tend to perpetuate segregation and isolation and operate to the disadvantage of planned change and mobility within the majority community.

Middle-class blacks, in contrast to the poverty level or low-income families, are often employed as teachers, businesspeople, technicians, and in professional occupations as doctors, lawyers, and preachers. Middle-class blacks often take exception to any school efforts to teach using the black dialect or black dialect textbooks; they feel that such an effort is dishonest and perpetuates both the stereotype and the use of nonstandard English. Family life among upper-working and middle-class black families is similar to that of other middle-class populations. Years of education and income again contribute substantially to life style.

Poverty-level black families since Reconstruction days have been dominated by the female. Subjected to stereotyping by the film industry and the media as lazy, dumb, and shiftless, the black male in the city or in rural areas has had a difficult time obtaining work. More than other minority members, the black male has been ruled by the LIFO system (last in, first out) and has suffered from an almost complete lack of freedom to choose employment. Unskilled, and the most visible of the minorities, the black male has been denied access to housing, employment, schooling, and recreation. Strategically, the male has held a weak economic position and has often granted control of the family unit along with the purse strings to the female. The female's independence and dominance has resulted in the male's absence from the home a great deal of the time, so that poverty-class black family life has been described by sociologists as unstable. Black students from poverty-level families have often been denied a healthy relationship with male figures or with male authority.

School curriculum and black Americans. The basic curriculum has omitted the cultural contributions of many minority Americans, but none has suffered at the hands of the historian in the same way as the Negro race. In a 1968 publication, Katz commented about the Negro's right to history:

> The distortion of the Negro's past has always had a purpose. The assertion that the Negro has no history worth mentioning is basic to the theory that he has no humanity worth defending.
>
> Historians have habitually ignored Negro contributions to most phases of American life, particularly the exploration of the new land and our great post-Civil War industrial growth.
>
> American Negroes have played a hitherto unheralded part in the history of the last Western frontier.
>
> Americans are unaware of Negro gallantry in defense of the nation during wartime.
>
> But American Negro history is important for other reasons. It provides a greater truth, a fully dimensional picture of America. Part of our denial of justice to the Negro has been our consistent distortion of his positive role in our society.[22]

For most Americans it is difficult to conceive that the school would purposefully subvert, hide, or destroy a student's culture. Yet, many black students, deprived of their personal statement concerning reality, developed a sense of inferiority. The black experience in American society has been substantially different from the experience of immigrant groups. Forbes[23] suggested that schools need to develop techniques for working with black communities. Among his suggestions are the following:

1. School and room environment should reflect the heritage of the community. Library resources should be oriented to the needs and interests of the student's cultural background.
2. Teachers should have training in speaking and understanding the dialect and should use ESL techniques. (Note Chapters 2 and 5. This particular statement by Forbes has been subject to a great deal of opposition by middle-class blacks.)
3. Effort should be extended to teach students about their African background, including possibly the teaching of African languages.
4. Prominence should be given to black authors, musicians, and artists in the curriculum.
5. Encouragement of dance skills should be included in the curriculum.
6. Adults living in the community should be used as resource persons.
7. Cultural heritage should be treated as an integrated part of the curriculum.
8. Curriculum content should be relevant to the students in each community (community-oriented).

Forbes expected the school to develop the motivation of the black student. Through conscious efforts of teachers to teach culture-oriented studies, he believed that this could happen.

The American Indian community

The story of the American Indians contributes to the shame of the school. As with other minority groups, American Indians have been denied their personal statement in history. The actuality of this denial has been documented by Turner:

> Without involving the spectre of conspiracy, I say that there has been among whites a planned destruction of the past or at any rate, all of it that did not illustrate the national mythology.
> This attempted destruction of the African and Indian pasts can also be understood as a consequence of our physical subjugation of these peoples: the victors write the histories; the vanquished are rendered historyless. It was this and something more. In the white man's opinion, oral history was non-history, a bundle of foolish superstitions without authority or value. Worse, such traditions seemed to be the very things which stood most in the way of the psychological subjugation of Blacks

and red men. Thus the history of the New World was to be begun again, this time from the top down: written history from the white point of view, fixing its attention on economic trends, trade agreements, election processes, military engagements, and diplomatic entanglements.

The long-silenced voices of the Blacks and of the Indian have risen to challenge the words of the textbooks. And to these has been added the wordless voice of the land itself, crying out against the continued despoilment of it, threatening to turn finally upon the despoilers and swallow them whole like the vagina dentata of Indian legend.

But by this time these school children (that is, we ourselves) were all but incapable of reading the emerging record of the substratum of New World history. Our minds and ears were closed; oral history still seemed less than authentic; and the histories of the Afro-Americans and Indian less important on the world stage than the Plymouth Rock-Washington litany.[24]

Whereas most minority Americans emigrated from their native land to improve their life style or, as with the black American, migrated from farm to city, the American Indian migrated to protect himself and to gain personal and group security. The land the Indian owned was always the *stake*. The Indians constantly sacrificed land title for survival. Today, as a race, the American Indian is almost extinct.

White society developed stereotyped expressions about the Indian. The literature was filled with negative comments about the Indians' warlike nature, brutality, drunkenness, and even cowardice. Their generosity, culture, and agricultural and technological skills went unsung. Armstrong pointed out that Indians have no written record of their heritage, but that a rich oral history is available:

> From childhood an Indian learned the art of public speaking. This art was employed and developed in tribal council speeches, in peace negotiations with other tribes, in coup-counting speeches, in public ridicules, in religious ceremonies, in story tellings, in war preparations and actions, in tribal clubs, and in treaty-making with the white man.
>
> The Indians' was a thoroughly oral culture, elaborated only by pictorial material, such as winter counts. With the coming of the white man—explorers, trappers, soldiers, government agents—a written record began to emerge of the extraordinary gift of speech which the Indian had long possessed. Primarily in minutes of treaty negotiations, in diaries, in memoirs, in anthropologist's notebooks, the Indian's words were preserved—and often soon forgotten.[25]

The recording of Indian oral history has produced a rich source of early American "continental" history. Statements like the following document the Indians' misery and ghetto-like existence:

> I have heard talk and talk, but nothing is done. Good words do not last long unless they amount to something. Words do not pay for my dead

people. They do not pay for my country, now overrun by white man.
. . . Good words will not give my people good health and stop them
from dying. Good words will not get my people a home where they
can live in peace and take care of themselves. I am tired of talk that
comes to nothing. It makes my heart sick when I remember all the good
words and broken promises. . . .

You might as well expect the rivers to run backward as that any man
who was born a free man should be contented when penned up and
denied liberty to go where he pleases.

Let me be a free man—free to travel, free to stop, free to work, free
to trade where I choose, free to choose my own teachers, free to follow
the religion of my fathers, free to talk and think and act for myself—
and I will obey every law, or submit to the penalty.[26]

The American Indian was not granted citizenship until 1924. How
do you think an Indian child would feel to learn that the American
Indian was not considered a "person"? Although able to be charged
and penalized for the commission of a crime, the American Indian
(until an 1879 decision by Judge Elmer S. Dundy) was denied the
right of habeas corpus. How would this affect the student's achievement motivation? That decision was "buried" in old legal records,
and the Indian rarely was granted the rights of other strangers in their
lands.

Indian community members who are willing to discuss the need
for an "Indian history" point out that even when history has been
recounted, too often the textbook obscures the diversity of Indian
culture. There is a history worth recording about each of the tribes
and no one history can do justice to the story. The Bureau of Indian
Affairs operates the vast majority of schools for Indian children, but
there are Indian children attending urban schools and like their multicultural classmates, their enculturation needs may outweigh their need
for acculturation. The Indian community is growing in urban areas
primarily because many Indian Americans expect that the city will
offer employment opportunities. But like the other newcomers to the
city, the Indian lacks work skills, education, and proficiency in English.
Many American Indians are also unused to the competitive structure
of city life.

The Asian American community

Snubbed and ostracized by white society, Chinese and Japanese
Americans were forced to develop their own communities. "China-
towns" and "Little Tokyos" became economically and socially self-
sufficient in many large cities across the nation. Often described as
crafty, treacherous, and subversive, called the "yellow peril"[27] Asian
Americans withdrew from American society into their own ghetto.

Unlike the black, Mexican, or Indian Americans, Asian Americans retained a strong sense of personal and group identity.

Recently Chinese Americans astonished much of the nation when they protested the desegregation of their San Francisco schools. Chinese parents were asking, how will traditional Chinese culture survive if Chinese students are forced to attend schools outside Chinatown? Many Chinese Americans can trace their roots to the Gold Rush years. Like other immigrant groups, they emigrated to take advantage of the economic opportunities in America. The Chinese were employed in the mining camps, in agriculture as stoop laborers, and by the railroad. Willing to accept less than "American" laborers, the Chinese found jobs plentiful. But as the labor shortage ended, the Chinese were subjected to violent assaults on their person and their belongings. In 1882 Congress bowed to labor's demands and passed the Chinese Exclusion Act.

The Japanese migration movement occurred after the passage of the Exclusion Act. The Japanese became heir to both the prejudice and the jobs of their fellow Asians. In 1907 the Japanese government entered into an agreement with the United States to discourage Japanese citizens from emigrating. Japanese Americans were somewhat more successful than the Chinese; perhaps they adapted more easily to the new society. They adjusted in school and satisfied their own cultural needs with after-school training. Japanese seemed to accept the acculturation process. But with the outbreak of World War II, the Japanese population was subjected to unimaginable cruelty and finally interned in relocation centers, even though many had citizenship rights. Stone and DeNevi commented about the result of that confinement:

> A significant result of the wartime encampment was that those of
> Japanese descent who were born and raised in America became aware
> of the vulnerable position they occupied, outside of American society
> yet not able to identify with Japan and its society.[28]

Since the end of World War II, Asian American communities have expressed dual and sometimes conflicting goals: to establish themselves as "full Americans" with complete citizenship rights or to develop Chinese or Japanese styles of life within their own communities.

Multicultural Students, the School, and Problems of Poverty

All these groups live in the city. So, too, do poor white children, Puerto Rican children, and many others. Children are powerless. Children of the city have divergent problems. They represent a pluralistic community, a multicultural society, and they themselves are bicultural.

Fifty-five percent of Americans have less than $10,000 a year income.[29] There are at least 10 million children who live in poverty. The majority of these children reside in urban areas and attend the 20 largest school districts in the country. These children lack health care. Preschool programs serve one child out of ten. Many urban working mothers are away from home 10 hours per day. Their children are often called "latchkey" children, left to the care of older siblings or fend for themselves. These children are in need of hot meals, supervision, and companionship.[30] The urban community and the problems associated with poverty are interrelated. Harrington has observed that

> The impoverished are better off than their predecessors in misery; but relatively speaking, in terms of hope and economic opportunity, their plight is much worse.
>
> About a third of American youth today drop out of education before they leave high school. They have an unemployment rate of 15 percent (and it is almost double that for Negro dropouts).
>
> The Department of Labor projections on the educational attainment of the work force in 1975 are even more revealing. In 1964 the Senate Subcommittee estimated that a young worker needed fourteen years of schooling—two years beyond high school—in order to have a really good chance for economic opportunity. But in 1975, when the skill requirements for the available decent jobs will presumably be much higher, more than one-fourth (26.6 percent) of the workers twenty-five to thirty-four years of age will be without a high school diploma. This society apparently plans for them to be either unemployed or janitors, i.e., poor.[31]

The population of blacks aged 18 to 24 enrolled in college was 18 percent compared with 25 percent for whites. The proportion of blacks aged 20 to 24 having completed high school was 72 percent in 1974, up from 65 percent in 1970, while the total for whites last year was 85 percent.

One often hears that the trouble with "poor" people is that they do not believe in work. A study by Goodwin of 4,000 poor and non-poor persons identified that the "work-ethic" was as strong among the poor as among middle-class individuals. The major difference between the two groups studied indicated that the poor lose self-confidence as a consequence of their inability to succeed in the work world.[32]

The significance of this situation for the school is vast. There must be

> Sensitivity to the problems of the poor vs. "blaming" the poor for "their own problems."

Knowledge that chronic illness often plagues the poor family, contributing to absence from school.

Understanding that older children are needed to babysit if adult family members are to work.

Acceptance that teenaged children may be able to obtain work and contribute to the family well-being when adult members cannot obtain work.

Realization that many states keep their welfare grants so low (to provide incentive!) that welfare children are dying of starvation.

Recognition that low self-esteem of the adult family members affects their children's self-confidence and self-concept.

Political leadership rather than the school must resolve the problems of poverty, but the school is the most accessible institution within the urban community and therefore has the opportunity to act responsibly toward the people in the community. Daily contact with children provides access to the family. Teachers, as highly trained professionals, are capable of perceiving needs and suggesting and initiating supportive services from other specialists and institutions. The school can offer some types of job training and work experience programs in which students receive school credit for work experiences; the school can allow its facilities and equipment to be used (auto maintenance, sewing machines); the school can accommodate preschool, before school, and after school child care; the school can manage food programs for children; and the school can identify needed health services.

Prejudice, stereotyping, and the urban classroom

Each of the multicultural groups living in the city faces somewhat similar problems in terms of low income, urban problems, and prejudice. Prejudice seems to be the unwelcome stranger at the classroom door. The challenge of prejudice has underpinned almost every question in this chapter. An understanding of the causes and consequences of prejudice is critical for urban teachers. As you read about the problem of prejudice, consider and respond to the following questions:

To what extent is the use of linguistic descriptors (*greaser, beaner, dago, kike, white cracker, Jap, nigger*) reflective of the ego needs of the speaker?

Name stereotypes, visual and verbal, developed and nurtured by the mass media.

How many expressions can you think of to describe a particular minority group? Would you use those expressions face-to-face with the persons so designated? Why not?

How does the use of verbal rationalizations such as "you're different" or "my best friend is . . ." give the speaker away?

What makes some individuals deny personal membership in a minority group?

Why are some members of minority groups "super" sensitive?

Does humor in the form of dialect jokes foster or nurture stereotypes?

Would "victims" of prejudice be likely to band together?

The urban community responds sometimes shyly, sometimes with distrust, toward the urban teacher because it is natural for human beings to be somewhat hesitant in relationships with individuals who are strange. It is strangeness that sometimes fosters prejudice. Allport defined prejudice as. "A feeling, favorable or unfavorable, toward a person or thing, prior to, or not based on, actual experience."[33] Ethnic prejudice is defined as ". . . an antipathy based upon a faulty and inflexible generalization. It may be felt or expressed. It may be directed toward a group as a whole, or toward an individual because he is a member of that group."[34]

The definition of prejudice contains two essential components: an *attitude* of favor or disfavor, and an overgeneralized *belief*. The individual rationalizes his belief in favor of his attitude, thus accommodating his beliefs to his attitudes.

Are all people prejudiced? Jahoda called prejudice a social attitude and disease that is *learned* in order to fulfill personal needs. Both Allport and Jahoda found that less than 20 percent of the population was free of prejudice. Prejudice is used as a crutch to bolster the individual's ego and self-esteem. Bigots perceive evil because they despise themselves. They reject their own weakness and deny their own ambitions because of a personal fear of failure. Secure individuals are less prejudiced than individuals who are insecure.[35]

People who have a poor education are more likely to be prejudiced than those who are highly educated. Individuals secure in their social position are less likely to be prejudiced than those who are insecure. The blue collar worker fearful that the new immigrant group may displace him on the job is more likely to be prejudiced than the white collar worker secure in a clerical or service occupation. Groups of individuals cut off from outside stimulation or contact with others are more likely to be prejudiced than those individuals or groups with many interactive relationships. Individuals who have moved up the social ladder too fast to form new patterns of behavior and relationships with others may feel insecure, and as they attempt to "keep up with the Joneses," they may act prejudicially toward the group from which they came.

Does the process of socialization nurture prejudice? Clark stated that the white immigrant driven by group insecurity migrated to new lands and then proceeded to exploit the land, resources, technology, and each subsequent new group.[36] Various authors, notably McWilliams, Tuck, and Clark, have related the socialization process on the American frontier to the exploitation of each new immigrant group. As groups succeeded socially and financially and changed jobs or as new jobs became available, new groups arrived to fill the void. Tuck described the labor contractors who went to Mexico to recruit cheap labor and offered them the Impossible Dream. The flow of immigration of Mexican-Americans (and other immigrant groups) coincided with the development of the railroads, cotton, citrus, and sugar. It has been said often that each group carries its culture in a suitcase. The successful immigrant in America has been the one who could not be recognized as an immigrant. He has conformed in speech, dress, ideals, values. Thus, once again, the urban teacher comes face to face with the controversy of acculturation vs. enculturation.

Are there degrees of prejudice? Allport identified five degrees of negative action that describe the range of possible prejudicial behavior.[37]

Antilocution. People express, verbally, their prejudices with friends of the same mind.

Avoidance. Even though it may be inconvenient, the prejudiced individual may go out of his way to avoid contact with the object(s) of his prejudice.

Discrimination. The prejudiced individual makes personal decisions that exclude the individual or group in question. These decisions usually are related to employment, housing, social and political rights, education, and recreation. When discrimination is institutionalized, it may be called *segregation.*

Physical attack. Attacks upon the person, group, or their personal possessions occur during a heightened emotional situation.

Extermination. The maximum expression of prejudice occurs when the group in question is lynched, massacred, and so on.

Perhaps the gravest danger inherent in the nature of prejudice is that it seems to be contagious, and in a world that is progressively smaller, the social consequences of prejudice can be less tolerated.

How might prejudice affect the urban teacher's judgment? Tony was meeting with his high school counselor. The counselor had reviewed Tony's cumulative record card from junior high school. In junior high school, when Tony was first tested for intelligence and achievement, he could speak very little English. (He was born in Puerto Rico.) His score was therefore quite low. In senior high school Tony was absent when the tests were given. At the interview the counselor asked Tony about his hobbies and which class he liked best in high school. Tony hesitantly responded that he enjoyed his auto shop class the most and that recently he had become interested in metal sculpturing. From this interview the counselor recommended to Tony that he should consider a trade school, and that he was not oriented for and would not profit from a college experience.

What happened?	*How was it interpreted?*
Tony did poorly on a group intelligence test and on an achievement test.	Tony was stupid.
Tony was absent from school when the tests were given in senior high school.	Tony purposefully missed school.
Asked about his hobbies and what he liked best at school, Tony responded, metal sculpture and auto shop.	Tony is "skilled with his hands"; he is not academically oriented.

What happened?	*Why did it happen?*
Tony did poorly on a group intelligence test and on an achievement test.	Tony could not read or speak English; the tests were unfair.
Tony was absent when the tests were given in senior high school.	Tony was ill.
Asked about his hobbies and what he liked best at school, Tony responded, metal sculpture and auto shop.	Tony was shy but felt compelled to respond. His auto shop teacher worked individually with students and spoke Spanish. Tony was appreciative. He had learned welding in auto shop and became interested in tinkering with metal sculptures. He was really more interested in academic pursuits.

The counselor in this incident focused his attention upon certain preconceived signs. He *selected* the evidence, *accentuated* the signs, and then *interpreted* the evidence. In making his judgment, the counselor sorted out all other evidence that would be inconsistent with what he was looking for. Allport made the following conclusions about the prejudiced personality:

> . . . the cognitive processes of prejudiced people are in general different from the cognitive processes of tolerant people.
> . . . the prejudiced person is given to two-valued judgments in general. He dichotomizes when he thinks of nature, of law, or morals, of men and women, as well as when he thinks of ethnic groups.

He is uncomfortable with differentiated categories; he prefers them to be monopolistic. Thus his habits of thought are rigid. He does not change his mental set easily, but persists in old ways of reasoning— whether or not this reasoning has anything to do with human groups. He has a marked need for definiteness; he cannot tolerate ambiguity in his plans. When he forms categories he does not seek out and emphasize the true "defining" attribute, but admits many "noisy" attributes to equal prominence.[38]

Contrast the experience of Tony with the experiences of these eighth-grade students:

Ms. Ames, an eighth-grade English teacher, reviewed the results of a group achievement test. She shared the results with the class, explained each of the subcategories, and related the class members' scores to other students' scores, nationally. Ms. Ames commented that students must learn to speak, read, and write standard English in order to be considered literate. She amplified her explanation with an example about two teenagers applying for the same "boxboy" job. The class discussed who would get the job— and for what reasons. Next, Ms. Ames devised the following strategy to motivate her students:

The students were divided into seven groups; each group was composed of five students. Three students in each group were to pretend to be interviewers. The other two students in the group were interviewees. The interviewers were to decide which company they represented, the personnel policies and skills needed by their firm, and the questions they would ask of the interviewees. After the interviews the five students would sit down and evaluate the validity of the questions and the interviewees' responses.

This strategy was tried on two successive days until all students had the opportunity to be both interviewer and interviewee. A final class evaluation concluded with seven groups sharing their questions and their problems, in terms of the interviewees' responses. With the teacher's assistance, the class then made a master list of attributes that prospective employers seemed to look for and a list of "no-nos" for prospective employees. Using both lists, Ms. Ames taught communication skills. One of the class tasks was to design an employment form to obtain personnel data, and the students practiced filling it out.

Ms. Ames was not overwhelmed by the results of an achievement test, nor would she have applied the results of an intelligence test that was inappropriate. She recognized her students' needs, and facilitated their recognition of their own learning needs and goals. She proceeded to teach to accomplish those goals without prejudice.

How can prejudices be changed? Prejudiced individuals may change their behavior because they are forced to conform to new people or to a new situation. Some prejudices are changed as a result of public opinion and newly accepted values. Prejudice may be eliminated by psychotherapy; the bigot, however, rarely consults a psychoanalyst. Prejudice is also eliminated through direct personal experience. Sociologists define four stages of relationship for personal experiences: sheer contact, competition, accommodation, assimilation.

Legislation has had the best record for changing prejudice because it creates a public conscience and a standard for expected behavior. Through legislation new folkways are developed. As the folkways are assimilated, the emergence of new values changes old prejudices. (However, there is often a tremendous gap between the enactment and the enforcement of the legislation.)

Is the urban community prejudice-free? The urban community, which is in fact many communities, is confronted with cultural clash in the educational setting and in the everyday experiences of life in the city. To the extent that the urban community is poor and uneducated, it is more prone to prejudice than other communities. However, since urban cultures have continuous contact and many direct interactive experiences, prejudice may be less rampant than with other groups living in isolated and poor environments.

Stereotyping. Stereotyping affects the thinking of minority individuals as well as the thinking of the majority group (see Chapter 2). A study by six teenaged minority youths in a Los Angeles city high school, sponsored by the National Endowment for the Humanities, revealed that many teenaged students believed in stereotypes. The survey disclosed that young people tended to use words like "nigger," "honky," "greaser," and "Buddha-head." The research conducted at Dorsey High School found that minority students have a "particular interest in racism," and identified the following feelings:

Asians have high moral values, are more interested in helping their race as compared to other racial groups and are hard workers.
Blacks are easygoing, have rhythm, stick together, and like to wear loud clothes.
Whites are usually unfriendly toward minorities, try to use minorities to their own advantage, tend to be pushy in order to get their way, feel they are superior to other racial groups and are usually more prejudiced than other groups.[39]

Some educators feel that minority stereotyped thinking is a natural consequence of television (films, radio), which reinforces an image of a group that has been stereotyped.

The film industry has failed Black people not by casting the Black women as fat Black women but by failing to create a wide variety of roles reflecting the diversity and complexity of the Black experience in America.[40]

Chicano educators objected to a television program ("Chico and the Man") which presented a stereotypic view of Chicano youth. Vahac Mardirosian, director of the Los Angeles Hispanic Urban Center, stated the objections of the educators:

> The title of the program demeans Mexican youth by casting the Chicano in an inferior role.
> The program ridicules the character and language of Chicano young people.
> The program content reinforces a simplistic perception of the Mexican life style.[41]

The considered opinion of both educators and members of the urban community seems to be that programs or films that support a stereotyped view of a minority group may be "funny" to the "in" group, but unfunny and inaccurate in perception and representation of the race or culture being depicted.

Since teachers in urban schools are in most cases members of the majority community, how they act, what they say and espouse, and the resources they choose for the classroom are all "suspect" by a multicultural community. The teacher is a stranger, and members of the urban community often feel uncomfortable in the teacher's presence. Sensitivity or strangeness between community and teacher may be related to cultural experiences or it may be related to socio-economic status. Both majority and minority groups may be afflicted by prejudicial attitudes, but urban specialist teachers should be attuned to detecting attitudes and sensitivities related to interpersonal behaviors.

Community involvement

In school life, community involvement accomplishes important goals:

> Teachers and community become acquainted, and prejudicial attitudes are less likely to affect parent-teacher-student relationships.
> School security improves as the community becomes concerned with and involved in the school program. (The Normandie School cited in Chapter 1 is indicative of the positive effects of community involvement.)
> Education assumes greater importance when the community becomes involved and participates in school life.

The Cloward and Jones study indicated that "the value of education is heightened for parents who visit the school or who participate in Parent-Teacher Associations. Furthermore, the impact of involvement in the school upon definitions of the importance of education tends to be greater in the lower and working-classes than in the middle-class."[42]

Community involvement in school life must be initiated by educators because, as a consequence of many years of noninvolvement, minority communities have felt insecure and distrustful of the school. Educators in the past did not respond positively to community participation. Creative ideas for motivating community involvement include the "dig-in" cited in Chapter 2, the community walk where teachers and administrators rang doorbells to become acquainted, and utilization of community members as resource individuals for teaching skills related to specific occupations, such as classroom and laboratory assistants, clerical aides, and language specialists.

Community and educational decision making

Educational decision making may relate to the following kinds of policy decisions:

Personnel Decisions. Who should be hired? Who shall be retained? How shall personnel be evaluated? What positions should receive priority? Which specialists are needed?

Curriculum Decisions. What should be taught? When should it be taught? How shall it be taught?

Instruction Materials. What shall we choose? What will receive priority—teachers' materials or students' materials? Will print and nonprint items be encouraged? Should machinery (hardware) be bought?

Financial Support. Which programs will be encouraged through financial support? Should teachers receive a cost of living raise? How much should be spent on materials? What shall be the policy concerning repairs and maintenance?

All communities are concerned about their schools, and most individuals consider themselves fairly "expert" about the schools. This occurs because to varying degrees all individuals have had school experiences. A critical question currently relates to who should control the schools—the community or professional educators? Some communities, urban and suburban, advocate participatory decision making in some aspects of the school program; other communities desire control over policy decisions that affect their schools. Parsons defined a *community-controlled* school as one ". . . in which parents, students or residents who form a self-defined 'community' previously lacking control exert extensive decision-making power over the policies of the school or schools serving that community."[43]

A plan for participatory decision making was initiated in California. In each school, elementary and secondary, community advisory councils were mandated by law. Advisory councils were composed of parents of children attending the school, residents of the community with no children in the school, teachers and classified employees. The majority members of each council were elected by the community. Teachers and classified employees elected their own representatives. Each principal was allowed to appoint several community members to the council based upon needed "expertise." Principals were ex-officio members of the councils.

The councils' original mandate was to determine community goals for their schools. These goals were then to be submitted to the school district. Each school district was to develop a district philosophy, goals, goal indicators, program objectives, and priorities based upon school-community goals as defined by the individual school advisory groups. Advisory councils were to meet at least once a month to discuss community priorities, problems, and to be "informed" about school problems and needs. As originally conceived, the council's role was advisory. Principals were to consult and to consider the council's position before making policy decisions. The councils generally would be involved in broad policy matters but not consulted about specifics, such as teacher evaluation or curriculum matters. These broad decisions involved the following kinds of questions:

Should the school establish an early childhood program?

If the school were to develop a reading laboratory, would parents volunteer to assist?

Is the community interested in multi-age grouping and nongraded primary classrooms?

Should parent-teacher conferences be established for student evaluation instead of using a report card?

A recent controversy in Los Angeles, typical of other large cities, focused upon a key control problem. Some school advisory groups advocated defining standards to evaluate school administrators. Such a plan would mean that in each of Los Angeles's 625 schools, different standards could be conceived for the evaluation of the school administrator. Los Angeles Superintendent William Johnston maintained that if such a plan were to go into effect, the following consequences might occur:

Advisory councils would influence the caliber of persons named as principals.

Advisory councils could control the content of educational programs.

Principals lacking social effectiveness or social attractiveness (or appropriate dress standards as conceived by the community) might be deemed unacceptable despite a record of outstanding educational practices and knowledge.

Accountability would be difficult to maintain with varying standards in each school.[44]

The issue in Los Angeles, as in New York, Philadelphia, and other cities, involved degree and intensity of community involvement in school life. Many citizens desire greater involvement in and decision-making power over the specifics of their children's education.

Although parental participation in the schools has a long history in the United States, it has not been concerned with the "specifics" or "power" decisions. Some of the best schools in the country have had virtually no parental input. Large city school districts have operated with a central board of education responsible for all decision making. The superintendent, responsible to the board, implemented the decisions. Policy flowed, so to speak, from the top down. It was precisely because of this pattern, which was characteristic of the decision-making process, that many minority communities were unhappy and claimed that changes in the classrooms never occurred.

In an effort to make local schools *accountable* to the parents of the community, many have advocated community control of the schools. Under a community control plan, the parents in a small community would organize themselves into a local board of education. The local board would be responsible for making all decisions that related to the school and would operate to involve the parents of the community in the life of the school. Advocates of the plan theorize that parental involvement will lead to better student achievement. Local or community control of the schools means a redistribution of decision-making power. Educators have been fearful of the concept of community control because they are concerned that they will be left out of the participatory decision-making system and relegated to employee status. To promote a middle ground or compromise between centralized and community control, some educators have advocated the decentralization of decision making. Under decentralization systems, school programs could be adjusted to meet community needs. Major decision-making policies would be in the hands of the professional educators, but parental background and culture would be influential in restructuring the system.

Community control advocates have been most active in minority communities because of the disadvantaged position of minority students in the schools. Its proponents claim innovative programs and flexibility will solve feelings of frustration and inadequacy on the part of minority students (and parents). In New York City, experimental programs have produced high voter turnout at school board elections and higher school attendance. However, some opponents of community control are fearful that local control systems will intensify segregation. Experimental programs involving decentralization as well as community control seem to indicate that shared concern by parents and educators for children's education can result in positive practices and prosperous schools, but both professional educators and communities need practice in sharing responsibility.[45]

What Should Educators Do?

Four major areas of adjustment and change are suggested here to improve conditions in the schools:

> Urban educators should develop understanding and knowledge about the sociocultural and historical backgrounds of the students they teach (a student perspective).
>
> Urban educators should develop personal skills to meet students' needs.
>
> School programs should be designed to be commensurate with student and community needs and goals.
>
> Educators should develop ways to involve the community in school life.

A student perspective

The development of understanding and knowledge about students' unique histories can be achieved in a variety of ways. Colleges and universities offer special workshops and institutes as well as planned courses that facilitate understanding and sensitivity about specific cultural groups. Teachers can plan a reading program of their own to develop an acquaintanceship with the literature, research, and history that affect their teaching situation. School-community workshops can be developed to accomplish joint understanding and definition of goals. Attendance at cultural events within the community will also develop understanding and perspective. To enhance students' self-concept and need for self-identity (the concept of enculturation), teachers should seek answers to the following questions:

> What is the unique history both in the United States and elsewhere of each cultural (ethnic) group? How does that history affect the student? How can the teacher assist students to learn about and appreciate their own history?
>
> Why did the group or individuals immigrate, migrate? Can the teacher guide students to appreciate the similar needs and reasons for immigration and migration of others?
>
> What are the unique contributions and accomplishments of each

group (political, cultural, technological, and so on)? How can students learn about them?

In what ways is each group unique (special skills, language, celebrations)? In what ways is each group similar to all other groups (problems)?

How have prejudice and discrimination affected the group?

How can prejudice and discrimination be eliminated?

Teachers also need to be cognizant of the diversity within cultural subgroups. For example, the Chinese American student may speak English, yet react socially to traditional Chinese culture; in the same classroom another Chinese American student may speak Chinese but react socially in what may be considered typical majority ways of behavior. *Each student is different;* therefore, criteria statements that attempt to pigeonhole an individual or a group should be regarded with suspicion.

Professional education

Students and parents should be continually assured that *teachers believe students can succeed.* For teachers to develop optimism and confidence in their own ability to facilitate student success, there must be understanding that teaching competence is developmental. Continuing education to refine humanistic, subject matter, and professional skills is indispensable to teaching effectiveness. Professional education should relate to the personal needs of the teacher and to the teaching situation.

Many school faculties design their own in-service programs. Successful in-service programs are planned to meet specific cognitive and affective objectives. For example, the following objectives could comprise an in-service program:

Cognitive objectives	Teachers will identify reading skills related to teaching reading in a content field.
	Teachers will identify advantages of teaching reading in content fields.
	Teachers will identify alternate activities (other than reading) to gain information.
Affective objectives	Teachers will participate in role playing, small-group discussions, and interviewing activities in order to gain information for problem resolution.
	Teachers will demonstrate to a colleague multisensory activities in their own classrooms.

Goals for the in-service program could include the following:

Teachers will gain an understanding of the advantages of teaching reading in content fields.

Teachers will experience multisensory activities such as role playing and recognize the impact of such an experience upon learning; teachers will use activities other than reading in their own classrooms.

Teachers will learn alternative means to accomplish objectives. They will use a range of activities to teach all subjects during the school day.

Competency themes for continuing education should relate to urban teaching. These themes might include the following:

Interpersonal and Interactive Effectiveness. Role playing, buzz groups, and team activities can be used to develop the teacher's humanistic skills.

Teaching Skills. Specific skills related to school needs, such as the teacher's language facility in languages other than English or reading diagnostic skills, are teaching skills. These skills may be related to specific subject fields.

Research Skills. The urban teacher should survey practitioner research about "what works" in the urban school. Experienced teachers can suggest research themes that focus on methods rather than theory.

Development of Curriculum Materials. Teachers can design needed materials for the classroom that are substantive in nature and relevant to the students and the environment.

Strategy Versatility. Preservice and in-service education that focuses on the range of teaching options available to accomplish goals will assist in strategy versatility. (If one technique doesn't work, try, try again!)

Specific school programs

Although state and federally funded special programs (Higher Horizons, Head Start, ESL) have been successful in urban areas, the real potential for improving student skills will occur in the local school when teachers and parents work together to utilize what they know about the children. A club format has been used successfully by some elementary and junior high schools as a vehicle to interest students in special studies and to involve the community in school life. The club design serves two functions: (1) It is a means to interest students in new areas of achievement, and (2) it is a means to dwell on existing accomplishments and motivate overall school success. The club programs operate during the school day for one or two afternoons per week. Teachers and community people, with the assistance of older students or university students, act as club leaders. Clubs focus on a variety of skills, interests and hobbies: mathematics games, costume design, marketing, sing and strum, folk tales, set design, banking, paint and sculpture, drama, gardening, drill and drum.

The mathematics games club develops new games to teach specific math skills in the classroom; club members "play" games to meet their own skill needs. The folk tales club invites senior citizens of the community to share Old World (and New World) folk tales. Students are also encouraged to tell folk tales their parents have told them. The club reads and listens to folk history. Many groups in the community as well as librarians can provide human and material resources for the club. Some enterprising teachers record oral folk tales and transcribe them into booklets for classroom use to read and listen to in learning centers. The drama club provides another means to develop language skills. Appropriate plays can be found in most libraries, although quite often students and community members are interested in writing their own productions. Sometimes members of the community can be encouraged to play adult parts in the production, which is ultimately staged for the students of the school and the community. The costume design club members learn to use sewing machines and patterns. The club may furnish the costumes needed for the drama club production. Interested adults in the community may sew along, teach, and assist the students. The costume design club may also furnish uniforms for the drill and drum team. Set design is another club that can be supportive of the drama club productions. Students learn carpentry and painting skills. Skilled workers in the community can often be convinced to demonstrate specific skills and contribute paint and nails. Lumber can be found at the "throw-away" site of any new building.

The banking club members study business problems, law, and economics related to everyday problems in the community. Sometimes students begin with the highly motivating game of Monopoly to learn business concepts. Business leaders in the community may be invited to discuss their "beginnings," their problems, and their successes. The fresh fish and poultry store owner, the shoe repairman, and the banker all make interesting guests. The marketing club may focus on home economics, nutrition, and supermarket shopping. Similar to the banking club, emphasis is on practical problems and mathematics skills. Mothers, retail clerks, and nutritionists can contribute to the organization of the club.

The gardening club, which one school tagged the "sodbusters," can teach methods of plant propagation and supply the classrooms of the school with science exhibits and the school grounds with new plants. A green school environment encourages many members of the community to care about their school. The sing and strum club is a departure from the typical music club. Guitar lessons are provided. Folk and rock music are encouraged. Since more singers than guitar players are needed, the proportions usually work out quite well. Students can be encouraged to write their own music or at least write their own words to existing music. The drill and drum team is another means to develop school morale and community involvement. The community may be encouraged to assist the costume design club to provide this group with uniforms. Music reading, singing, and marching can be taught to the beat of the drum. Painting and sculpture, using vermiculite, clay, plaster, and old hangers can provide a whole new school environment. One group designed a six-foot statue to greet people as they entered the school grounds. School buildings and walls can be festively (and meaningfully) decorated. Cultural history can be researched and expressed. Community members as well as historians and art and museum specialists can be enlisted for aid.

Educators can develop appropriate school programs by diagnosing students' needs and recognizing community priorities. Research studies have also contributed information about students that yields programming directives. For instance, social class dialect research has yielded information categorizing oral language problems: verb problems, pronoun problems, and syntactic problems. The implication for program development should be the development of teaching strategies that focus on improving children's oral language skills. Loban's study of high school students reported that high language proficiency students developed language skills earlier and to a greater degree of competence than did students from low socioeconomic groups. High proficiency students used a larger number of transformations and more adverbial clauses, and made more accurate use of relational words.[46]

A special program designed to improve children's discussion techniques was implemented in 1972–73 in South Whittier, California, by Oxstein.[47] The school was located in a low-income community; 36 percent of the community was Spanish-surnamed; the mobility rate was 40 percent, and a large percentage of the community received Aid to Families with Dependent Children. The fourth-grade children in this study were taught discussion techniques using a small-group organizational plan. After repeated experiences, the teacher observed the following behavioral changes: development of leadership techniques by discussion leaders and the development of conversational skills such as "sticking to the subject"; content assumed greater importance to the children; idea vs. mechanics of discussion assumed greater importance; students developed oral evaluative and synthesizing skills.

Objective means measured student growth. Two instruments

quantified the effects of the procedures: Bales' Interaction Process Analysis, and the Project Potential Group Test of Creativity to measure the fluency of verbal expression.

	Experimental group	Control group
Pretest responses	766	659
Mean score	24.70	21.96
Posttest responses	1,249	708
Mean score	40.3	23.6
Difference between pre- and posttest	483	49
Average gain per student	15.58	1.64

The results of the program were impressive and demonstrated that students profit from well-conceived programs which concentrate on skill needs. Techniques used in the program are discussed in Chapter 4. The study also directs attention to the need for more "teacher" research to test methodological procedures rather than theoretical research.

Community involvement

Invite the community in; let them help you. Walk around your school. Meet people. Say hi. Talk about *their* school. Go over on weekends and look around. Get the children to take care of *their* school.

Talk to the teenaged kids. Tell them, if you wreck the school, you're just taking away from your younger brothers and sisters.

Tell people if you see something in someone's house or yard that belongs to the school—tell us. Because *you're* being ripped off. Then it's our job to go over and talk to the people.

You got to teach children to take pride in *their* school.[48]

The foregoing were the remarks of a Los Angeles, California, school principal who successfully curbed vandalism at his school. (Statistics for the Normandie School were cited in Chapter 1.) He commented that children and even adults have to be taught to "care." He believes that teachers and administrators often have tunnel vision; they drive to school and back home each day without ever really seeing what is around them.

Earlier in this chapter some creative ideas were suggested to achieve community involvement, but quite often it is the mundane efforts that achieve results. The effective urban specialist seems to be acquainted with the people in the community in a natural, ordinary way, similar to the teacher in a small rural or suburban community. Too often teachers believe that the school belongs to the profession, and if a community shares a similar belief, then nobody takes the trouble to watch or become involved. The principal's advice to new urban teachers and administrators is to "reach out" to people and they will respond; to elicit involvement, and to become involved.

Summary

The urban community is composed of a multicultural population that is predominantly poor. That population is affected by the urban environment, by technology, and by society's social stratification system. The newcomer to the city today experiences a life far different from that of the immigrant of earlier times.

Minority communities denied access to institutional life and decision making in the majority society may develop clannishness, militancy, and their own forms of social and religious life, political leadership, and sources for economic survival. Problems in the urban school may be a result, in part, of the complexity of instructional planning for a diverse student population. The problem of students who speak languages other than English has not been their lack of English-language skills, but rather that no one at school was equipped to understand the students. Too often the minority child returned home from school defeated, frustrated, and belligerent. Cultural-linguistic factors as well as socioeconomic factors inhibit an accurate assessment of the minority student's ability when achievement and intelligence testing is dependent upon English-language skills. Tests that reflected a monocultural society resulted in the "tracking" and labeling of minority children as disadvantaged.

Voices in the urban community are distressed. Some are expressing dissatisfaction with historical omission and disregard. They do not consider themselves "Johnny-come-latelies"; many are stating to white society: "You are the latecomer, the immigrant; I was here first." Some voices in the urban community have asked: Should only black teachers teach black children? Should only Chicano teachers be allowed to teach Mexican children? The voices are demanding bilingual programs of instruction, community involvement and decision making in planning instruction, cultural and historical integration of instruction, and respect and dignity for all members of the community.

The urban family is interested in education and anxious for its children to succeed. Parent lack of involvement can often be attributed to lack of time, resources, and embarrassment because of personal inadequacies. School-community cooperation requires direct contact between home and school, with the teacher taking the initiative. To establish effective relationships and build true understanding, the teacher must look beyond immediate perceptions and discard stereotyped thinking. Surface evaluation resulting from inadequate evidence too often results in prejudicial judgments. Teachers and community must develop a common language to communicate ideas and feelings.

Recognition of and opportunity for the expression of the student's primary culture and language is a stated goal of the urban community. The development of literacy skills through creative student activities and the setting of reasonable standards for student success are of primary importance to the urban community. The development of student self-concept through the cultivation of student interest and opportunity for democratic decision making instead of the use of child "management" techniques is viewed by the community as a responsibility of the urban school. The development of new and creative ways to involve parents in the life of the community and new ways to utilize school facilities, resources, and environment may assist the urban family to overcome the burden of poverty. An alliance between the urban home and the urban school could eradicate illiteracy in our society.

Low-income groups as well as educational researchers appear to agree that it is the school's responsibility to "adjust" to the needs of social groups if equitable education is to be provided. Opportunity for high-level positions await minority individuals; however, tragically few are able to avail themselves of these opportunities. The problems of maintaining themselves and their families throughout the school years inhibits both the aspiration and the achievement. Social mobility for each immigrant group in American history was dependent upon a "new wave" of immigration to feed the pecking order. Many believe that no new wave of immigration can or will occur. If minority groups are restricted to low-level positions due to inadequate preparation in the schools, the urban crisis will engulf our total society.

Changes in teachers, schools, and society are important if the urban community is to achieve its human potential. Some of these changes involve the inclusion of new practices and the exclusion of others. Here are some desirable changes:

1. Involvement of the urban family and community in the classroom.
2. Involvement of the urban community in instructional planning.
3. Involvement of a variety of individuals as models of appropriate behavior. (Expose the children to success.)
4. Reinforcement of these behavioral models through planned experiences and activities.
5. Recruitment of teachers and aides who are knowledgeable about and empathetic to the students they are to teach.
6. The use of instructional teams and cross-aged grouping to facilitate teaching and learning.
7. The use of a testing system that is free of bias so that students are not screened out or "tracked" as a result of dialect or language differences.

8. Realization by school personnel that ability to learn is affected by social forces. (The teacher is a significant "other" person in the young child's life and therefore affects achievement, behavior, and beliefs.)

Notes

1. WILLIAM S. MILLER, "Comments," *Phi Delta Kappan*, December 1974, p. 255.
2. ROBIN M. WILLIAMS, JR., *American Society, A Sociological Interpretation* (New York: Knopf, 1951), p. 22.
3. LEWIS MUMFORD, *The City in History* (New York: Harcourt Brace Jovanovich, 1961).
4. RAYMOND C. HUMMEL and JOHN M. NAGLE, *Urban Education in America* (New York: Oxford University Press, 1973), p. 54.
5. ROBERT J. HAVIGHURST and BERNICE L. NEUGARTEN, *Society and Education* (Boston: Allyn and Bacon, 1967), p. 12.
6. HAROLD M. HODGES, JR. "Peninsula People: Social Stratification in a Metropolitan Complex," in *Education and Society,* ed. W. Warren Kallenback and Harold M. Hodges, Jr. (Columbus: Merrill, 1963).
7. MICHAEL HARRINGTON, *The Other America* (New York: Macmillan, 1962).
8. DAVID RIESMAN et al., *The Lonely Crowd* (New Haven, Conn.: Yale University Press, 1950).
9. WILLIAMS, *op. cit.,* chap. 5.
10. *Ibid.,* p. 91.
11. ROBERT COLES, quoted in "School Storm Centers, Boston" by Donald W. Robinson, *Phi Delta Kappan*, December 1974, p. 263.
12. RICHARD A. CLOWARD and JAMES A. JONES, "Social Class: Educational Attitudes and Participation," in *Education in Depressed Areas,* ed. A. Harry Passow (New York: Teachers College, Columbia University, 1963), p. 193.
13. *Ibid.,* pp. 202–204.
14. *Ibid.,* p. 215.
15. *Ibid.,* p. 212.
16. JOAN MOORE, *Mexican Americans* (Englewood Cliffs, N.J.: Prentice-Hall, 1970), pp. 131–132.
17. CAREY MCWILLIAMS, *North from Mexico* (New York: Greenwood Press, 1968), p. 207.
18. Y. ARTURO CABRERA, *Emerging Faces: The Mexican-Americans* (Dubuque: William C Brown, 1971), p. 61.
19. LYNN LILLISTON, "A School Says Si to Bilingual Education," *Los Angeles Times,* March 31, 1974.
20. DONALD W. ROBINSON quoting Robert Coles in "School Storm Centers, Boston," *Phi Delta Kappan*, December 1974, p. 264.
21. ROBIN M. WILLIAMS, JR., *Strangers Next Door* (Englewood Cliffs, N.J.: Prentice-Hall, 1964), pp. 252–253.
22. WILLIAM LOREN KATZ, *Teachers' Guide to American Negro History* (New York: Quadrangle, 1968), pp. 6–8.
23. JACK D. FORBES, "Working with the Afro-American Pupil," in *Teaching Multi-Cultural Populations—Five Heritages,* ed. James C. Stone and Donald P. DeNevi (New York: Van Nostrand Reinhold, 1971), pp. 89–93.
24. Frederick W. Turner, III, in *I Have Spoken,* compiled by Virginia Irving Armstrong (Chicago: Swallow Press, 1971), pp. xii–xiii.

25. *Ibid.*, p. xix.

26. CHIEF JOSEPH, in *I Have Spoken*, compiled by Virginia Irving Armstrong (Chicago: Swallow Press, 1971), p. 116.

27. JAMES C. STONE and DONALD P. DENEVI, "Asians in America—Asian-Americans of the Third World Political Alliance," in *Teaching Multi-Cultural Populations —Five Heritages*, ed. James C. Stone and Donald P. DeNevi (New York: Van Nostrand Reinhold, 1971), pp. 373–374.

28. *Ibid.*, p. 374.

29. The median income for black families was $7,808 in 1974, an increase of 7.4 percent over 1973, but, after adjusting for the effects of inflation, actual purchasing power of black families declined 3.2 percent. Median income for white families in 1974 was $13,356. (*Statistical Abstract of the United States 1974*, Bureau of the Census, Washington, D.C., July 1975.)

30. Select Committee on Equal Educational Opportunity, United States Senate, *Justice For Children* (Washington, D.C.: U.S. Government Printing Office, 1972).

31. MICHAEL HARRINGTON, "The Politics of Poverty," in *Poverty: View from the Left*, ed. Jeremy Larner and Irving Howe (New York: William Morrow, 1968), pp. 26–27.

32. LEONARD GOODWIN, *Do The Poor Want To Work?* (Washington, D.C.: Brookings, 1972).

33. GORDON W. ALLPORT, *The Nature of Prejudice* (Garden City, N.Y.: Doubleday, 1958), p. 7.

34. *Ibid.*, p. 10.

35. MARIE JAHODA, "What Is Prejudice?" *Look Magazine*, May 24, 1960.

36. KENNETH CLARK, *Prejudice and Your Child* (Boston: Beacon Press, 1963).

37. ALLPORT, *op. cit.*, pp. 14–15.

38. *Ibid.*, pp. 170–171.

39. JEAN DOUGLAS MURPHY, "Racial Stereotyping Found Among Youth," *Los Angeles Times*, August 8, 1972.

40. J. K. OBATALA, "Blacks on TV: A Replay of Amos 'n' Andy?" *Los Angeles Times*, November 26, 1974.

41. VAHAC MARDIROSIAN. "Under Fire: Chico and the Man—Chicano Educators Object," *Los Angeles Times*, September 30, 1974.

42. RICHARD A. CLOWARD and JAMES A. JONES, "Social Class: Educational Attitudes and Participation," in *Education in Depressed Areas*, ed. A. Harry Passow (New York: Teachers College, Columbia University, 1963), p. 210.

43. TIM PARSONS, "The Community School Movement," in *Myth and Reality*, ed. Glenn Smith and Charles R. Kniker (Boston: Allyn and Bacon, 1972), p. 299.

44. JACK MCCURDY, "School Chief Opposes Key Control Proposal," *Los Angeles Times*, December 9, 1974.

45. An interesting commentary about community control of schools can be found in an article by Joseph Featherstone, "Community Control of Our Schools," *New Republic*, January 13, 1968.

46. W. LOBAN, *Language Ability: Grades Ten, Eleven and Twelve*, Project #2387, University of California, Berkeley, 1967.

47. JUNE DEBODE OXSTEIN, "The Relationship of Instruction in Small Group Process Techniques to Classroom Instruction and Verbal Expression of Fourth Grade Pupils." Unpublished doctoral dissertation, University of Southern California, Los Angeles, 1975.

48. THEODORE ALEXANDER, Lecture to Teacher Education Class #401, January 13, 1975.

Workshop III

In the same way wrongs that afflict society are seldom willed by anyone or any group, but are by-products of acts of will having other objects; they are done, as someone has said, with the elbows rather than the fists. There is surprisingly little ill-intent, and the more one looks into life the less he finds of that vivid chiaroscuro of conscious goodness and badness his childish teaching has led him to expect.

Charles Horton Cooley, *Social Organization*, p. 400.

There are many signs and symbols of prejudice. Sometimes the language an individual uses gives him away. Sometimes prejudice can be detected in textbooks through misrepresentation and sometimes it is detected because of errors or omissions. Urban communities are concerned about the fairness and validity of instructional materials used in the classroom. For this reason, this workship directs your attention to the evaluation of instructional materials and the use of the classroom environment.

In your previous observations of behavior (Workshops I and II), did you detect *individual* characteristics? Did you generalize or make inferences about the behavior you witnessed? Workshop III requires that you distinguish among individual behaviors, role behaviors, and cultural behaviors.

Parental involvement in school life benefits the school, the children, and the profession. How does the school elicit parental involvement? In some instances parental involvement is reactive rather than planned or voluntary; the "News Item" story will illustrate. If you were a teacher, principal, or parent, how would you react?

The Language of Prejudice

OBJECTIVE: Interpret prejudicial behavior.

Can you detect prejudice? Describe an incident you witnessed in which you believe that the persons involved acted or spoke prejudicially. Who was involved? Describe the reaction. Did you detect preferential treatment—stereotyped thinking or language—or the use of a rationalization? What motivated the incident? If you had been involved, how would you have resolved the situation?

Cultural, Role, and Individualistic Behaviors

OBJECTIVE: Differentiate among the following behaviors: cultural, role, individual.

Distinguish among the following behaviors. Decide which behaviors reflect culture, role interpretation, or the individual. Some behaviors may be a combination.

1. Kim tugged at his tie and patted his hair slick.
2. Ishi lowered his eyes when he spoke to an adult.
3. The boys refused to assist in the preparation of the food.
4. Mary is always giggling.
5. Sam carries a schoolbag to school.
6. Although Brad was badly hurt, he appeared stoic.
7. Maria carefully straightened her skirt to hide her knees.
8. Girls wear blouses; boys wear shirts.
9. Sue ate at the cafeteria using a fork with her left hand and a knife with her right hand. She used the knife to assist her fork.
10. As the men greeted each other, they shook hands. The women joining the group smiled.
11. Tony was punctual in all his assignments.
12. Barry was aggressive in the classroom but not on the playground.

Local Control

OBJECTIVES: Express personal attitudes and beliefs; develop understanding of self.

The Rialto community includes four elementary schools, a junior high school, and a senior high school that borders the community. The area has had a long history of conflict with the school district. Upsetting to the community has been the low achievement level of the children; the high percentage of high school dropouts, which residents attribute to the youngsters being counseled out of school; and the widespread feeling that even those youngsters who graduate have not been prepared to succeed and live a life to which they would aspire.

The community's militant and moderate residents are pressing for local control of the schools. Their goal is to make the local schools accountable to them. They want the power to make decisions con-

Answers

1. Role. Individuality may also be expressed.
2. Cultural behavior.
3. Role. Cultural behavior also possible.
4. Individualistic behavior.
5. Individualistic behavior.
6. Role. Individualistic behavior also possible.
7. Role.
8. Role.
9. Cultural behavior.
10. Role and cultural interpretation is possible. In the United States women frequently do not shake hands.
11. Individualistic behavior.
12. Individualistic behavior.

cerning personnel, curriculum, and instructional materials. They are also determined to control the purse strings. The crucial issue in the conflict is the decision-making power related to personnel hiring and firing.

The school district has attempted various experiments in the area including federally funded compensatory educational projects, bilingual training for teachers, and summer workshops for students. Still the community feels that the majority of the teachers are disinterested in minority children, lack empathy, and teach down to them. Teacher turnover in the area has been excessively high.

If local control is achieved, the area would remain segregated; however, residents are quick to assert that since desegregation has progressed at a snail's pace, it would be far better for the community to control its own schools and ensure a better education for its children.

Professional groups are upset over the conflict. Their concern focuses upon the desire to hold decision-making power over matters that affect their professional activities. Teacher groups state that the profession should make educational decisions concerning curriculum and instructional materials, types of in-service programs that they will need, and the services they will provide to their clients. Basic to their argument are the questions concerning professional negotiation. Will teachers negotiate with the local community or the central district? How will job security be preserved if local control is granted?

Since both teachers and those who favor decentralization desire to make the educational decisions, how can conflict be averted? What are the options open to the teaching profession today? To what extent would it disturb you if your school were controlled by the local community?

News Item, Free Press, Thursday, January 11, 1976

OBJECTIVES: Compare personal perception with others; develop insight into community perception.

Students at Robert McKenzie High School in Lodgetown were searched for weapons upon their arrival at school on Wednesday. The search by police was made upon the request of the principal, Norbert Ames, following an incident between black and white students during the lunch hour on Tuesday. Parents were enraged that police had been called in and that students had been searched. Many faculty members, the *Free Press* learned, felt the principal overreacted. It is now feared that this incident may spill over into the community, influencing the junior high school and the four elementary schools in the area. Until Tuesday's incident, Lodgetown has been free of racial strife.

Mona Keppel, English teacher at the high school, described the incident for the *Free Press*.

> There was an especially long lunch line on Tuesday. The service seemed to be extremely slow. Students are taking final

exams and everyone is a bit edgy. Bill Randolph, a black student, was carrying his lunch tray. As he passed the line, he taunted Rod Emery, a white student. Actually, I think the boys are friends. Rod got angry and stuck out his foot. Bill tripped, dropped his tray, and came up swinging. The two boys exchanged blows and epithets.

It was at this point that other students joined in the melee, with black students taking Randolph's side and white students taking Emory's side.

The disturbance was ended by physical education teachers who manned a bull horn demanding cessation, and then waded in and pulled the groups apart.

When asked by the *Free Press* how many students were involved, Ms. Keppel estimated, "Perhaps about 10." Ms. Keppel had not been aware of any weapons used by the students.

The enrollment at the high school is 2,500. The ethnic composition of the school and community is 30 percent black, 70 percent white. Community meetings have been called by concerned parents at each of the elementary schools and the junior and senior high schools for this evening at 8 P.M.

What do you think will be the consequences of the situation?

How would you decide what had happened?

If you were a parent in that community, what would you expect of the school?

Advisory Council

OBJECTIVES: Attend parent-teacher function; describe interactions.

Attend an advisory council meeting. To what extent is the council representative of the ethnic composition of the community? Describe the meeting. Consider some of the following questions in your description:

How many people attended the meeting?

How many people expressed opinions?

What issues caused conflict?

Were conflicts resolved? In what ways?

Who initiated discussion?

How were decisions made?

Characterize the interactions: friendly, tense, cooperative, antagonistic. Cite evidence for your characterization.

School and Community

OBJECTIVE: Develop personal perspective concerning cooperative behaviors between school and community.

Describe parent-community involvement in your school.

Describe changes that would heighten the involvement, cooperation, and participation of parents in school life.

School Population and School Environment

OBJECTIVE: Develop cultural and ecological perspective and sensitivity.

Survey the ethnic composition of your school community for students, faculty, and staff. Describe the school environment that relates positively or negatively to the ethnic population of the school. (Refer to Chapter 1 if you need assistance with the term *school environment.*)

Students and Instructional Environments

OBJECTIVE: Develop an ecological perspective concerning the pattern of relations between students and instructional environments.

Describe the instructional materials in the classroom that relate to human relations.

Describe possible changes in the materials that would enhance the understanding of children about one another.

Enumerate student strengths.

Enumerate activities to utilize those strengths in classroom instruction.

Content of Materials

OBJECTIVES: Examine instructional materials for content omission and historical inaccuracies.

How have textbooks or films erred in descriptions about people or historical events resulting in the deprecation of the minority student?

How can books or films create good attitudes and images?

How is your school utilizing the students' cultural heritage?

How can your school reinforce the students' cultural heritage?

Suggested Readings

A recipe to develop a historical, ecological, and sociocultural perspective about the students you teach requires a little pinch of history, sociology, literature, and education. Mix well and enjoy!

General

Allport, Gordon W.: *The Nature of Prejudice* (Garden City, N.Y.: Doubleday, 1954) Social Psychology.

Bradburn, Norman, Seymour Sudman, Galen Gockel, and Joseph Noel: *Side by Side: Integrated Neighborhoods in America* (New York: Quadrangle, 1971) Sociology.

Cartwright, William H., and Richard L. Watson, Jr., eds.: *The Reinterpretation of American History and Culture* (Washington, D.C.: National Council for Social Studies, 1973) History.

Epstein, Charlotte: *Intergroup Relations for the Classroom Teacher* (Boston: Houghton Mifflin, 1968) Education.

Kane, Michael B.: *Minorities in Textbooks* (New York: Quadrangle, 1970) Education.

Mack, Raymond W.: Prejudice and Race Relations (New York: Quadrangle, 1970) Sociology.

McWilliams, Carey: *Brothers Under the Skin* (Boston: Little, Brown, 1951) History.

Report of the National Advisory Commission on Civil Disorders (New York: Bantam, 1968) Education.

Rose, Peter I.: *The Subject Is Race* (New York: Oxford University Press, 1968) Education.

Stone, James C., and Donald P. DeNevi: *Teaching Multi-Cultural Populations* (New York: Van Nostrand Reinhold, 1971) Education.

Mexican Americans

Burma, John H., ed.: *Mexican Americans in the United States* (Cambridge, Mass.: Schenkman, 1970) General.

Cabrera, Y. Arturo: *Emerging Faces: The Mexican Americans* (Dubuque: Brown, 1971) General, Education.

Galarza, Ernesto: *Merchants of Labor: The Mexican Bracero Story* (San Jose, Calif.: Rosicrucian Press, 1965) History, Sociology.

————: *Spiders in the House and Workers in the Field*. (Notre Dame, Ind.: University of Notre Dame Press, 1970) History, Sociology.

————, Herman Gallegos, and Julian Samora: *Mexican Americans in the Southwest* (Santa Barbara, Calif.: McNally & Loftin, 1969) Sociology.

Gonzalez, Rodolfo: *I Am Joaquin* (Toronto: Bantam, 1967) Literature.

Grebler, Leo, et al.: *The Mexican American People: The Nation's Second Largest Minority* (New York: Free Press, 1970) Sociology, History.

Heller, Celia S.: *Mexican American Youth: Forgotten Youth at the Crossroads* (New York: Random House, 1966) Sociology.

Lewis, Oscar: *Five Families* (New York: Mentor, 1959) Sociology.

Litsinger, Dolores: *The Challenge of Teaching Mexican American Students* (New York: American Book, 1973) General, Education.

McWilliams, Carey: *North from Mexico: The Spanish-speaking People of the United States* (Philadelphia: Lippincott, 1949) History.

Manuel, Herschel T.: *Spanish-speaking Children of the Southwest: Their Education and the Public Welfare* (Austin: University of Texas Press, 1965) Education.

Matthiessen, Peter: *Sal Si Puedes: Cesar Chavez and the New American Revolution* (New York: Random House, 1969) History.

Moore, Joan W.: *Mexican Americans* (Englewood Cliffs, N.J.: Prentice-Hall, 1970) Sociology.

Moquin, Wayne, Charles Van Doren, and Feliciano Rivera: *A Documentary History of the Mexican Americans* (New York: Bantam, 1971) History.

Nava, Julian: *Mexican Americans Past, Present and Future* (New York: American Book, 1969) History.

Parkes, Henry Bamford: *A History of Mexico* (Boston: Houghton Mifflin, 1960) Historical heritage.

Paz, Octavio: *The Labyrinth of Solitude: Life and Thought in Mexico* (New York: Grove Press, 1961) General, History, Sociology.

Robinson, Cecil: *With the Ears of Strangers: The Mexican in American Literature* (Tucson: University of Arizona Press, 1963) Literature.

Rumano, Octavio, ed.: *El Espejo—The Mirror: Selected Mexican American Literature* (Berkeley, Calif.: Quinto Sol Publications, 1969) Literature.

Samora, Julian, ed.: *La Raza: Forgotten Americans* (Notre Dame, Ind.: Notre Dame Press, 1966) Sociology.

Tebbel, John, and Ramon E. Ruiz: *South by Southwest: The Mexican American and His Heritage* (Garden City, N.Y.: Doubleday, 1969) Historical heritage, History.

Tuck, Ruth: *Not With the Fist—Mexican Americans in a Southwest City* (New York: Harcourt, Brace, 1946) History, Sociology.

Valdez, Luis, and Stan Steiner, eds.: *Axtlan.* (New York: Knopf, 1972) Literature.

Vasquez, Richard: *Chicano* (Garden City, N.Y.: Doubleday, 1970) Literature.

Black Americans

Baldwin, James: *Nobody Knows My Name* (New York: Dell, 1961) General, History, Sociology.

Banks, James A., and Jean D. Grambs: *Black Self-concept* (New York: McGraw-Hill, 1972) Education.

Blaustein, Albert P., and Robert L. Zangrando, eds.: *Civil Rights and the American Negro* (New York: Washington Square Press, 1968) History.

Botklin, B. A., ed.: *Lay My Burden Down: A Folk History of Slavery* (Chicago: University of Chicago Press, 1945) History.

Brown, Claude: *Manchild in the Promised Land* (New York: New American Library, 1965) Autobiography.

Carmichael, Stokely, and Charles V. Hamilton: *Black Power* (New York: Vintage, 1967) Sociology.

Clark, Kenneth: *Dark Ghetto* (New York: Harper & Row, 1965) Sociology.

Cleaver, Eldridge: *Soul on Ice* (New York: McGraw-Hill, 1968) Literature, Sociology.

Drake, St. Clair, and Horace R. Cayton: *Black Metropolis* (New York: Harcourt Brace World, 1945) Sociology.

Ellison, Ralph: *Invisible Man* (New York: New American Library, 1947) Literature.

Grambs, Jean, and John Carr, eds.: *Black Image: Education Copes with Color* (Dubuque: Brown, 1972) Education.

Haley, Alex, and Malcolm X: *The Autobiography of Malcolm X* (New York: Grove Press, 1966) Autobiography.

Halsey, Margaret: *Color Blind* (New York: Simon and Schuster, 1946) Literature, Sociology.

Hansberry, Lorraine: *The Movement: A Documentary of the Struggle for Equality* (New York: Simon and Schuster, 1964) History.

Hughes, Langston: *New Negro Poets, U.S.A.* (Bloomington: University of Indiana Press, 1964) Literature.

————, Milton Meltzer, and C. Eric Lincoln: *A Pictorial History of the Negro in America*, rev. ed. (New York: Crown, 1968) History.

Katz, William Loren: *Teachers' Guide to American Negro History* (New York: Quadrangle, 1968) Education.

King, Martin Luther, Jr.: *Where Do We Go from Here: Chaos or Community?* (New York: Bantam Books, 1967) General, Sociology.

Kvaraceus, William, John S. Gibson, et al.: *Negro Self-concept* (New York: McGraw-Hill, 1965) Education.

Larkins, A. Guy, and James P. Shaver: *Race Riots in the Sixties* (Boston: Houghton Mifflin, 1973) History, secondary.

————and ————: *The Police and Black America* (Boston: Houghton Mifflin, 1973) History, secondary.

Lindenmeyer, Otto: *Black History: Lost, Stolen, or Strayed* (New York: Avon, 1970) History.

Myrdal, Gunnar: *An American Dilemma* (New York: Harper & Row, 1944) History, Sociology.

Quarles, Benjamin: *The Negro in the Making of America* (New York: Collier Books, 1964) History.

Randall, Dudley: *The Black Poets* (New York: Bantam, 1971) Literature.

Rose, Harold M.: *The Black Ghetto* (New York: McGraw-Hill, 1971) Geography.

Rustin, Bayard: *Down the Line* (New York: Quadrangle, 1971) Literature.

Sloan, Irving: *The Negro in Modern American History Textbooks* (Washington, D.C.: American Federation of Teachers, AFL–CIO 1968) History.

Wright, Nathan, Jr.: *Black Power and Urban Unrest* (New York: Hawthorn Books, 1967) History, Sociology, Political Science.

Wright, Richard: *Black Boy* (New York: Harper & Row, 1937) Literature.

American Indian

Armstrong, Virginia Irving, comp.: *I Have Spoken* (Chicago: Swallow Press, 1971). History.

Astrov, Margot, ed.: *American Indian Prose and Poetry* (New York: Capricorn, 1962) Literature.

Aurbach, Herbert A., ed.: *Proceedings of the National Conference on*

American Indian Education (Kalamazoo, Mich.: Society for the Study of Social Problems, 1967) Sociology.

Borland, Hal: *When the Legends Die* (Philadelphia: Lippincott, 1963) Literature.

Brown, Dee: *Bury My Heart at Wounded Knee: An Indian History of the American West* (New York: Holt, Rinehart & Winston, 1970) History.

Cahn, Edgar S., ed.: *Our Brother's Keeper: The Indian in White America* (New York: World, 1970) History.

Deloria, Vine, Jr.: *Custer Died for Your Sins: An Indian Manifesto* (New York: Avon, 1969) History, Sociology.

————: *We Talk, You Listen: New Tribes, New Turf* (New York: Macmillan, 1971) Sociology.

Forbes, Jack D., ed.: *The Indian in America's Past* (Englewood Cliffs, N.J.: Prentice-Hall, 1964) History.

Kroeber, Theodora: *Ishi in Two Worlds* (Berkeley: University of California Press, 1961) Literature.

Marriott, Alice, and Carol Rachlin: *American Indian Mythology* (New York: Crowell, 1968) Literature.

Momaday, N. Scott: *House Made of Dawn* (New York: Signet, 1968) Literature.

Underhill, Ruth: *Red Man's America: A History of the Indians of the U.S.* (Chicago: University of Chicago Press, 1953) History.

Asian Americans

Chinese

Barth, Gunther: *Bitter Strength: A History of the Chinese in the United States 1850–1870* (Cambridge, Mass.: Harvard University Press, 1964) History.

Chiu, Ping: *Chinese Labor in California* (Madison, Wis.: State Historical Society, 1963) History.

Chu, Daniel, and Samuel Chu: *Passage to the Golden Gate: A History of the Chinese in America to 1910* (Garden City, N.Y.: Doubleday, 1967) Sociology, History.

Hsu, Francis L.: *The Challenge of the American Dream: The Chinese in the United States* (Belmont, Calif.: Wadsworth, 1971) Sociology.

Lee, Calvin: *Chinatown, U.S.A.* (Garden City, N.Y.: Doubleday, 1965) Sociology.

Lee, Rose Hum: *The Chinese in the United States of America* (Hong Kong: Hong Kong University Press, 1960) Sociology.

Sandmeyer, Elmer C.: *The Anti-Chinese Movement in California* (Urbana: University of Illinois Press, 1939) History.

Sung, Betty Lee: *Mountain of Gold* (New York: Macmillan, 1967) History.

Japanese

Bosworth, Allan R.: *America's Concentration Camps: The Shocking Story of 110,000 Americans Behind Barbed Wire in the U.S.* (New York: Bantam, 1968) History.

Daniels, Roger: *The Politics of Prejudice: The Anti-Japanese Movement in California and the Struggle for Japanese Exclusion* (Berkeley: University of California Press, 1962) Sociology, History.

DeBary, W. T., et al., eds.: *Sources of the Japanese Tradition* (New York: Columbia University Press, 1958) Sociology.

Hosokawa, Bill: *Nisei: The Quiet Americans* (New York: Morrow, 1969) History.

Kitano, Harry L.: *Japanese Americans: The Evolution of a Subculture* (Englewood Cliffs, N.J.: Prentice-Hall, 1969) Sociology.

McWilliams, Carey: *Prejudice: Japanese-Americans: Symbol of Racial Intolerance* (Boston: Little, Brown, 1945) Sociology.

Okada, John: *No-No Boy* (Rutland, Vt.: Tuttle, 1957) Literature.

Okubo, Mine: *Citizen 13660* (AMS Press, 1946) Pictorial history.

Sansom, George B.: *Japan: A Short Cultural History* (New York: Appleton, 1962) History, Sociology.

Spicer, Edward H., et al.: *Impounded People: Japanese Americans in the Relocation Centers* (Tucson: University of Arizona Press, 1969) History, Anthropology.

Children in the urban school: learning styles and learning problems

Mr. Block is teaching geography. He has a large hanging map of the United States displayed. He is using a pointer to identify the location of large bodies of water and mountain ranges. Then he points to the location of several large cities. He asks his class to hypothesize why large cities developed in certain areas of the United States. While some of the students in Mr. Block's classroom seem to be completely absorbed in what he is saying, others appear bored. Harry is staring out of the window; Michele is surreptitiously writing a letter; Bill does not seem to be able to sit still. When Mr. Block asked the students to respond, it was obvious that there were varying degrees of attention and comprehension.

The students in Mr. Block's classroom learn in a variety of ways. This seems simple enough and quite understandable; however, let us explore this further. Does *each* student learn in a variety of ways *or* does each student have a unique way of learning? Can a teacher detect both *when* a student is learning and *how* he learns? If Bill has a specific style for learning that can be isolated, should Mr. Block translate everything into that mode to increase the likelihood and capacity of Bill's intellectual development?

As we look into another classroom, Bill, Michele, and Harry are playing different roles. The teacher is Ms. Ames and the students are participating in the job interview activity (Chapter 3). Harry, a prospective employer, is diligently questioning a fellow student about his capabilities. His face is animated and he expresses himself well.

Michele is filling out a personnel form and Bill is being interviewed for a job at a department store. Are these the same students who appeared sluggish, disinterested, and dull?

We can all remember during our own formative school years a specific teacher who really made an impression. Is it possible that this teacher's classroom style corresponded with our own learning style? If so, should the teacher's style be matched with the student's learning style? Should the school provide opportunities to learn in a variety of ways? How would that concept change the organization of our schools?

To describe an individual's "characteristics," we must consider cognitive, affective, and psychomotor abilities. These abilities will also be influenced by age, sex, social class, cultural group, and place of residence. All these characteristics affect the individual's readiness to learn, motivation to learn, and efficiency in learning. Other forces that seem to affect learning in the school setting have to do with the nature of the learning task, the social setting for learning (the environment), the teacher's characteristics and teaching style, the nature of the learning group (peer group), and any other forces outside the school that tend to constrain or to nurture the learning environment.

In What Ways Is Each Child Unique?

Each individual may have a particular style of learning. The style may be physical (the person prefers "to do"), visual (the person must "see" before he learns) or auditory (the person must first "hear" in order to learn). Urban schoolchildren are unique in their multicultural heritage. Some cultural characteristics affect the ways in which children respond and learn in the school environment. These characteristics contribute to the child's unique nature. A number of research studies have been directed toward isolating cultural characteristics that relate to listening behaviors. Hall discovered a number of cultural differences:

> My friends, who were also my subjects, soon began to talk about how hard it was to know whether Americans were "tuned in" or not. When my subjects felt sufficiently at ease to talk freely, they said that we were rude. I slowly learned that how one indicates that one is paying attention is different for each culture.

Hall described his experiences working with Navajo Indians:

> I was fortunate in having friends who were good models for interacting with Navahos. A small point, but one which I learned was crucial to the entire tone of a transaction, is the way the Navahos use their eyes. Unlike middle-class whites, the direct open-faced look in the eyes was

avoided by Navahos. In fact, Navahos froze up when looked at directly. Even when shaking hands they held one in the peripheral field of the eyes, letting the message of the other person's warmth and pleasure at seeing a friend seep through a long-clasped, but delicately held, hand.

I ultimately learned that to look directly at a Navaho was to display anger. . . . Another Navaho taboo was the use of the name as a form of direct address. Nor were voices ever raised—except in anger.[1]

Briere, a linguist at the University of Southern California, developed a test of proficiency in English as a second language to use with American Indian children and noted cultural biases that affect language testing. As Briere analyzed the answer sheets on which the children had responded, he discovered that their responses were indicative of the "flight of geese" pattern that typically appears on Indian pottery or rugs. The children had obviously become tired during the test, but instead of quitting, each child at the moment of tiredness had resolved his dilemma by responding in a sequential, patterned fashion. If the point of tiredness occurred at question 20, then that question would be answered "A," question 21 would be "B," question 22 would be "C," question 23 would be "D" and then the pattern would begin anew.

Since individualistic behavior was not typical of the children, when they were tested in a classroom they would get up and help their classmates. Community responses were preferable. Cooperative behavior was common. Briere noted that cooperative behavioral responses were also typical of the Mexican American students with whom he had worked.

Children's storybooks normally are filled with pictures and stories about animals. For American Indian children, animals have great importance in their cultural and religious life. For instance, to the Hopi Indians, snakes have divine qualities; for the Navajo Indians, bears have great importance. The symbolic significance of animals in American Indian cultural life makes animal stories inappropriate for many teaching purposes.

Navajo children are consistently poor in their responses to either the Goodenough Draw a Man test or the Goodenough Completion test. Inquiry yielded cultural information that explained their behavior. The Navajo believe that every design must have a "break" in it to allow the soul to escape. If a Navajo child completed a design, his soul would be entrapped. Briere also noted communication distances (proximics) preferred by American Indian and Mexican Americans. Navajo adults disliked the Caucasian closeness of stance, preferring to be farther apart for normal conversation. Mexican Americans were just the opposite; they preferred closeness. The Anglo stance is too far away and uncomfortable for their normal conversation.[2]

As Hall studied black culture, he discovered cultural responses that governed eye contact, body motions, speaking and listening distances, hand movements.

> Basically, the informal rule for black culture goes somewhat as follows: If you are in the room with another person or in a context where he has ready access to you there are times when there is no need to go through the motions of showing him you are listening because that is automatically implied. When blacks interact with whites the differences in how one communicates that he is paying attention can cause great difficulty. One of my black assistants, working as a draftsman, got into trouble with his engineer boss who wanted to tell him something. Following his own culture, my assistant continued working at his drafting table without looking up, thus giving the engineer no visible or audible sign that he was listening. The man finally said, "John! Are you paying attention to me?" At which point John looked up and said, "Of course."
> When I discussed eye behavior with a black colleague he observed, "When I punish my boy *I look at him,* and when I look at him *I'm mad.* I look at his eyes and they grow big and he *knows* I'm mad."[3]

Leonard Olguin, a California bilingual specialist, in a talk to Los Angeles City teachers, discussed Spanish cultural habits that affect the relationship between classroom teacher and Spanish-speaking child.

> Mexican children are taught that it is disrespectful to direct their eyes into the eyes of an adult.
> The Spanish language is protective of the speaker, thus, the Spanish speaker when asked, "Who broke the dish?" would respond: "It broke itself" or "The dish itself fell from my hand." If asked why he was late to school, the teenaged student might respond, "The bus passed me by" rather than "I missed the bus."[4]

The influence of culture on language habits has been detailed by many researchers. Labov refuted the notion that black ghetto children were verbally deprived and explained the growth of that myth:

> The concept of verbal deprivation has no basis in social reality. In fact, Negro children in the urban ghettos receive a great deal of verbal stimulation, hear more well-formed sentences than middle-class children, and participate fully in a highly verbal culture; they have the same basic vocabulary, possess the same capacity for conceptual learning, and use the same logic as anyone else who learns to speak and understand English.[5]

Facts used to support the verbal deprivation theory have included the following:

> Urban black children do poorly in all the basic skill subjects.
> Urban black children average two years behind the national norm in reading.

The performance of black urban ghetto children becomes worse the longer they are in school. (cumulative deficit theory)

It has also been noted by sociolinguists that *any* group segregated from majority society will do poorly in the basic skill subjects when compared on national norm scales.

Labov asserted that psychologists who developed the deprivation theory based their assumptions on interview techniques which disregard the influence of a possibly hostile interview environment. For example, an interviewer who is usually white and adult, with a threatening stance (confrontation) because he literally towers over the young child, is very threatening to a black child. Labov's interview technique differed substantially from that of others. First, using a black interviewer who lived in and was knowledgeable about the Harlem community, he tried a standard interview session. He discovered the same limited verbal capacity and monosyllabic behavior as reported by other researchers. But at the second interview, the interviewer changed his tactics. This time, interviewing the same eight-year-old boy, he brought along to the interview session the child's best friend and some potato chips, and he sat in a chair that reduced his overall height by some 2'8". He introduced some "naughty" words during the interview and then proceeded to listen to the two boys as they competed for the verbal floor. Labov's conclusions about the speech of black urban children is reflected in the following statement:

> We see a child bathed in verbal stimulation from morning to night. We
> see many speech events which depend upon the competitive exhibition
> of verbal skills; sounding, singing, toasts, rifting, louding—a whole
> range of activities in which the individual gains status through his use
> of language. We see the younger child trying to acquire these skills
> from older children—hanging around on the outskirts of the older peer
> groups, and imitating this behavior to the best of his ability. *We see no
> connection between verbal skill at the speech events characteristic of
> the street culture and success in the schoolroom.*[6]

Cohen and Cooper summarized research findings about the language of urban black children and its relationship to reading instruction. Their report refuted seven fallacies about urban black children that have characterized them and affected classroom instruction.

1. *The urban black child is less verbal than the middle-class child.* The research of Labov refuted this characterization. Cohen and Cooper stated: ". . . people who find themselves in a threatening, degrading social context tend to keep their mouths shut. When the environment provides positive reinforcement of verbal output, the

organism is verbal; when it provides negative reinforcement, the organism shuts up."[7]

2. *The urban black child has little verbal interaction with adults who are important to him.* The authors cited the research of Kagan (1968) and Horner and Gussow to refute the characterization. Horner and Gussow used a radio transmitter (sewed into the child's clothes) to record informal verbal interactions in the child's home environment. Cohen and Cooper concluded that urban black children have appreciable verbal interaction with adults significant to them.

3. *Nonstandard English (black English) is inferior in linguistic form to standard English.* The research of Dillard (1970) and Cohen and Cooper were cited to refute the characterization. The research indicated that black English was as complex in form, highly structured, and developed as standard English.

4. *Differences between standard English and black English require the black child to translate written standard English into black English in order to communicate.* The researchers refuted the contention that language output is directly related to language input. The research of Ramsey, described in Chapter 5, demonstrated that comprehension for beginning readers was no greater for students who listened to standard English than for those who listened to black English; the use of black English does not appear to affect the "translation" process.

5. *The urban black child is disadvantaged conceptually and in the use of vocabulary; these two factors interfere with learning to read.* Beginning reading books use an extremely limited vocabulary. Even a child with limited verbal repertoire has "enough" vocabulary to handle primary reading books.

6. *The improvement of oral language patterns will improve developmental reading skills.* Cohen and Cooper cited Rystrom (1968 and 1970) and others: reading is not directly related to speaking. Good oral language does not necessarily guarantee good reading.

7. *Auditory discrimination is affected by poor articulation and affects the development of phonic skills.* The research of Cohen and Cooper indicated no direct relationship between encoding and decoding. Discrimination of word sounds can be taught independently of articulation.[8]

The research of Johnson in the Chicago area and in the Watts area of Los Angeles indicated that teachers need to change their attitude about nonstandard English. He corroborated the Cohen and Cooper review and stated that classroom teachers attributing false characterizations to black children have then based their classroom strategies on *false* assumptions, such as:

Student use of nonstandard English limits the student's cognitive development.

Black children are nonverbal.

Nonstandard English lacks a consistent pattern; black dialect is therefore a sloppy speech.

Black children do not "hear" the sounds of standard English.

Standard English *can replace* the black dialect.

Johnson recommended the use of second language teaching techniques (note Chapter 2) to assist black children learn standard English. His suggestions included:

> The identification of points of language interference. (How does black English differ, systematically, from standard English?)
>
> Identification of the differences for children to "see" and "hear."
>
> Opportunity for children to *discriminate* between the nonstandard dialect and the standard speech.
>
> Opportunity for the children to reproduce standard speech.[9]

Some research studies have related learning-style differences to socioeconomic status. Sigel, Anderson, and Shapiro detected differences that affect reading instruction. Lower-class black preschoolers were less able to objectify and deal representationally with materials. The researchers concluded that lower-class children lacked the requirements to move from egocentric and subjective behavior to an objective and representational mode. The lower-class children preferred to categorize objects based upon use and interdependence, whereas the middle-class children categorized objects based upon common physical attributes.[10]

Ramirez studied the cognitive style of Mexican-American students. His subjects tended to be what some researchers refer to as "field-dependent" individuals. Their behavior reflected conformity rather than autonomy; they were controlled by their environment instead of controlling their environment. Ramirez suggested that classroom instruction should be compatible to the field-dependent approach of his subjects.[11]

A Crisis of Identity

Ralph Ellison wrote an extremely moving novel about a young man's search for identity. In the prologue, he stated:

> I am an invisible man. No, I am not a spook like those who haunted Edgar Allan Poe; nor am I one of your Hollywood-movie ectoplasms. I am a man of substance, of flesh and bone, fiber and liquids—and I might even be said to possess a mind. I am invisible, understand, simply because people refuse to see me.
>
> Nor is my invisibility exactly a matter of a biochemical accident to

my epidermis. That invisibility to which I refer occurs because of a peculiar disposition of the eyes of those with whom I come in contact. A matter of the construction of their *inner* eyes, those eyes with which they look through their physical eyes upon reality.[12]

Ellison was reacting to what he felt was an ambiguous existence for black Americans. The adaptation to the realities of American social, economic, and political life has often caused a *crisis of identity* for multicultural populations living in urban areas. But the social reality for black Americans has certainly been more difficult than for other groups.

The *self-concept* of the individual is based upon who he believes himself to be (which is based upon the individual's concept of who his family is) and who he believes he will be in the future. The sense of future orientation is formulated as the individual perceives the recognition and esteem of others (teachers, peers, family). The individual's concept of self is reflected in his personality and the ways in which he directs his actions to reciprocate the perceived expectations of others. The individual's self-concept is comprised of all of the following:

A personal concept of identity

The individual's attitudes

The individual's vision of his environment

The individual's personal goals as well as his success in achieving those goals

A self-assessment as the individual compares himself to others and includes the individual's perceived evaluation by others

In a study reported by Bronfenbrenner, children's behavior was influenced by the *lack* of parental concern rather than the attractiveness of the peer group. Bronfenbrenner and his colleagues characterized 766 sixth-grade children as either "peer-oriented" or "adult-oriented," depending upon the number of weekend hours the children spent with either peers or adults. To analyze how the children became either peer- or adult-oriented, the researchers analyzed the child's perception of peers, family, self. They concluded that, in general, ". . . the peer-oriented youngster was more influenced by a lack of attention and concern at home than by the attractiveness of the peer group." The peer-oriented children also seemed to hold "rather negative views of themselves and the peer group. They also expressed a dim view of their own future." The peer-oriented group admitted engaging in more antisocial behavior than the adult-oriented group.[13]

Bronfenbrenner concluded that children who received little parental attention were seldom reinforced for curiosity and achievement.

They were not accustomed to a "reward" for their own thinking or efforts. They were accustomed only to negative attention when they did something wrong; therefore, their personal environment was unresponsive to them.

In an early compilation of research about the self-concept, Wylie noted that the self-concept was a consequence of the following:

Parent-child interaction
Social interaction other than parent-child
Body characteristics
Counseling and psychotherapy
Lobotomy
Experimentally induced success and failure
Learning

The following behaviors, according to Wylie, are dependent upon the self-concept:

Performance in learning tasks
Self-regard and adjustment
Self-acceptance and acceptance of others
Self-regard and ethnocentrism or authoritarianism
Self-regard and level of aspiration[14]

In reviewing a number of experiments that induced success or failure, Wylie noted that under certain conditions, subjects changed their self-evaluations after being subjected to experimentally induced success or failure and that it was more likely for subjects to rate themselves higher after success than downward after failure. Also observed was the tendency for subjects to react in the following ways after failure:

Devalue the source of the failure information
Fail to recall low evaluation accurately
Blame others
Attempt behaviors that have brought satisfaction in the past
Exhibit anxiety reactions[15]

Many psychologists have assumed from their studies that the self-concept is antecedent to cognitive behavior and is attributable to the influence of motivation.

The concept of "experimentally induced success or failure" has great implications for the instructional process, for it is apparent that where the school environment previously may have played a role in defeating the culturally different student, it could be used to change and strengthen the self-concept of the child. Many urban teachers deliberately plan teaching strategies to develop, strengthen, or change the self-concept of their students.

The following excerpt, written by a sixth-grade girl in a Los Angeles City urban school, is an example of a creative language lesson planned to enhance the self-concept of the students.

> I am someone who is not a him, her, we, they, but I am me. I want to be treated as an individual. I am somebody that is clean not dirty. I am somebody who is not sad. I care for others. I am somebody who loves my mother, father, sisters, brother. I am somebody who loves anyone and everyone no matter what race or color. I am someone who wants to be a SOMEBODY.
>
> —Elicsha Babers[16]

In past years the development of the self-concept was left to chance. The school is second only to the home in its influence on the child; for that reason, urban teachers today are designing instructional strategies which involve students in activities with older children and adults to ensure ego development and success. (Review the section on modeling in Chapter 2 and the strategies for modeling in Chapter 5.)

Biber and Minuchin studied the impact of school philosophy on children's self-image and self-identity. Some aspects of their research are particularly relevant to urban school children. The researchers differentiated between *traditional* and *modern* schools, defining the two in terms of school environment and educational program. In the *traditional* school, the teacher was the central figure who established all learning tasks; the children carried out the tasks according to standards established by the teacher. The textbook and the syllabus determined the curriculum. In the *modern* school, the curriculum was diversified, with creative arts as a built-in feature. Emphasis was on student exploration and discovery. The teacher's role was that of a knowledgeable adult guide. Rules were developed by the children with the teacher to satisfy school "living" needs. The rules were considered flexible.

Some selected findings of Biber and Minuchin that relate to children's self-concept include the following:

Children's Attitudes Toward Authority. Children in the *modern* school were rational and objective and did not find the authority figure threatening. Children in the *traditional* school responded continually to rules, regulations, and infractions. They were deeply involved in the consequences of transgression. They were authority-oriented.

Children's Self-image. Children in the *modern* school saw themselves, their qualities, and their interests in differentiated terms. They focused on current interests and personalities.

Children in the *traditional* school characterized themselves impersonally and tended to look at their own development in terms of established roles for the future.

Family Influence. Boys from traditional family environments were particularly assertive about their sex roles. Girls from modern family environments were particularly open and exploratory.

Interaction of School and Home. When school and home hold consistent orientations (modern or traditional), the effect on the child's self-concept and value system is cumulative and powerful.

School Philosophy, Consistency. Greater impact on child development exists when the school presents an integrated environment throughout the school day.[17]

Reviewing self-concept research as it relates to the urban child, it is apparent that school performance is dependent upon the child's feeling of self-worth and self-esteem. The individual who lacks confidence cannot perform adequately in the classroom or on the job. There seems to be a relationship between high achievement and a positive self-concept. (The reverse may also be stated: there seems to be a relationship between a positive self-concept and future achievement.) Acceptance of the relationship between school achievement and a positive self-concept compels teachers to find ways in which students' self-identity and self-image can be enhanced. Research also indicated that the school can be used as a setting to foster a positive self-image as well as to promote student growth. Coopersmith and Feldman suggested the following classroom practices to build self-concept and self-esteem:

1. Teacher *acceptance* of the child. (To understand this concept, review teacher tactics in Chapter 2.) Teacher *trust* of the child. The teacher relinquishes some control to the child to govern his own actions. The teacher offers students opportunity for *choice*. Students learn to make decisions that affect themselves.

2. The teacher sets *limits* that indicate his expectations to the child. The limits are clear and rational statements of behavior. The teacher sets *guidelines* in order for students to interpret the limits. The teacher *enforces* the limits and guidelines. The implementation of the limits and guidelines is practiced in an authoritative and democratic rather than authoritarian manner (review Lippitt and White research in Chapter 2.)

3. The teacher expresses an *optimistic outlook* that is interpreted by the child as acceptance, respect, and expectance of success. The teacher indicates a design for success. The design is a *realistic plan* with appropriate actions that students can perform. The

teacher develops *responsibility*. The child is forced to take personal responsibility for his own growth.[18]

Several researchers have called attention to the positive characteristics of urban children. Both Briere and Olguin have identified specific features about Indian and Mexican American children. These factors have included:

Cultural Warmth. The "personal" nature of culture, the affective orientation. This is also true of Asian American children.

Language. Individual welfare is a natural instinct of Spanish-speaking individuals. The language protects the person.

Early Maturity. Children become independent at an early age, caring for themselves and younger siblings. Dressing and washing are performed by the child. Young children also run errands for the family and perform home chores.

Practicality. The practical (what works?) is utilized rather than the theoretical.

Family Lineage. Who you are is more important than what you have achieved. The Mexican father will introduce his sons as my Baron 1, Baron 2, and so on. In the introduction of two strangers, the speaker does not mention "position" or "status," only names and relationship to self.

Cooperative Behavior. Children are accustomed to looking out for each other and helping each other.

Community. The community is characterized as happy; a great deal of informal language takes place in the community as does laughter and music. The community is responsive.

For a number of years Riessman researched some of the positive characteristics of disadvantaged children. Based upon his findings, the following list was compiled to summarize some of the unique characteristics of urban students.[19]

Verbal ability	Extremely verbal in out-of-school situations. Articulate in conversation with peers. Descriptive, expressive, colorful use of slang.
Attitude toward education	Positive attitude about education; value education as a means for personal achievement. However, a negative attitude often exists about the institution of the school.
Cooperativeness and mutual aid	This characteristic is a result of the extended family.
Avoidance of competitiveness	Informality and humor prevail in out-of-school relationships and carry into the classroom.

Freedom from self-blame	The student wastes little time crying over "spilled milk."
Lessened sibling rivalry	Children enjoy each other's company and derive security from the extended family.
Enjoyment of music, sports, games, cards	Greater enjoyment seems to be derived from creative and expressive activities.
Emotional expressions	Children express anger and other emotions readily. They lack emotional deviousness.
External orientation	Rather than introspective outlook.
Spatial perspective	Rather than temporal perspective.
Expressive orientation	Rather than instrumental orientation.
Consent-centered	Rather than form-centered mental style.
Problem-centered	Rather than abstract-centered approach.
Physical and visual style	The student may be a slow learner, but this is not to be confused with "dullness." It is descriptive of his learning approach.

Developmental Stages and the Learning Process: In What Ways Are All Children Alike?

Many learning as well as behavioral problems arise because the teacher is not cognizant of the student's developmental level. Some psychologists, particularly Piaget, believe that children learn most efficiently when instruction corresponds with the child's developmental level. Other psychologists theorize that optimal learning is achieved when instruction is adjusted to the next higher developmental level (Kohlberg). This supposition is based on the assumption that the individual is motivated to learn when he feels a wee bit of anxiety or dissonance. It is important to remember that the purpose of most teaching strategies is to increase the student's level of abstract thinking.

Piaget's stages of development

Theories about the nature of child development have influenced parental care and discipline, health care for children, and teaching approaches in the school. Behavioristic, maturational, and psychoanalytic theories have influenced American parents and the schools during the twentieth century. The studies of Jean Piaget into the nature of children's thinking and the development of intelligence have shaped many teaching models in recent years. Piaget identified four stages in the development of thinking.

Prelanguage stage (0–2 years). The sensorimotor stage is vital to later development of thought. The baby develops substructures important for later actions. The baby demonstrates intelligence *prior* to speech. The baby begins to learn the principle of invariance. By the end of the first year, the baby is able to search for a vanished object. He begins to coordinate his actions and reversibility commences. During this stage the baby has learned through experience concepts of space, time, causality, and intentionality.

Preoperational stage (2–7 years). The child moves from the universe of direct action to the universe of representation. This is the stage Piaget calls conceptual intelligence. Thinking is concrete. The child structures reality in terms of concrete actions, overt or mental. The child participates in imitation and symbolic play. True language begins and is indicative of representational thought. Intuitive thinking begins at about age four. The idea of conservation begins during this stage.

Stage of concrete operations (7–11 years). In this stage the child resolves most of the problems of conservation. The child performs simple reasoning as it relates to concrete manipulations. His logic implies an understanding of a pattern of relationships, identity, and simple reversibility. The first concepts used by the child are preconcepts. They are action oriented, concrete rather than abstract. The child has difficulty recognizing stable identity when there is contexual change.

The child links preconcepts by transductive means that are neither inductive nor deductive. Reasoning proceeds from item to item to conclusion without reversing thought. There is no guarantee that the process is arrived at logically. Items are juxtaposed rather than connected by causal relationships. During this stage the child is unconcerned with logical proof and has difficulty distinguishing between play and reality. Concrete operations are performed in the immediate present. The child begins with his own reality; therefore, the structure of content cannot be set in advance.

Stage of propositional operations (11–16 years). Skill in scientific reasoning increases during this stage. The child is no longer limited to concrete reasoning about objects. He now manipulates data into statements of meaning. He organizes the concrete by classifying, seriating, and corresponding and can use the results of these operations by formally casting them into propositions which he then subjects to logical operations including inference, implication, identity, conjunction, and disjunction. Formal operations are both outcome and outgrowth of concrete operations. The child performs combinatorial operations that involve proportions. He now reasons hypothetically. "If-then" types of operations are apparent.

Piaget related the solving of a problem with the child's ability to coordinate his actions while focusing on a solution. Thinking begins with simple action; later the operations become internalized and represented symbolically. Unlike habits, actions are reversible; once the child is able to handle a particular operation, he is also able to reverse it.

Piaget's concept of egocentrism has special meaning for this text. Flavell defined it this way:

> It denotes a cognitive state in which the cognizer sees the world from a single point of view only—his own—but without knowledge of the existence of viewpoints or perspectives and, a fortiori, without awareness that he is the prisoner of his own.[20]

The preoperational child, according to this viewpoint, is unable to perceive others as having a different viewpoint than his own. He is not role-oriented to others. He is unaware and indifferent to other reasoning constructs and unwilling to participate in retrospection. Egocentric thought is unreflective because only consciousness of his own reasoning process and the desire to justify and to accommodate his reasoning process to others forces the child to be reflective. Through repeated and forced social interactions the child is able to relinquish his egocentrism and subject his thinking to argument and disagreement.

Piaget stated that as each developmental phase commences, egocentrism increases; then slowly, when the child can deal with new cognitive action, egocentrism subsides. The concept of egocentrism is somewhat a restatement of Piaget's equilibrium model, wherein each new cognitive development subjects the individual to disequilibrium. Egocentrism proceeds through the sensorimotor stage into the concrete-representational stage and finally occurs in the adolescent in the form of a desire to reshape reality through his own omnipotence.[21]

Since curriculum design (what to teach, when to teach it, in what order, to what depth) is dependent upon a conceptual framework, psychologist Irving Sigel studied Piaget's theory to determine its applicability in the classroom. Important elements from Piaget that Sigel felt classroom teachers should be aware of included the following:

Children acquire knowledge through different cognitive modalities at different developmental levels. This means that where the preschool child might learn through imitation or acting out, the older child might talk it out.

Cognitive growth, although a continuous process, proceeds with spurts and plateaus. The teacher needs to recognize that developmental levels are not fixed but develop, adapt, modify. It is a dynamic process.

Language is the key mode of communication. Language is a tool to express thoughts. Language is not thought; therefore, children must develop skill in expressing thoughts to convey meanings. Since they do not know *all* the words, they have to borrow what they need in accordance with their developmental level. This is particularly significant when teaching bilingual children, since it is difficult to know how many words they know and the significance they place on concepts expressed by the teacher.

Children are egocentric and express egocentricity in thought and language. The social environment teaches children the meaning of cooperation and objectivity. For the teacher, this is significant because the classroom environment needs to be used as a laboratory for interaction and interchange of thought and cooperative endeavors; otherwise children do not progress from egocentrism to sociocentrism.

Development proceeds in an orderly sequence. This is significant to the teacher because unless a child is "ready" for what is to be taught, the teaching time will be wasted. The teacher must be cognizant of the varied stages and the behavioral indications of each stage.

Sigel also cautions teachers that children may not develop in all areas at the same time; they may be in one stage conceptually and in another stage in a different area.[22]

The application of these principles in the classroom provides guidelines concerning physical setting, content, choice of experiences, activities, interaction, and the teacher's role.

Physical setting. The classroom environment should be set to conform to the child's developmental level. Young children require an environment that allows them to move, explore, manipulate, construct, imitate. Therefore, the physical arrangement needs to be supportive of these activities; the environment is arranged to foster interaction.

Content. Children need to be constantly challenged (confronted) with their own illogical thought in order to progress to the next conceptual stage. Choice of content must be based upon the child's conceptual level. Primary children (K–2) use words such as *more, less, few, many, long ago;* yet these abstract, quantitative expressions lack significance for them. The teacher's task should be to determine the conceptual level and provide appropriate content and experiences to allow children to build their own "meanings."

Experiences. Since children progress from the concrete to the abstract, experiences must be chosen appropriately. Very young children learn to group and classify by manipulating differently shaped objects. Teaching about the "long ago" becomes more significant if children can see the same city street, uncrowded, with horse and buggy transportation, and compare it to the crowded street of today, clogged with automobiles.

Activities. The choice of activities must be purposeful and sequentially planned. The activities should involve children in interaction with others. Situations should be created that allow children to experiment, manipulate, question, hypothesize, and compare findings with others.

Interaction. No concept in the Piagetian theory is as significant as interaction. Children need opportunity to interact with their physical and social environment. Children need to use language and experience verbal interaction. The teacher plans physical, social, and conceptual confrontations to develop interactive experiences.

Teacher's role. The teacher needs to be a diagnostician, strategist, guide, and evaluator. The teacher should be constantly alert—observing, assessing, arranging the environment, providing the confrontations.

The research of Lawrence Kohlberg indicated that the growth of moral character progresses sequentially based upon moral reasoning and application to action. The influence of Dewey and Piaget is apparent in Kohlberg's stages. Kohlberg, in an address to the National Council for the Social Studies, acknowledged his debt to both men:

> In stating my goals . . . I wish to acknowledge my debt to the greatest modern educational psychologist and philosopher, John Dewey. In 1895, Dewey said: "Only ethical and psychological principles can elevate the school to a vital institution in the greatest of all constructions —the building of a free and powerful character. Only knowledge of the order and connection of the stages in psychological development can insure the maturing of the psychical powers. Education is the work of supplying the conditions which will enable the psychological functions to mature in the freest and fullest manner." The educational implications of Piaget's work in cognitive stage development and my work in moral stage development may be best understood as outgrowths of this statement of Dewey.[23]

According to the moral development theory, children move from egocentric behavior, where they make decisions based upon personal needs and wants (and avoidance of punishment), to the stage of being "good" and conforming to authority, and then finally to the stage of moral reasoning, where rules and agreements are based upon negotiation, respect, and trust. The individual does not skip stages. There is a relationship between chronological age and level of reasoning. Kohlberg has identified six stages of moral development at three levels:

Chronological age	*Moral development level*
Preadolescent	Preconventional level
Adolescent	Conventional level
Adult (less than 20 percent of adult population)	Movement toward postconventional levels

Kohlberg's moral stages

The preconventional level. The individual reacts to punishment and obedience. Children respond to cultural rules and labels, such as good, bad, right, wrong. They interpret these concepts in terms of their own personal orientation. What will be the consequences to them? (punishment, reward?) The level is divided into two stages. At stage I, the individual orientation is sensitive to punishment and obedience. Individuals reach a decision based on their perceptions of authority and respond to personal consequences of punishment, reward, or exchange of favors. At stage II, the orientation is instrumental-relativist. Individuals may be responsive to the needs of others if they interpret them as ultimately affecting their own needs. Concepts of fairness, equality, reciprocity are interpreted in a practical manner. Loyalty, gratitude, and justice are not necessarily considered. Kohlberg poses a moral dilemma to demonstrate the individual's responses at these two levels. His subject is a middle-class boy, and the dilemma is as follows:

> Before the Civil War, we had laws that allowed slavery. According to the law if a slave escaped, he had to be returned to his owner like a runaway horse. Some people who didn't believe in slavery disobeyed the law and hid the runaway slaves and helped them to escape. Were they doing right or wrong?[24]

At stage I, Kohlberg's subject would respond: "They were doing wrong because the slave ran away himself. They're being just like slaves themselves trying to keep 'em away." When asked whether or not slavery was right or wrong, he would respond: "Some wrong, but servants aren't so bad because they don't do all that heavy work."

The subject responded in this way at age 10, but at age 13, when asked the same question, he responded in the following manner:

> They would help them escape because they were all against slavery. The South was for slavery because they had big plantations and the North was against it because they had big factories and they needed people to work and they'd pay. So the Northerners would think it was right but the Southerners wouldn't.[25]

The conventional level. Individuals are capable of moral reasoning that involves the consideration of family or peers. Individuals consider it important to maintain the existing social order. At stage III of this level, the individual's orientation is a consequence of the aspiration to please others and thereby reap their approval. The individual judges others by an interpretation of the other's intent (he means well). At stage IV, the individual is concerned about personal duty and makes decisions that correspond to the maintenance of authority, rules, and the existing social order.

Kohlberg's subject, now nineteen, responds to the slavery question at a stage IV level of development:

> They were right in my point of view. I hate the actual aspect of slavery, the imprisonment of one man ruling over another. They drive them too hard and they don't get anything in return. It's not right to disobey the law, no. Laws are made by the people. But you might do it because you feel it's wrong. If fifty thousand people break the law, can you put them all in jail? Can fifty thousand people be wrong?[26]

Kohlberg's subject still defines "rightness" in terms of obedience to the law. One wonders how many people in Germany during the 1930s were frozen at stages II, III, or IV levels of moral development!

The postconventional, autonomous, or principled level. Moral values and principles are incorporated into moral reasoning. Values and principles have validity and application independent of the authority of groups. The individual's orientation is to universal principles; moral reasoning is comprehensive.

At stage V, the individual's orientation is related to a recognition that rights are based on a social contract within society. "Rightness" is determined by the society of which the individual is a member. Actions are based on laws that are critically examined and agreed upon; however, laws can be changed. The individual is aware of the relativistic nature of personal values. Emphasis is placed on "procedural rules" and the "legal point of view." At stage VI, the individual reasons and makes decisions based on ethical principles. The universal principles of justice, reciprocity, equality of human rights, and respect for the dignity of others serves as a basis for reasoning and applies to all mankind.[27] To differentiate between stage V and stage VI, Kohlberg quoted Martin Luther King's stage VI statement:

> One may well ask, "How can you advocate breaking some laws and obeying others?" The answer lies in the fact that there are two types of laws, just and unjust. One has not only a legal but a moral responsibility to obey just laws. One has a moral responsibility to disobey unjust laws. Any law that uplifts human personality is just, any law that degrades human personality is unjust. An unjust law is a code that a numerical or power majority group compels a minority group to obey but does not make binding on itself. This is difference made legal.[28]

Research using Kohlberg's stages demonstrated that teenaged students can understand all stages below their own moral developmental level and sometimes the stage immediately above their own level. Kohlberg recommended confronting students one stage in advance of their own level. He described an experiment by Moshe Blatt in ghetto schools, suburban schools, and working-class white schools. Each classroom of junior high or high school students contained children at three developmental stages. Blatt had students at the two lowest stages confront each other. They would then move on to a confrontation with those at the third stage. The classroom discussions yielded moral development change, with each class moving to the next higher stage of development. Classes attained a minimum of 15 percent to a maximum of 66 percent upward movement.[29]

The research of Leon Festinger provides insight into the way an individual forms a decision and acts upon it. Festinger asserted: "There is a consistency between what a person knows or believes and what he does."[30] He found that an individual's opinions and attitudes exist in groups or clusters and are usually consistent. His theory of cognitive dissonance merits consideration as teachers plan strategies for moral development.

Festinger defined *consonance* as consistency and *dissonance* as inconsistency. His theory is based upon the following premise:

The human organism tries to establish internal harmony, consistency, or congruity among his opinions, attitudes, knowledge, and values. That is, there is a drive toward consonance among cognitions.[31]

Cognitive dissonance exists immediately after a decision has been made whenever there is a choice between two or more alternatives. The research indicated that the positive features of the rejected choices and the negative features of the chosen alternative are dissonant with the knowledge of the action taken. At the same time, the negative features of the rejected alternatives and the positive features of the chosen alternative are consonant with the knowledge of the action taken.[32]

Two important implications of the Festinger study indicate that, in the presence of dissonance, some individuals will seek new information in an effort to achieve consonance or attempt to avoid new information which may be likely to increase the dissonance. Cognitive dissonance may lead to behavioral and opinion change. Festinger also noted that some individuals cannot tolerate dissonance. This type of individual puts forth great effort to reduce dissonance. Individuals with low tolerance for dissonance tend to polarize the issues as they formulate beliefs. According to Festinger, if developmental growth is to occur, the individual must be confronted with cognitive dissonance. Kohlberg described a similar condition as *disequilibrium.*

Learning Styles: Can a Teacher Detect
How a Child Learns?

Students differ both in their learning problems and in their learning needs. These differences may be related to dissimilarity in life styles. The experiences of the urban student are obviously different from the experiences of the student who lives in a small town or a suburban community. But, however much students may differ, there are also many similarities. The theoretical approach of Piaget and Kohlberg emphasized similarities in terms of cognitive development.

Developmental theories are useful because they direct attention to immediate as well as future needs. A good theory specifies where the child is and where he will be going. Educational practitioners utilize the theory when they diagnose the student's developmental stage and then prescribe appropriate learning activities to facilitate long-term growth. At Carnegie-Mellon University, a teaching plan was developed to utilize the theory of moral development. The plan was composed of four parts.

Confronting a Moral Dilemma. The teacher presents the moral dilemma to the class, and assists the students to clarify and define concepts or aspects of the dilemma.

Stating a Position. Students are encouraged to state the problem and take a value position. Students need to decide what to do and why to do it. The teacher assists students by giving them enough time to think about it, to write down their ideas, or to brainstorm together. The teacher asks the students to express an opinion about the dilemma. This can be done by a show of hands—"How many believe. . . ." The purpose of the show of hands is to determine whether or not an actual difference of opinion exists in the classroom. If it does not, then a new dilemma should be chosen by the teacher.

Testing the Reasoning. Students meet in small groups to develop their defense or "best" reasons for action. Groups may be chosen in one of two ways: Each member of the group may *agree* with every other member and can then work out appropriate action; or group members may be in *disagreement*. The group must discuss its disagreement and choose the two best reasons for each position.

Reflection on a Reason for a Position. The final step of the teaching process is the evaluation or summary of what has transpired in the discussions. The reasons are presented. The teacher does not attempt to achieve consensus but rather tries to facilitate thinking about whether or not there is a "right" answer. The teacher may or may not decide to present additional reasons to the students (that they had not presented). Achievement of the "best reason" or "the answer" is not an objective.[33]

The teacher's role is that of a facilitator who maintains a moderately structured classroom for the discussion. The teacher encourages students to talk and reason. When the teacher contributes to the discussion, the contribution should lead to more student discussion rather than acting to close out student reasoning. The teacher must remember that moral development occurs because students come into contact with other students at a higher level of development. It is this confrontation that leads them upward. Teacher diagnosis of students' moral development stage occurs during part two of the teaching plan when the teacher encourages students to state the problems and the appropriate action. Such a teaching plan may actually take several days to accomplish.

Some psychologists and educators studying individual differences have observed the ways in which different individuals process information. Recent behavioral studies have focused on the ways in which students approach a learning task, the strategies they employ in working through the learning situation, the ways in which students organize information to group and sort, students' demonstration of ability, and students' indication of preferences. Perhaps because the researchers have studied individual ways of "operating" in a variety of situations, they have not developed a consistent terminology to define "cognitive style." But psychologists have concluded that each individual *generally* has a consistent, patterned learning style and that "style" is identifiable.

The child's ability to conceptualize from overgeneralized labeling to discrete and abstract concepts is developmental. The young child may label helicopters, airplanes, and hummingbirds "birds," and anything on four legs may be labeled "dog." As the child develops, his perception becomes specific and differentiated. Although it is recognized that the ability to conceptualize is developmental, teachers have detected vast differences among children of the same age and of the same IQ. To study and describe cognitive activity, researchers have directed attention to "cognitive style." Kagan, Moss, and Sigel have defined it as "A term that refers to stable individual preferences in mode of perceptual organization and conceptual categorization of the external environment."[34]

These researchers began studying adults who were asked to sort, group, and respond to a number of stimulus arrays (pictures of human figures). Their subjects produced concepts whose orientation the researchers classified as either egocentric or stimulus-centered. Concepts labeled *egocentric* were based upon the individual's personal reactions to the stimuli, such as "People I like" or "People who like me."[35] *Stimulus*-centered concepts were based upon the external stimulus, such as "men," "soldiers," "women with skirts on." Conceptual categories also were identified by the researchers. These included analytic-descriptive, inferential-categorical, and relational. Responses within these categories included the following orientations: In the *analytic-descriptive* category, the subject might refer to attributes shared by the grouped stimuli, such as "people holding something," or "people with their left arms up." In the *inferential-categorical* category, these concepts would involve an inference assumed by the subject about the stimulus group, such as "people who help others," or "poor people." In the *relational* category, the subjects would assume a functional relationship among the grouped stimuli. The subjects might respond: "Murder scene—he shot this man," or "People arguing with each other."[36]

The researchers concluded that relational responses required the least amount of analysis, whereas the analytic-descriptive responses required greater conceptual analysis. The relational category was considered passive in the subject's acceptance of the entire stimulus, whereas the analytic response was considered an "active" conceptual analysis.

The educational implications of this study suggested by the researchers included the observation of primary children as they learn to read. Reading specialists have long been aware that an analytic attitude seems to facilitate the decoding process. "To notice the differences between 'cat' and 'bat' and 'dog' and 'bag' requires differentiation and analysis of the stimulus."[37] The researchers also pointed out that boys have greater difficulty than girls with the reading process and that boys of normal IQ with reading problems are typically restless and impulsive. The classroom application of this theory would seem to direct teachers to design learning tasks that will develop the student's analytic capability, thereby diminishing some future reading difficulties.

Another outgrowth of this research related to the greater difficulties experienced by lower-class children and by boys with the reading process pertains to what Yando and Kagan refer to as the psychological dimension of reflection vs. impulsivity.[38] This dimension identified the tendency for children to respond to learning problems either impulsively or reflectively. (Chapter 2 discussed research related to the teacher's ability to modify the tendency toward impulsivity. Chapter 5 suggests strategies that increase the dimension of reflectivity.) Many errors in the classroom in reading responses and in computation skills may be attributed to the student's orientation to respond impulsively. Yando and Kagan suggested learning tasks that would provide specific training in scanning strategies for impulsive responders.

Heider proposed a method to modify the impulsivity of a group of lower-class seven- and nine-year-old white boys. The researcher manipulated four conditions in the experiment in order to determine whether any of the conditions would affect both student errors and response times:

1. Control condition in which the subject was given standard instructions.
2. Forced delay in which the subject was told to delay his response until he heard a chime.
3. Increased motivation in which the subject was told he would be rewarded if he made few mistakes.
4. Task strategy instructions in which the subject was given two instructions about how to perform the task.

In a prior study, Heider had found evidence that ". . . class differences in habitual strategies of information processing might originate in differing motivations concerning intellectual performance but, once established, may not be readily changed by manipulation of motivation."[39] Her later study confirmed this evidence and Heider determined that *only* the task strategy instructions significantly reduced errors. Heider concluded that methods of information processing could be taught and that they could be influential in modifying impulsivity among lower-class children. The Heider study is significant because its classroom application can be readily accomplished. Providing students with a model for problem solving and teaching them how to solve the problem has been effective in many urban classrooms.

Oxstein used a variation of the task-instructions technique in a fourth-grade classroom where the majority of the students were Mexican American. The study focused on improving discussion techniques and the development of cooperative group behavior. The class sessions were divided into four parts: (1) teacher provided content instructions, description of task or game; (2) discussion or "game" session; (3) evaluation or debriefing; and (4) overall review of content.

During the first module, Oxstein presented information to the children about speaking patterns for small discussion groups. Then, the children were divided into groups and participated in a small-group discussion. During the debriefing stage, the children commented that their discussions were inhibited due to the lack of a leader, to not knowing whether to raise their hands before they talked, and to the fact that not all members of each group had participated.

Since the children had specified the need for a leader, during the second experience the researcher appointed a leader and a recorder for each discussion group. The job of the recorder was to tally each time a person spoke. The researcher gave the leaders "special" instructions. Two of the leaders were asked to be "facilitators," to make comments such as, "That's a good point, Ted." The other discussion leaders were instructed to be "obstructors." They were to talk as much as possible, complain, and generally badger their groups. As expected, during the debriefing stage it was revealed that in the groups with "facilitating" leaders, all went well. The other groups were frustrated and few had participated. The teacher then revealed the planning that had occurred and provided information about the role of cooperative leaders and how cooperative behavior affects others.

Midway through the experiment, the researcher introduced "tokens" to induce and reward cooperative group behavior. When each member of a group participated and group goals were accomplished, the group as a whole would be rewarded with some tokens. Later in the semester the tokens were exchanged for prizes or games. During successive sessions the children defined obstructive and facilitative behavior. They developed awareness of behaviors that caused group frustration or cooperation. By the end of the experiment the children had improved in both group interaction skills and verbal expression.[40]

These studies raise many interesting questions for urban teachers. Does the cognitive style of the urban student influence what he *chooses* to learn? Does the cognitive style of the urban student influence the *effectiveness* of how he learns? How does teaching methodology affect learning? Should teachers consciously attempt to modify the student's cognitive style? Sigel and Coop raised the possibility that cognitive style may represent the individual's preference and as such may be a deeply ingrained habit: "The source of these habits, however, is still open to question. They may well be habits that are analogous to defense mechanisms, where children employ certain styles in the service of coping with anxiety or some other adaptation procedure."[41]

David Hunt used a psychological theory to arrange a social environment to "fit" students' learning needs. Hunt and his associates

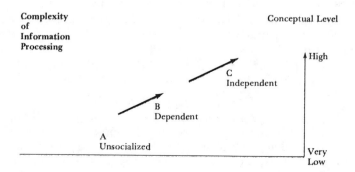

characterized three stages of personality development:[42] The individual changes from an immature, unsocialized being (stage A) to a dependent, conforming being (stage B) and finally to an independent, self-reliant person (stage C). (How do these stages compare with Kohlberg's stages of moral development?) Hunt described his model in this way:

> The Conceptual Level developmental model is an interactive theory of development which considers developmental progression or growth to be determined both by the person's present developmental stage and by the environment he experiences.
>
> To progress from Stage A to Stage B the individual must understand and incorporate the cultural rules. Since rules are learned best when they are clear the ideal environment to foster development to Stage B is therefore a clear, consistent, highly structured one.[43]

As the individual progresses from stage B to stage C, Hunt would moderate the structure to encourage self-expression and autonomy. High structure is indicative of an authoritative environment controlled by parent or teacher. Low structure would be indicative of subject control of his own environment (personal responsibility) or a student-centered teaching approach.

Stage A   High structure
Stage B   Moderate structure
Stage C   Low structure

To classify the student's conceptual level, Hunt had the subjects react to a stimulus that required some cognitive work in the response. Hunt used a paragraph completion test. The subject would respond with a few sentences that would indicate his reaction. The responses would be coded from 0 to 3; the code corresponded to the developmental stages. Next, Hunt matched the subject's conceptual level with the instructional environment.

Hunt experimented to investigate the effect of high structure using the lecture method and low structure using the discovery method on children of low and high conceptual levels. His research indicated that low conceptual level students performed significantly better with high structure (lecture method) than with low structure (discovery method). Hunt's conceptual-level system seems to discriminate among behavioral patterns characteristic of different levels of integrative complexity. The following example may illustrate the application of Hunt's system in a high school classroom:

> In an American government class the students were discussing an ordinance being considered by the city council. The ordinance proposed to ban public nudity on city beaches. The students expressed their viewpoints. Pam Sears, who just happened to have an American flag pinned to her collar, expressed the viewpoint that nudity would destroy our country because it was an expres-

sion of permissiveness. Bob Edwards was a proponent of nudity on specified sections of the ten miles of public beaches. He expressed the viewpoint that others have the right to go to the beach and not see nudes. "I support that, I don't want to make other people behave my way, nor do I want to be required to behave just the way others think I ought to."

Pam Sears' viewpoint represents an extremely deterministic interpretation of what would happen if nudity were allowed on any of the public beaches. Her thinking seems to be categorical—if this happens, then that will occur; there is no room for conflicting opinions or alternatives. In Hunt's conceptual-level system this kind of thinking would be representative of low complexity (stage A). Sears would appreciate a highly structured environment where rules are specific. Bob Edwards appears to be the opposite sort of individual. His integrative complexity would be high. His system is less deterministic. He appreciates alternate viewpoints, interpretations, and conflict. He seems to be able to accept alternate resolutions of conflict. In Hunt's conceptual-level system he would be representative of stage C and would appear to appreciate a low-structured environment where

Characteristics of stages and matched instructional environment

Stage (Conceptual Level)	Characteristics	Environment
C	Self-responsibility Multiple alternatives Capacity for integration	Low structure Discovery approach Example—rule Student-centered
B	Authority-oriented Concerned with rules Categorical thought	High structure Lecture Rule—example Teacher-centered
A	Self-protective Immature self-centeredness No alternatives	

SOURCE: David E. Hunt et al., *From Psychological Theory to Educational Practice: Implementation of a Matching Model* (Washington, D.C.: Educational Resource Information Center, U.S. Office of Education, April 1968), ED 068 438, 34p.

individuals learn by example rather than by specific rule making. (Review the information about the prejudiced personality in Chapter 3. Classify the prejudiced personality using Hunt's conceptual-level system.)

Joyce defined three tasks for the classroom teacher who wishes to use the Hunt conceptual-level system:

1. Diagnose the student's level of development. Utilize a problem such as the nudity issue discussed in the government class, listen to the students as they express their personal viewpoints, compare what the students said with Hunt's characteristics, and classify the students' conceptual level.
2. Create an environment that corresponds to the complexity level of the subject. The classroom learning environment must "fit" both the chronological age of the students and the subject or grade level to be taught.
3. Prescribe an optimal environment for personality growth to increase the integrative complexity of the students. If students are at a low conceptual level, choose appropriate teaching strategies. However, it is important to provide instruction that leads to the next higher conceptual level. In the case of the Sears and Edwards dispute, it may be valuable for the students to work together in a small group to explore their differences. Perhaps the students should choose their own teaching strategies. Sears would probably choose an input technique that allowed her to view a film, read a textbook, or listen to a tape or lecture. Edwards would probably choose an interactive strategy that permitted him to work with others or "do his own thing."

In reviewing Hunt's research, Joyce theorized about the application of the system. He stated that "the world of the person of low complexity . . . is evaluative and becomes rigid . . . and is very different from the real world of a person of high complexity . . . who accepts the responsibility for creating rules in new situations, and who can easily build conceptual bridges between himself and problem situations."[44] Hunt's work would therefore indicate that the low conceptual level individual would have difficulty in a free-choice environment. Discussion techniques with individuals of low complexity might be extremely difficult and inappropriate. For optimal growth, students should be matched, environmentally, with the characteristics of their own worlds. However, the teacher's task is to provide an environment that will also encourage integrative development—that is, growth from one level of complexity to the next higher level. Therefore, learning tasks should be arranged so that individuals experience confrontations which will force some negotiation about rules.[45]

Summary

The urban child rarely performs well during formal test situations. Teachers therefore need other kinds of information upon which to base their diagnostic assumptions (note Chapter 2). Piaget's theory provides insight into the process of thinking. The sequence of developmental stages is influenced by maturation, by action, and by experience. Each stage prepares the way for successive stages. To progress to more advanced stages, children need time to practice and repeat concepts in a variety of contexts. It is in this way that teachers can facilitate the process.

Many individuals would like a diagnostic system that fits the student into a category so that the teacher could then say: "Ah ha! He is at this level and needs blankety-blank and he will/will not progress until. . . ." Tests do provide diagnostic information, but some tests are of questionable validity. The purpose of this chapter was to examine research that would serve as a guide to the urban teacher for inferring developmental stages on the basis of observing students at play, at work, as they ask questions, and as they are presented with problems which invite decision making. Using observation skills as well as objective test evidence, the teacher can choose, plan, and evaluate teaching strategies and activities for the urban classroom.

Underpinning this chapter is a basic philosophical question: Do teachers have the ethical right to induce the modification of students' cognitive style? Do teachers have a choice? Dewey in 1895 seemed confident that education should provide the environment and direction for sequential cognitive and moral development. Kohlberg in an address to social studies teachers criticized the "hidden" curriculum that teaches conformity to authority and competition for status. In reviewing the Kohlberg theory and the classroom application of his work, we might well question the effectiveness of teaching techniques that didactically attempt to "teach" concepts such as loyalty, respect, justice, honesty.

Three questions were considered in this chapter: In what ways is the urban student unique? In what ways are all students similar? Is it possible to identify an individual's learning style?

In the first section the work of sociologists and sociolinguists characterized cultural influences that affect the learning process. Some learning-style differences were related to socioeconomic status. Both the strengths and weaknesses of urban children were explored. Researchers refuted the concept of verbal deprivation, and common fallacies that have both characterized urban black students and plagued educational practices were exposed. Research related to the individual's self-concept concluded that the student's image of self affected personality, learning performance, and aspiration level. Suggested practices for improving the student's self-concept included a number of teacher behaviors: providing acceptance and trust, setting limits and guidelines, providing a responsive environment, relinquishing control, and granting decision-making responsibilities to the child.

The second section of the chapter presented the developmental theories of Piaget and Kohlberg, with the application of the theories by other researchers. Piaget's developmental theory suggested that instructional activities could be coordinated with the child's cognitive level. Kohlberg's moral development theory suggested that learning activities could be arranged at a level just above the child's developmental stage.

The third section of the chapter reviewed learning styles. The purpose of this section was to develop teacher sensitivity to students' individual learning approaches. The implications derived from the research on learning style seemed to indicate that students' cognitive style influenced learning ability, learning effectiveness, and student choice of learning activities. Some researchers investigated the feasibility of modifying style preferences in order to develop the student's information-processing capability. Understanding style preferences would assist the classroom teacher to analyze student error and performance on tests as well as performance and responsiveness during verbal activities. Application of the cognitive style research has diagnostic and prescriptive implications. Urban teaching suggestions derived from the research included these: Develop students' analytic capability to diminish some reading difficulties; moderate students' response time to develop reflectivity rather than impulsivity; teach methods of information processing using task instructions.

Notes

1. EDWARD T. HALL, "Listening Behavior—Some Cultural Differences," from *Language and the Language Arts*, ed. Johanna S. DeStefano and Sharon E. Fox (Boston: Little Brown, 1974), p. 131.

2. EUGENE BRIERE, interview between Briere and the author, January 27, 1975.

3. HALL, *op. cit.*, pp. 132–133.

4. LEONARD OLGUIN, "The Red Brick and Adobe Wall," speech presented to Los Angeles City School District teachers, May 1968.

5. WILLIAM LABOV, "The Logic of Nonstandard English," in *Language and the Language Arts*, ed. Johanna S. DeStefano and Sharon E. Fox (Boston: Little Brown, 1974), p. 135.

6. *Ibid.*, p. 143; emphasis added.

7. S. ALAN COHEN and THELMA COOPER, "Seven Fallacies: Reading Retardation and the Urban Disadvantaged Beginning Reader," *The Reading Teacher*, October 1972, p. 39. See also J. KAGAN, "His Struggle for Identity," *Saturday Review*, December 7, 1968, pp. 80–88; V. HORNER and J. GUSSOW, "John and Mary: A Pilot Study in Linguistic Ecology," in *Functions of Language in the Classroom*, ed. Courtney Cazden, et al. (New York: Teachers College Press, 1972); J. DILLARD, *Black English in the United States* (New York: Random House, 1970); R. RYSTROM, "Effects of Standard Dialect Training on Negro First Graders Being Taught to Read," Report Project No. 81053, U.S. Department of Health, Education, and Welfare, 1968.

8. COHEN and COOPER, *op. cit.*

9. KENNETH R. JOHNSON, "Teacher's Attitude Toward the Nonstandard Negro Dialect—Let's Change It," *Elementary English*, 48, 2 (February 1971), 176–184.

10. IRVING E. SIGEL, LARRY M. ANDERSON, and HOWARD SHAPIRO, "Categorizing Behavior of Lower and Middle Class Negro Preschool Children: Differences in Dealing with Representation of Familiar Objects," *Journal of Negro Education*, 35 (1966), 218–229.

11. M. RAMIREZ, III, "Implications of Cultural Democracy and Cognitive Styles for Evaluative Research," paper presented at American Education Research Association, April 1972, and reported in *Psychological Concepts in the Classroom*, ed. Richard H. Coop and Kinnard White (New York: Harper & Row, 1974), p. 257.

12. RALPH ELLISON, *Invisible Man* (New York: Signet Books, 1947).

13. URIE BRONFENBRENNER, *Two Worlds of Childhood* (New York: Russell Sage Foundation, 1970).

14. RUTH C. WYLIE, *The Self-Concept* (Lincoln, Neb.: University of Nebraska Press, 1961), p. 118.

15. *Ibid.*, p. 198.

16. A sixth-grade student in the class of Mrs. Linda Ellis, 32nd St. School, Los Angeles, California, March 1974.

17. BARBARA BIBER and PATRICIA MINUCHIN, "The Impact of School Philosophy and Practice on Child Development," a study supported by the National Institute for Mental Health (Grant #M1075), as reported in *The Unstudied Curriculum: Its Impact on Children*, ed. Norman V. Overly (Washington, D.C.: Association for Supervision and Curriculum Development, 1970), pp. 27–52.

18. STANLEY COOPERSMITH and RONALD FELDMAN, "Fostering a Positive Self-concept and High Self-esteem in the Classroom," in *Psychological Concepts in the Classroom*, ed. Richard H. Coop and Kinnard White (New York: Harper & Row, 1974), chap. 7.

19. FRANK RIESSMAN, "The Overlooked Positives of Disadvantaged Groups," in *Culture and School*, ed. Ronald Shinn (Scranton: Intext, 1972), chap. 16.

20. JOHN J. FLAVELL, *The Developmental Psychology of Jean Piaget* (Princeton, N.J.: Van Nostrand, 1963), p. 60.

21. JEAN PIAGET, "The Attainment of Invariants and Reversible Operations in the Development of Thinking," trans. Marianne L. Simmel, in *Readings in Human Development*, ed. Harold W. Bernard and Wesley C. Huckins (Boston: Allyn & Bacon, 1967), pp. 136–149.

22. IRVING E. SIGEL, "The Piagetian System and the World of Education," in *Studies in Cognitive Development*, ed. David Elkind and John Flavell (New York: Oxford University Press, 1969), pp. 465–488.

23. LAWRENCE KOHLBERG, "Moral Development and the New Social Studies," *Social Education*, May 1973, p. 369.

24. *Ibid.*, p. 372.

25. *Ibid.*, p. 373.

26. *Ibid.*, p. 373.

27. The six stages of moral development have been adapted from three sources: Norman V. Overly, ed., *The Unstudied Curriculum;* two articles by Kohlberg, "The Moral Atmosphere of the School," ASCD, 1970, and "Moral Development and the New Social Studies," *Social Education*, May 1973. (Reprinted with permission of the National Council for the Social Studies and Lawrence Kohlberg); and "Teaching Strategies for Moral Dilemmas," by Galbraith and Jones, *Social Education*, January 1975.

28. KOHLBERG, "Moral Development and the New Social Studies," p. 373.

29. *Ibid.*, p. 375.

30. LEON FESTINGER, *Theory of Cognitive Dissonance* (New York: Harper & Row, 1957), p. 1.

31. *Ibid.*, p. 260.

32. *Ibid.*, p. 261.

33. RONALD E. GALBRAITH and THOMAS M. JONES, "Teaching Strategies for Moral Dilemmas," *Social Education*, January 1975, pp. 16–22.

34. JEROME KAGAN, HOWARD A. MOSS, and IRVING E. SIGEL, "Psychological Significance of Styles of Conceptualization," in *Basic Cognitive Processes in Children*, ed. J. C. Wright and Jerome Kagan, *Monographs of the Society for Research in Child Development*, 28 (2, serial no. 86), 1963, pp. 73–112.

35. *Ibid.*, p. 76.

36. *Ibid.*, p. 76.

37. *Ibid.*, p. 111.

38. REGINA M. YANDO and JEROME KAGAN, "The Effect of Teacher Tempo on the Child," *Child Development*, 39 (1968), 27.

39. ELEANOR ROSCH HEIDER, "Information Processing and the Modification of an Impulsive Conceptual Tempo," *Child Development*, 42 (1971), 1276–1281.

40. JUNE DEBODE OXSTEIN, "The Relationship of Instruction in Small Group Process Techniques to Classroom Instruction and Verbal Expression of Fourth Grade Pupils," unpublished doctoral dissertation, University of Southern California, 1975.

41. IRVING E. SIGEL and RICHARD H. COOP, "Cognitive Style and Classroom Practice," in *Psychological Concepts in the Classroom*, ed. Richard H. Coop and Kinnard White (New York: Harper & Row, 1974), p. 265.

42. DAVID E. HUNT et al., *From Psychological Theory to Educational Practice: Implementation of a Matching Model* (Washington, D.C.: Educational Resource Information Center, U.S. Office of Education, April 1968), ED 068 438, 34p.

43. *Ibid.*, p. 6.

44. BRUCE JOYCE and MARSHA WEIL, *Models of Teaching* (Englewood Cliffs: Prentice-Hall, Inc., 1972), p. 306.

45. *Ibid.*, p. 308.

Workshop IV

In this chapter you have read about differences and similarities among children that influence teaching and learning in the classroom. None of the differences among children was related to the concept of IQ. Variations in development and learning styles among children require diversity of teaching methods and materials. In some cases, moderating students' learning approaches will help them become more effective and efficient learners. The purpose of this workshop section is to assist you to detect differences and to decide what to do about them.

The Playground Teaching Episode

OBJECTIVE: To characterize cognitive level using Piaget, Kohlberg, and Hunt.

It was recess time. The only playground equipment available for use were some balls. The students began to play a type of "sock" ball. They divided into teams and play commenced. After a few minutes a ball was socked just inside the first base line. The first baseman ran for the ball and then ran with it back to his base. He did not tag the runner, but he arrived at the base before the runner did. An argument developed as to whether or not the runner was out without being tagged. The children crowded around the first baseman, with his team taking his side and the other side refusing to accept the "out." The verbal hostility soon turned into physical combat, with children pushing and hitting each other. A teacher arrived, blew a whistle, and shouted, "Who started this?" The children ceased fighting and stared at the teacher.

Do you believe that the children should be punished? why? Characterize the cognitive level of the children; use Piaget, Kohlberg and Hunt.

Speaking Spanish Not Allowed

OBJECTIVE: To classify levels of moral development.

Rick taught in a probation camp school. He was Mexican, but no one was aware of it. On his first day in class a small group of students gathered in the back of his classroom; they were laughing and speaking Spanish. Rick knew that speaking Spanish was not allowed at the school. The rule had been made because other students had complained that the Mexican students were always talking about them. Other students came into the classroom. They looked up at Rick expectantly as they listened to the Mexican students talking. Rick knew that if he reported the Mexican students, they would be severely punished. Yet if he did not report them, it was likely that the students would report *him*, and he could lose his job. What should Rick do?

The following comments were made by students. Use Kohlberg's stages to classify levels of moral development.

1. Rick should take his chances. It would not be right for him to report the students even though they were breaking a rule.
2. Rick ought to talk about the rule in class with all the students. The rule is unjust; it should be changed. It is ethically unenforceable.
3. Since the rule states, "No Spanish allowed," Rick does not have a choice. It would not be right for him to break the rule.

Moral Development

OBJECTIVE: Read to gain knowledge about alternative approaches for moral education; contrast approaches and viewpoints.

Douglas Superka, "Approaches to Values Education," *Social Science Education Consortium Newsletter*, Boulder, Colorado, November 1974.

Special Issue on Moral Education, *Phi Delta Kappan*, June 1975.

Short statements such as these are difficult to interpret. In the classroom the teacher should ask for statement clarification and explanation so that students have the opportunity to express their thoughts fully.

3. Stage I.
2. Stage V or VI.
1. Stage III or IV.

Answers

Cognitive Style Theories

OBJECTIVE: Read to gain knowledge about cognitive style theories.

The research of Garza and Ames contradicts the Ramirez field-dependence theory of Mexican American cognitive style. Read the Garza and Ames study and cite the conflicting evidence.

Garza, Raymon T., and Russel E. Ames: "A Comparison of Anglo and Mexican American College Students on Locus of Control," *Journal of Consulting and Clinical Psychology*, 42 (December 1974), 919.

Read the studies of Witkin and his associates. Compare Witkin and associates' global-analytic styles of field articulation to the Kagan, Moss, and Sigel concepts of cognitive style.

Witkin, H. A., R. B. Dyk, H. D. Paterson, D. R. Goodenough, and S. A. Kays: *Psychological Differentiation* (New York: Wiley, 1962).

Witkin, H. A., D. R. Goodenough, and S. A. Kays: "Stability of Cognitive Style from Childhood to Young Adulthood," *Journal of Personality and Social Psychology*, 1 (1967), 291–300.

Conceptual Categories

OBJECTIVE: Using statements, categorize conceptual style according to the research of Kagan, Moss, and Sigel.

Categorize the following statements using the three categories:

Analytic-descriptive
Relational
Inferential-categorical

1. I saw a number of windmills on farms in Holland.
2. All Germans are arrogant.
3. Children attending inner city schools are poor.
4. There was a loud crash; two cars hit each other.
5. There was a loud crash; probably a couple of female drivers.
6. I heard a loud crash and saw a group of boys dragging a load of scrap metal.

Answers

1. Analytic-descriptive.
2. Inferential-categorical (stereotyped thinking).
3. Relational (the relationship is assumed.)
4. Relational.
5. Inferential-categorical.
6. Analytic-descriptive.

Modify Cognitive Style

OBJECTIVE: Apply cognitive style information; diagnose students' problems; alter teaching method.

Students read an information sheet that presented factual details about Ashanti family life in Ghana. Family members' roles and chores were compared to those of rural farm families in the United States. In the discussion which followed it was apparent that the students failed to make distinctions between life on a United States farm and the Ashanti life style. A second group of students studying the same information was able to chart the information categorizing the facts: Ashanti family roles, U.S. farm family roles, Ashanti life style, U.S. farm life style. The second group of students could be described as "analytic" in their approach to the problem. How can you develop an analytic style in the first group of students?

Ego-satisfying Behaviors

OBJECTIVE: Observe student(s) satisfying ego needs; identify examples of student competence; identify contributing and/or inhibiting factors; prescribe to enhance or modify behavior.

Activities that satisfy ego needs develop self-confidence, self-respect, security, and status. Possible examples include a task-oriented activity or skill the student completes successfully, or a peer teaching activity in which student demonstrates to or teaches another student(s). (Note Figure 2.4 in Chapter 2.)

1. Give examples of student competence.
2. Give examples of student need or difficulty.
3. Give examples of ways in which the teacher contributed to or inhibited student competence.

Answers

1. Ask very specific questions that will motivate the students to search out specific facts. (Where does the Ashanti farm family live? In what ways is the American farm family dwelling different from the Ashanti farm dwelling? (The Ashanti farmers live many miles from their farm; the U.S. farm family usually lives on its farm.)
2. Assist the students by providing a structure for them to "hang their facts on." Providing a chart such as the one used by the second group of students would facilitate analysis.
3. Assist the students to evaluate the significance of their contribution. As students respond, the teacher can indicate the relevance and validity of the information. (How does the contribution "fit?")

4. Give examples of contributing or inhibiting (other) factors that affected student competence.
5. What factors, tasks, behaviors, or experiences would you change to contribute to student(s) competence?

(Observation of these behaviors is not limited to the classroom.)

Learner-assertive Behaviors

OBJECTIVES: Observe student(s) performing learner assertive activities; identify examples of student competence; identify contributing and/or inhibiting factors; prescribe to enhance or modify behavior.

Activities that develop learner assertiveness require the following behaviors: questing, seeking, searching, defining, analyzing, conceptualizing, and evaluating. Examples include a task-oriented activity or project performed individually or with others in which student initiates, pursues, or reflects, demonstrating desired behaviors.

1. Give examples of student competence.
2. Give examples of student need or difficulty.
3. Give examples of ways in which the teacher contributed to or inhibited student competence.
4. Give examples of contributing or inhibiting (other) factors that affected student competence.
5. What factors, tasks, behaviors, or experiences would you change to contribute to student(s) competence?

Independent-oriented Behaviors

OBJECTIVES: Observe student(s) performing independent-oriented behaviors; identify examples of student competence; identify contributing and/or inhibiting factors; prescribe to enhance or modify behavior.

Activities that develop independence require the student to demonstrate the following behaviors: initiate (action), make decisions, express individuality, create, and demonstrate dependability. (Note Chapter 2, Figure 2.4.) One possible example might be a task-oriented activity or skill in which a student sets his own standard (goal setting), defines means, and demonstrates persistence.

1. Give examples of student competence.
2. Give examples of student need or difficulty.
3. Give examples of ways in which the teacher contributed to or inhibited student competence.
4. Give examples of contributing or inhibiting (other) factors that affected student competence.

5. What factors, tasks, behaviors, or experiences would you change to contribute to student(s) competence?

Group-satisfying Behaviors

OBJECTIVES: Observe students satisfying group behaviors; identify examples of students' competence; identify contributing and/or inhibiting factors; prescribe to enhance or modify behaviors.

Group-satisfying activities develop the following values: cooperation, rationality, responsibility, and respectfulness. (Note Figure 2.4, Chapter 2.) One possible example might be a task-oriented activity or project that requires participation as leader and/or group member.

1. Give examples of student competence.
2. Give examples of student needs or difficulties.
3. Give examples of ways in which the teacher contributed to or inhibited competence in group behaviors.
4. Give examples of contributing or inhibiting (other) factors that affected student competence.
5. What factors, tasks, behaviors or experiences would you change to contribute to student competence?

Signs of success, strategies for success

"I open the dror an thar
be a cockroach. My Momma
say git him. He bad."

The first-grader continued to describe the cockroach using the tape-recorder to preserve his story . . . "He be big and black and walk like he own the kitchen. I feel scared and my Momma, she mad." The teacher suggested that the student draw the cockroach, his mother, and himself. He did, and the teacher promptly pinned it upon the bulletin board. Underneath the picture appeared the statement: Sam and mother saw a cockroach.

Sam read the statement with the teacher's assistance. He was able to identify his own name and the words *mother* and *cockroach*. Next, Sam read the statement to his classmates. The teacher turned on the taperecorder for everyone to hear Sam's story. Sam grinned self-consciously. The teacher wrote on the blackboard: The cockroach is ———— and ————. The class guessed the missing words—*big, black*. The teacher asked: "How did Sam feel?" "Scared," they responded. She wrote: *Sam is scared*. The teacher asked: "How did Sam's mother feel?" "She mad." The teacher wrote on the blackboard: *Mother is mad*. Next the teacher transcribed the entire story underneath the picture so that it now read:

Sam and mother saw a cockroach.
The cockroach is big and black.
Sam is scared.
Mother is mad.

Teacher Behavior—Overt	Teacher Behavior—Covert
What did the teacher consciously do?	*What did the teacher consciously* not *do?*
Listened to Sam's story.	Made *no* grammatical corrections as Sam taped his story.
Taped Sam's story.	
Placed his picture on the bulletin board.	Made *no* comments about his story when his classmates listened to it.
Played the taped recording for Sam's classmates.	Made *no* value comments.
Wrote the story on the blackboard and cued the class to supply missing words.	

Why was the teacher successful? How did the teacher direct language instruction? Sam's teacher was aware that children bring to the classroom a wealth of language experiences. These experiences, as well as the child's feelings, need to be shared with others. Children gain confidence as they communicate in both oral and written form with their peers. The teacher exhibited respect, acceptance, and understanding by listening to and recording Sam's story. Sam and his classmates were encouraged to participate in oral language experiences because no value comments were made verbally or nonverbally concerning either the content of Sam's story or his grammatical structures. Since Sam's classmates would have no difficulty understanding Sam's story just as he told it, the teacher did not spoil the listening pleasure of the classroom members with unnecessary explanations. The teacher directed language instruction in the following ways:

1. Oral language was encouarged through the acceptance of the child's natural dialect.
2. The language within the child's own repertoire of experience was used to teach standard English and reading.
3. Standard phraseology was taught using the student's own vocabulary.
4. Oral language was correlated with the written language form.
5. Familiarity with the oral language was used to facilitate reading. (Only the verb form of be (is) could be expected to give the students a problem.)
6. Through individual reading of phrases as well as the complete "story" students practiced oral reading skills.
7. Reinforcement was achieved through the use of matching games as students matched the phrase on the blackboard with the phrase underneath the bulletin board picture.

Sam and his classmates were learning to read through the use of what teachers call the language-experience approach to reading. The teacher in the preceding episode had two major objectives: development of self-concept and self-identity, and development of communication skills.

Research reviewed in Chapter 4 identified a number of inter-related factors that affect the language skills of urban children: the primary language of the child, the child's attitude toward English, self-concept of the child, the child's ability to perceive contrasts, the teacher's attitude toward the use of nonstandard English. Since language and culture are so closely entwined, teachers who react judgmentally toward a child's oral expression (including the child's listening stance) may be communicating "bad language—bad child." Although Sam's teacher was effective, the techniques differed from those suggested by Johnson. How would Johnson's suggestions have changed the structure of the lesson? Can you identify the school success-oriented behaviors that the teacher achieved? How do you think other members of Sam's class will respond to the approach tactics of the teacher?

How does the urban teacher influence student learning? Good teachers are akin to good detectives. They have refined their observational skills and they use appropriate testing devices. By learning to identify and classify student behavior, the teacher is able to diagnose:

Student interest

Appropriate motivation for that student

How much the student has learned

How fast the student is learning

What the student remembers

The way in which the student applies information from one situation to another

Once the behavior is identified, the teacher can decide on its positive or negative effects. Assuming it to be positive, it is the teacher's task to judge whether a teacher response and/or a follow-up activity (or a related activity) will increase the likelihood of a desired goal. If the behavior is negative, the teacher must decide whether to ignore the behavior or take steps to correct it by strengthening an alternate behavior which in turn will act to suppress the undesirable behavior. Positive behavior is relatively easy to encourage and reinforce, provided the teacher recognizes it when it happens. The following incident will illustrate:

Tyrone chose a social studies book about the city. He read to himself. Later the teacher observed him as he shared a picture of the freeway system with a friend. The teacher observed the following: Tyrone chose a book to read; he read for a while by himself; he shared a picture with a friend; the two boys discussed the picture.

The teacher noted two areas of growth: communication skill development, interaction with a friend.

The teacher joined Tyrone and his friend and praised Tyrone for his choice; then she questioned the boys about the picture. She asked them whether or not they thought the city had freeways *many* years ago. The boys seemed confused. The teacher rephrased the question: "Do you think the city has *always* had freeways?" Still the boys were confused and did not respond. The teacher rephrased the question again. "Do you think the city had freeways when your fathers were little boys?" The boys smiled and responded, "Of course not."

The teacher, having recognized that the boys were having difficulty with indefinite quantitative concepts, had rephrased the question in order to clarify it. Next the teacher brought Tyrone and his friend a box of pictures about the city. The teacher suggested that the two boys sort the pictures into four groups using the headings Before, After, Many, and Few.

The urban specialist teacher is unique; instead of reprimanding the boys for talking (and reprimanding Tyrone for being out of his seat), the teacher withheld judgment, observed the behavior, and recognized positive growth. Next the teacher talked to the boys quietly, conference style, to determine interests and problems. The teacher discovered a conceptual deficiency and proceeded to fill the void and further encourage positive behavior and interest.

Consider the rest of the class. Children are not dumb; they saw Tyrone leave his seat and talk to his friend. They were also aware that Tyrone and his buddy were not loud and were in actuality discussing something in a textbook. Next they observed the teacher talking quietly to the two boys; they observed smiling faces, puzzlement, and responses. Finally, they observed the two boys sitting side by side "playing" a game. The two boys had "modeled" appropriate classroom behavior and the class accepted it. The teacher succeeded in encouraging not only the two boys, but the whole class.

Learning to recognize positive or negative behavior is relatively simple. The following list, which includes the four behavioral goals for urban teaching, suggests the kinds of activities to observe:

Negative directionality	*Positive directionality*
Destroys friend's wickiup (ego-satisfying)	Assists friend to build wickiup (ego-satisfying)
Fails to carry out his part of a group task (learner-assertive)	Suggests a group report about Indians and begins to search for resource books (learner-assertive)
Talks about developing a comic strip, but fails to begin (independent-oriented)	Creates a cartoon character and writes a script (independent-oriented)
Refuses to take responsibility during a group report (group-satisfying)	Joins the student council and presents a report (group-satisfying)

Tyrone's teacher recognized a positive approach pattern and proceeded to reinforce the positive behavior and provide circumstances in which the students (Sam and Tyrone) would model the appropriate pattern to others. The following lists identify signs of effective teaching and learning. As you work in the classroom and urban school environment, look for these signs.

Signs of Success

Affective behaviors that relate to the development of self-concept and self-identity

1. Increasing attendance pattern vs. an absence pattern.
2. Voluntarily identifies and demonstrates information and skills.
3. Voluntarily questions teacher and others to elicit information and clarify own thinking.
4. Accepts others' viewpoints during class or group discussion.
5. Accepts leadership and membership activities in work and play.
6. Voluntarily provides autobiographical information and insight; identifies future plans.
7. Chooses areas to direct work and play activities related to own ability and interests.
8. Voluntarily assists others in cooperative work and play activities.
9. Participates frequently in school-related activities during after school hours: club programs, sports, school government, choir, drama.
10. Self-evaluates own work and play activities; corrects own behavior.
11. Infrequent need for discipline or correction by teacher or others.
12. Infrequent use of sarcasm or hostile comments and exclamations.
13. Infrequent participation in "playing the dozens" (derogatory remarks about another's mother).
14. Accepts praise.
15. Voluntarily shares successes and failures.

Affective and cognitive behaviors that relate to the development of communication skills

1. Voluntarily reads to self or others; chooses library materials appropriate to interest and ability.
2. Voluntarily speaks, identifying information and values.
3. Listens attentively to others; responds to others.

4. Organizes ideas of self and others; voluntarily presents them.

5. Participates in school and class activities: debates, role plays, newspaper, choir, choral speaking, clubs, student council.

6. Responds to and complies with oral and written classwork.

7. Frequently completes written assignments and reports.

8. Shares successes and failures.

9. Frequently completes homework assignments.

10. Undertakes research or report assignments and follows through to completion.

11. Accepts leadership for group activities; takes responsibility.

12. Works cooperatively in group activities.

13. Frequently seeks and utilizes classroom resources: dictionary, encyclopedia, textbooks.

14. Self-evaluates own usage of written and oral language; corrects own pattern of usage.

Affective and cognitive behaviors that relate to the development of decision-making skills

1. Voluntarily identifies relevant information.

2. Voluntarily seeks information from others or utilizes resource materials.

3. Voluntarily identifies bias and value statements.

4. Accepts others' values, responds nonjudgmentally, examines own values; redefines relevant values.

5. Chooses and states specifics of problem focus.

6. Willingly debates or defends own commitment.

7. Organizes information (classifies); considers alternatives.

8. Uses organized units of information to predict or project consequences.

9. Chooses work activity or project, decides upon means to achieve, takes responsibility for completion.

10. Makes a rational decision; decides on a preference that is consistent with projected consequences and relevant values.

11. Chooses independent and group activities.

12. Acts as a leader and as a participant; works cooperatively.

Affective and cognitive behaviors that relate to process-oriented goals

1. Chooses an activity that does not have an immediate payoff.

2. Frequently sustains interest in an activity with multiple related goals.

3. Works cooperatively in group activities and accepts democratic procedures.

4. Chooses "thinking" activities. Engages in cause and effect thinking. Seeks alternatives; demonstrates knowledge of multiple causation.

5. Utilizes observational skills; engages in observational description, definition, classification.

6. Seeks to compare and contrast events, problems, values, situations.

7. Seeks to analyze, synthesize, and characterize information, problems, values.

8. Accepts uncertainty relating to problem solutions.

9. Accepts change in work activities, school program, classmates.

Signs of program success

1. Increasing circulation pattern of books in the school library.
2. Decrease of graffiti on school walls.
3. A weekend without a "ripoff."
4. Peaceful attendance of older brothers and sisters at after-school programs.
5. Cleanliness of school grounds.
6. Availability of equipment.
7. Parents' volunteering for and participating in school programs and after-school affairs.
8. Student participation in club programs.
9. Infrequent negative oriented telephone calls to school office.
10. Teachers' increasing attendance pattern vs. absence pattern.
11. Students' increasing attendance pattern vs. absence pattern.

Success occurs in the urban school because of the people who care to make it happen; it is a consequence of supportive behavior rather than ego-destructive behavior, communication of goals and progress step by step toward goals. Students in urban schools have needs that can be translated into strategy designs. The remainder of this chapter is organized to accomplish three objectives:

1. Identify urban teaching priorities, research related to the priority, and the criteria for choosing teaching strategies.
2. Correlate research theory with strategy application.
3. Illustrate specific strategies using a teaching episode or procedurally define the strategy.

Four teaching goal priorities have been identified for urban teachers: development of student self-concept, self-identity, and pride; development of communication skills; development of decision-making skills; and development of process-oriented behaviors. Teaching strategies can focus on objectives to achieve one or more of these goals.

Researchers have also provided information that can be used to guide the choice of teaching strategies. These guidelines suggest that a teaching strategy should develop the student's *analytic capability* by providing opportunities for conceptual development and conceptual analysis; additional research suggests that students' response time can be modified to *increase reflectivity* and decrease impulsiveness. In conjunction with conceptual development and conceptual analysis, researchers provide evidence which shows that students can be taught *how to use information to solve problems* if provided with a model and explicit instructions.

Each goal priority with its rationale will be presented separately; the great number of teaching strategies should demonstrate that teaching lessons can (1) integrate subject field content, (2) provide opportunity for social participation through the utilization of small-group organization, (3) induce decision making, (4) facilitate conceptual development, and (5) reward considered thought.

Priority 1: The Development of Self-concept, and Pride

In school urban children have the opportunity to experience acceptance and success. They can learn respect for themselves and others. They can be taught to feel competent, proficient, and powerful. Strategies that facilitate these achievements meet the following criteria:

1. Provide opportunity for students to observe appropriate behavior exemplified by teachers, other adults, and older children.
2. Provide opportunity and motivation for students to practice those observed behaviors.
3. Provide opportunity for students and teacher to cooperatively plan and set goals with well-defined academic standards, thereby allowing students to experience competence in academic achievement and skills.
4. Provide opportunity for students to observe the leadership behavior of older children and adults with whom they can identify culturally.
5. Motivate and involve students in decision-making activities that fulfill power identity needs.
6. Provide students with instruction materials whose content focuses on the lives, achievements, and problems of minority Americans.

Large-group strategy and directed discussion

A visit to a fifth-grade multicultural classroom provides an example of a teaching episode designed to satisfy self-concept needs. The teacher is teaching music; what other subjects are integrated within the lesson?

Using an autoharp, Ms. Jameson accompanied herself and sang the song "Let Me Live in My House (By the Side of the Road)" by Henry D. Kasin.[1] Next she distributed a copy of the song to her students. She asked the students to clap to the rhythm of the song as she sang it for the second time. After the students were asked to identify the song's signature (number of flats, rhythm, key), they read the song choral fashion by phrases. Then the students and Ms. Jameson with the autoharp accompaniment sang the song together. Ms. Jameson complimented them on how quickly they had captured the rhythm and sense of the song.

Ms. Jameson put her autoharp down and sat down with her students. (They were seated with their chairs arranged in a square.) "It's time to do some serious thinking," commented Ms. Jameson. She then proceeded to ask the following questions:

Who do you think was singing this song?
What kind of person was he? (What phrases in the song give us clues? Find the phrases in the song which tell us.)
What does the composer mean by the "judgment seat"?
Explain the phrase "They are good—They are bad—They are weak—They are strong—Wise—Foolish—so am I."
Why does the *race of men* go by?
If you were a composer, why would you write this song?

Ms. Jameson was careful to allow many responses from the students. She punctuated their comments with "Uh Huh!" "Why?" "Hmm," "Interesting," "Yes." The discussion period lasted twenty minutes; at no time during the discussion did Ms. Jameson ask a new question until the student responses appeared to be exhausted.

Teachers can elicit impulsive or reflective responses from students. Which did Ms. Jameson elicit? How do you know? How did Ms. Jameson encourage analytic conceptualizations? It may be helpful to review the Kagan, Moss, Sigel study about analytic and relational conceptualizations in Chapter 4. Do you believe that fifth-graders are sufficiently mature to respond to "Let Me Live in My House"? Would the teaching episode be successful with older and younger students? If you were Ms. Jameson, what would you do next?

Gaming strategies

These are particularly intriguing to urban students and provide appropriate means to develop all four of the teaching priorities. Often the urban student has had few opportunities at home to participate in board games. Games such as Monopoly can be used and modified in the classroom by teacher or students to teach content or to practice a skill. The students in a sixth-grade class, representing diverse cul-

"Let Me Live In My House"
(by the side of the road)

HENRY KASIN

(Henry D. Kasin, "Let Me Live in My House (By the Side of the Road)"
Los Angeles, Calif., 1965.)

tural groups in American society, were motivated to study about the problems encountered by immigrant groups as they arrived in the United States or changed area of residence within the United States. The teacher provided a gaming strategy to involve and commit the students to cooperative inquiry. The teacher identified the following objectives:

Cognitive levels: knowledge, comprehension, analysis, evaluation
Students will gather information about a specific minority group using the contents and indexes from texts to locate sources of information.

Students will practice note-taking, choosing appropriate information.

Students will exchange information reflecting and criticizing the historical importance, accuracy, and relevance of the data.

Affective levels: responding, valuing, organizing, characterizing
Students will participate in a group experience, discussing and exchanging information.

Students will respond in a leadership and group role.

Students will debate personal point of view as they choose relevant information.

Students will compromise as they work cooperatively to develop a game.

Students will empathize with the problems confronting minority groups as they choose relevant data and as they participate in the Immigrant Game.

THE IMMIGRANT GAME

(A game design researched and created by students.)

Materials: Butcher paper to draw a game board with any desired number of spaces.
Cardboard for chance cards.
Paper plate for a spinner, pointer attached with a brad.
Designations on spinner to read: 0, 1, 2, Chance, 3.

Object: To advance from start to finish before other players; to overcome all immigrant obstacles.

Rules: Player spins the spinner and moves or acts accordingly, moving 0 to 3 spaces or drawing a chance card.
If the player draws a chance card, he must follow its directions.
Play lasts until at least one player crosses the finish line.

Procedure: 1. Students will work in teams to research the experiences and problems faced by an immigrant group. Each team studies a different group within a specified historical time period: Puerto Ricans in New

York City, Irish in Boston, Mexicans in Southwest, freed or escaped slaves in northern United States, Chinese in California.

2. Each team will draw a game board on butcher paper and cut out 25 chance cards from cardboard.

3. Each team will write on each chance card a problem or good luck experienced by the chosen immigrant group. The problems or experiences must be appropriate to the group and the historical time period.

4. After the games are constructed, students exchange games for classroom "play."

Examples of Chance Cards:

1. Your car ran out of gas and you were stopped by the border patrol. You did not have immigration permits. Start over.

2. You tried to rent an apartment in New York City, but the manager was afraid of "your kind." Go back 3 spaces.

3. Congress passes the Exclusion Act, which prohibits your Chinese relatives from joining you. Go back 5 spaces.

4. You are a highly skilled seamstress and you have been hired to work in a clothing factory. Move ahead 2 spaces.

The joy of accomplishment that this class experienced in designing five games for their own classroom use cannot be expressed in educational terms. The morale building, the sense of togetherness, the esteem for their teacher, created a bond that will never diminish. The games were also shared with other classrooms. This type of a game design can be used at any grade level from grade 4 through senior high school. Board games can also be devised to reinforce reading skills.

How does the teacher evaluate a game?

Debriefing is the most important aspect of gaming. In the preceding design, after students had the opportunity to exchange games and to play, the teacher should ask the following types of questions:

What problems did the [Mexicans] face?

How did you feel when these things happened to you?

Why did the [Mexicans] come to the United States?

What alternatives did they have?

In what ways did each group face similar problems?

In what ways were the problems different?

It is extremely important to remember that since gaming is an output technique which motivates critical thinking, decision making, and communication, there is seldom one course of action or one answer to a problem. As in most teaching strategies, the lesson cannot be concluded until an evaluation (the debriefing stage) has occurred.

The Immigrant game provides a fine means for teacher evaluation and diagnosis of student progress. While the students were "researching," the teacher employed the "teacher facilitating behaviors" outlined for the small-group strategy (Chapter 2). When students asked for and needed instructional materials, the teacher provided them. When students were off the track, the teacher refocused their questing behavior. When students worked without the need for assistance, the teacher observed and listened. The teacher took notes of student interest, the types of questions they asked one another, ability to work cooperatively, dependence upon one another, ability to debate a viewpoint, compromise, and generalize. The teacher evaluated students' clarity and precision as they wrote their chance cards as well as their artistic design in creating a game board.

As students played the game, the teacher evaluated their ability to accept disappointment, and the trials and tribulations of game play, and the ways in which they handled success. During the debriefing stage, the teacher evaluated student ability to generalize and characterize the problems, similarities, and differences among all immigrant groups. Using the collected information, the teacher recognized student prejudice, interest, reading levels, and reasoning ability. The teacher was able to plan sequential follow-up activities to further student growth.

As you review the Immigrant game, evaluate it in terms of the criteria for the development of self-concept, self-identity, and pride. Do you believe that the teacher should have presented information about the different immigrant groups instead of utilizing the gaming strategy? If the teacher had utilized an input strategy and presented information to the students, how would it have changed the teacher and learner behaviors? How would it affect the learning environment and the instructional materials needed for the lesson?

Priority 2: The Development of Communication Skills

There are four components to communication: speaking, listening, reading, and writing. These four components are sometimes referred to (in the elementary school) as the language arts and encompass literature, composition, and language. The term *communication* is a far more accurate description of a basic priority for building teaching strategies in the urban school. Although some individuals do learn to speak a language without learning to read or write it, literacy is based upon the accomplishment of all *four* components of communication. Literacy is primary to satisfactory participation socially, economically, politically, and emotionally in both the responsibilities and pleasures of citizenship.

Urban specialist teachers confronted with the need to teach basic skills have found that the development of speaking and listening skills (sometimes referred to as "oracy" skills)[2] must precede the teaching of reading and writing skills. Very little research exists to provide teachers with either guidelines or techniques to assess oral language skill development. It is equally difficult for a teacher to determine when and if a student is listening. However, it is apparent that the student must feel comfortable and confident in the classroom in order to speak. Both the Lippitt and White and the Ryans studies cited in Chapter 2 established that authoritarian teacher methods discouraged active participation and talk in the classroom. If the classroom is arranged in a manner that discourages interaction, visual and verbal contact, then the quality of the language experience will be affected. The secondary school classroom, in particular, often inhibits effective communication. Some operational guidelines suggested by successful urban teachers to improve oracy skills include the following:

1. Arrange classroom furniture to encourage eye and voice contact. This is contrary to existing practice in many classrooms. If students are expected to hold a classroom discussion, allow them to arrange their chairs in a manner that will facilitate speaking and listening.
2. Provide both speaking and listening "models." (The teacher, of course, is the prime model.)
3. Provide speaking and listening "tools" of instruction such as tape-recorders, microphone, cassettes, language masters.
4. Create a variety of activities that provoke student involvement in speaking and listening to others. Suggestions include
   Drawing a picture, then talking about it
   Dramatics (making up plays, participating in role plays, dramatic representation, imitating others)
   Conflict problem resolution in small groups
   Interviewing
   Arranging a picture sequence of a story, then telling it to others
   Debating
   Choosing, then telling or defending the choice
   Singing "pop," folk or rock favorites, then changing the words
   "Sensitizing" encounters (closing eyes, touching and describing a contact, fantasizing)
   Listening to sounds, then describing them

Literally volumes of research have focused upon the teaching of reading in inner city classrooms, yet there is little agreement among researchers concerning the optimal age to begin reading instruction, how to teach reading, or even whether or not reading should be taught in the target language or the student's primary language. Alternatives for the classroom teacher include

Strategies that focus on the teaching of standard English prior to the teaching of reading

Strategies that rewrite the reading textbook, transforming it into the student's dialect

Strategies t̄ at utilize reading textbooks in the student's primary (native) language

Strategies that require instructional materials which neutralize dialect differences

Wolfram described the fourth alternative, and provided an example of the restructured reader.

Standard reader	Restructured reader
John's hat	The hat of John *or* John has a hat
John runs	John can run.
He asked if I came	He asked, "Can I come?"
He's big	He is big

Wolfram suggested that readers can be developed which are "culture-free" (dialect-free), meaning that the text would be "neutral" with respect to dialect. *Whenever possible,* the restructured reader would eliminate the following types of constructions: Possessive forms, contractions, plural forms, multiple negatives ("He doesn't have any toys.") and third person singular forms. The reader should also be constructed in the present tense. The textbook would utilize what Wolfram described as "avoidance strategy."[3]

Some urban teachers have felt that the second alternative (the use of dialect readers) would be more successful with dialect speakers. Dialect readers have been used to teach beginning reading skills. Once the initial decoding skills are attained and the child has developed self-confidence, then the transition to standard English readers is made. However, researcher Ramsey compared first-grade black children's comprehension skills as they listened to standard English and black English. Her investigation focused upon whether six-year-old black children would understand standard English as well as they were able to understand black English. The study involved the use of listening skills. Four short fables, free of cultural and sex bias, were recorded by a black speaker in both dialect and standard English. The children listened to the recorded stories. Following the listening experience, they were asked literal questions about the stories and were requested to retell the stories. Ramsey concluded:

> In only one aspect of the entire test did subjects who heard Negro dialect versions of stories outscore those who heard the standard English versions. This was in the number of interpretive statements included in retelling the stories. Though the difference was slight, it nevertheless was there.
>
> For the subjects involved in this study, it was possible to conclude that use of Negro dialect or standard English made no significant difference in ability to answer literal questions about the stories they had heard; sex and level of readiness did. When subjects retold stories, the number of literal statements made was significantly greater for those who heard the stories in standard English, but sex and readiness for instruction were not significantly related to performance of the task. The number of interpretive statements made was significantly greater for boys, but neither treatment nor readiness appeared to be significant factors. *These findings do not support the contention that materials should be developed in Negro dialect for reading instruction of those who speak the dialect.*[4]

Reading skills are developmental; oral language must precede written language development. Children whose primary language development has been other than standard English must have some special components, such as increased oral language skill development or self-identity development before formal reading commences. The Los Angeles Unified School District has had a Reading Task Force since 1970. This group has been responsible for the design of a developmental reading system.

The task force identified four sequential developmental stages for reading. The first stage emphasizes fundamentals focusing on multisensory and decoding skills and simultaneously developing vocabulary, comprehension, location, and study skills. The second stage reinforces and extends the skills developed in the Fundamental Stage. The third stage uses content areas for students to apply reading skills. The final stage further refines the student's ability to read complex materials in content fields. The task force structured the reading program so that the average learner would complete stage one by age 9, stage two by age 12, the third stage, Broad Application, by age 14, and the Advanced Reading Stage would correlate with high school course content and continue throughout the adult years.[5]

The Los Angeles program is probably the most ambitious undertaking that any district has ever initiated to combat the reading problems of urban children. Included in the program is a special component for black learners and a monolingual Spanish reading program The major objective of the black component is the development of standard English (oral language skills); the objective of the Spanish component is the facilitation of conceptual progression *in Spanish* for the Spanish speaker while simultaneously beginning oracy skills in English. The Spanish speaker uses reading textbooks in the Spanish language.

But a reading system is only as good as the teacher who uses it. Urban specialist teachers create natural, meaningful experiences to develop students' communication skills; and focus on the development of students' experiential base. Instruction is based upon the uniqueness of each student in terms of growth, ability, and learning style. Urban teachers consider it particularly important to involve each student actively in the learning process. Teachers do this through their knowledge of the individual's personal interests, their ability to communicate short-range objectives to each individual, and the manner in which they facilitate student involvement in planning appropriate activities. Since urban teachers believe that each individual is capable of educational progress, they provide constant encouragement and acceptance.

Strategies for teaching reading may be geared to three components: the instructional period, the reinforcement stage, and a free choice period. During the instructional period, the teacher may be meeting with students individually or meeting with students in small groups when their levels of performance and needs are similar. Students alternate throughout the reading program among the three components. In the beginning stages it is important to introduce the three components to the students. They must understand when it is their turn to meet with the teacher, have free choice, or practice a skill.

If the teacher uses the reading centers approach, then each center should be introduced to the children: the teacher should specify the purpose of the center, the equipment to be used, and the directions for each activity. It is these management techniques and organizational skills that will lead to success in the urban classroom. Standards for behavior must also be discussed. The use of each center or free choice activity may necessitate different behavioral standards. (Where shall materials be stored? Who should put them away? Where should students put their own papers when finished?) Since the urban classroom is large and there is often a great deal of absence, it is extremely important to develop a chart system that designates each student's responsibility throughout the reading program. Students should be able to find out, without disturbing the teacher, where they go first, second, and so on. If there is to be a choice of centers, it may be valuable to have students sign in at the center so that the teacher can record student interest and progress.

Instructional planning for a differentiated reading program may look like this:

Time	Directed instruction	Reinforcement	Free choice
1st 30 minutes	Group A and all its subgroups	Group B	Group C
2nd 30 minutes	Group C and all its subgroups	Group A	Group B
3rd 30 minutes	Group B and all its subgroups	Group C	Group A

But the chart does not exclude the possibility of individualization of instruction. The teacher may individualize reading instruction within the time block for directed instruction. Reinforcement skills will be differentiated for each individual.

Directed Instruction strategies focus on development of readiness skills, the decoding process, enrichment of vocabulary, comprehension skills, and location skills. Reinforcement strategies are designed to correlate with the directed reading lesson and the needed practice or reinforcement assignment for each individual. Free choice assignments are based on the reading process and ways in which to motivate interest. Choosing interesting activities for reinforcement is particularly important if the teacher is to maintain the necessary quiet for reading instruction. These activities may include word analysis exercises, word meaning exercises, detecting differences, finding similarities, illustrating, making dictionaries, compiling bibliographies, matching words, structural analysis exercises, rhyming exercises, answering specific questions, predicting outcomes, locating information and noting specific pages for the information, summarizing information, listing unknown words, writing letters, character sketches, writing advertisements and stories, taping an original story. Only teacher and student creativity limit the possible reinforcement activities. Centers for reinforcement were enumerated in Chapter 2. Free choice activities usually include a variety of reading games (puzzles, Bingo, matching, board games) and a library and writing center.

The development of speaking and listening skills requires special strategy designs. The next three teaching episodes will illustrate teaching strategies that develop communication skills along with other goal priorities.

Small-group discussion strategy

This teaching episode by a first-grade teacher, in a school where 70 percent of the students were Spanish-speaking, shows the development of reading readiness skills, communication skills, self-concept, and decision-making skills.

WHAT'S FOR BREAKFAST, LUNCH, AND DINNER?

The teacher displayed three charts. The charts were labeled in Spanish and in English: In the Refrigerator, In the Cupboard, At the Store. On each chart were cut-out pictures of foods and toys. The teacher divided the students into five classroom groups and read the following information to them, first in Spanish and then in English:

> There are five people in your family. Three of the people are children. The children take lunches to school. What can the mother make for breakfast and dinner? The mother went to the store and put seven items in her shopping cart. What do you think she chose? What would you choose if you were the mother?

In the refrigerator	In the cupboard	At the store
Hamburger meat	Catsup	Cookies
Cheese	Spaghetti	Milk
Corn tortillas—12	Cake mix	Cottage cheese
Peanut butter	Oatmeal	Corn flakes
Lettuce	Olives	Bacon
Celery	Corn chips	Orange juice
Apples—six	Beans	Tomato sauce
Eggs—four	Sugar	Candy
7-Up	Salt	Coloring book
Peas	Oil	Hamburger rolls
Mustard	Flour	Hot dogs
		Frozen vegetables
		Ice cream
		Bread
		Butter
		Pickles
		Tuna
		Toys
		Jelly
		Tomatoes
		Potatoes
		Onions

Each group was instructed to discuss the problem and decide what they would buy at the store, if they were the mother of the family. In addition, the students were given paper cut-outs of the items contained on the charts; each item was labeled so that students could identify it and read it. As each group made its decision, students would paste the appropriate cut-outs on a large sheet of newsprint. The teacher circulated while the students talked and worked. Finally, when decision making was concluded, the teacher had each group share its point of view and production. Sometimes the groups disagreed with one another.

During the next class day the teacher took the students on a walking trip to the market. At the market they identified "snack" foods, "party" foods, "holiday" foods, "breakfast" foods, fruits, vegetables, and so on. Back in the classroom, additional activities extended the students' conceptual development when they were given magazines and asked to cut out pictures to develop their own categories for classification.

This particular strategy developed all four urban teaching priorities and focused on analytic abilities, reflectivity, and information-processing skills. If you were the teacher, cite the teaching objectives and the teacher and learner behaviors. Compare your list with the urban teacher in the workshop section. The adaptation of priority 4, process-oriented skills, will suggest reading activities appropriate to extend the children's experiences after the use of this strategy.

Home involvement is important in every aspect of the school program, particularly as we consider communication skill development. There is a substantial difference in interpretation between "home involvement" and the concept of "homework." The urban specialist teacher seldom assigns homework because sometimes urban students do not have the tools with which to work. To involve the urban family in the learning activity, the teacher could send a magazine home with each child or the teacher could provide time during class for students to cut out pictures they could take home to paste (flour, salt, water) and to develop classification categories. A special note to the family (written in English as well as any other language that is necessary) should suggest family assistance with the project.

Directed discussion strategy, high school

This time we are observing in a tenth-grade high school English classroom. The class is studying about the nature of language. On the board appear two questions: How does communication differ from speech? Is communication language? The following is a shortened and paraphrased transcript of their discussion:

TEACHER. Who would like to make a statement or interpret the questions?

BILL. I don't think communication does differ from speech. Communication implies a language, a language system.

MARCY. Animals speak, but I don't think we would say that they have a language system.

RON. No. Animals may communicate, but I don't think that we could say that they speak.

TEACHER. Can you be more specific about that, Ron?

RON. Well, animals don't have names for things. I can tell from my dog's bark when a stranger is at the door, or when he has seen another animal, or when he smells something, or when my Mom has come home. He is communicating, but he is not speaking.

JILL. Baboons express emotions through the sounds that they make. I read once that baboons make about twenty different sounds which express either anger or excitement.

JUDY. People communicate in a lot of different ways that have nothing to do with language.

BILL. Do you think we would understand the communication if it weren't for the meanings of language?

JUDY. If someone yawns, you understand it all right! But it doesn't have to have an appropriate word meaning.

CHUCK. People communicate through gestures, movements, smiles, eyes; but I don't think that has anything to do with a language system.

ALMA. Members of the same species often have special ways of greeting each other. I've noticed that dogs seem to have a special approach pattern; they stalk each other; smell; then if they know each other, they wag their tails.

BEA. I think all animals have a sort of alarm system for telling their young about danger.

TEACHER. How can we decide if there is a difference between communication and language?

CARLOS. I think we would have to decide if there is a system involved that expresses meanings to a specific group of people.

RON. Animals have a system of communication.

CARLOS. Man's responses aren't necessarily automatic. We learn a language system.

TEACHER. How shall we go about studying the nature of language?

MARY. Why don't we work in groups and study different cultural groups and find out the origin of their language?

BOB. We would also have to study to see if there were special sounds and rules.

BILL. Pronunciation also.

TEACHER. OK. Then that is how we will go about it.

As you read this episode, did you characterize the teacher as reflectively oriented or impulsively oriented? What kinds of responses did the students make? How were the students grouped? How did the teacher achieve student planning? The teacher in the foregoing episode was facilitating the development of two concepts: language, communication. On successive days the class would research the system of a language. The teacher's overall objective was that students would learn that language and behavior are a reflection of the individual's culture.

Communication skill development occurs from kindergarten through the high school years. As a teaching priority it is just as important in the high school classroom as it is in the elementary classroom. Although teaching objectives will differ and concepts may be quite a bit more sophisticated in the high school classroom, the teaching method could be similar. Compare the preceding teaching episode with the one that follows.

Directed discussion strategy, elementary school

We are observing now in a third-grade classroom. The students are looking at two pictures displayed in the front of the classroom. One of the pictures indicates two boys fighting; the other picture depicts two girls playing jacks.

TEACHER. What are these pictures about?

MARIA. The first picture is about a fight.

TOM. The second picture is about playing.

TEACHER. You are good observers. Fighting and playing are both examples of what scientists call "behavior." What do you think is meant by the word *behavior*?

SAM. Does it mean anything that people do?

SELMA. Animals do things too. I've heard my mother say she doesn't like my dog's behavior.

TED. I think it means animals and humans because they both do things.

TEACHER. It sounds like you agree that behavior is "doing." Can you think of another word to use for "doing"?

BILLY. "Doing" is the same as "acting."

KATHY. I guess maybe we could say "actions" instead of "doing."

TEACHER. That is very good thinking, class. Now I have another puzzle for you. What kinds of actions or behavior can you describe?

ROBERT. You can describe anything that you can see.

SELMA. You can also describe things that you hear.

JUAN. Can't you also describe what you think?

TEACHER. Explain that, Juan.

JUAN. Well, like right now. We are thinking. We know what thinking is. Isn't thinking a kind of action, too?

TEACHER. Juan has brought up something very important. Let's look at two new words. (The teacher writes two words on the board:

covert, overt.) Juan was trying to describe *covert* actions. Can you think of some other covert actions?

SYLVIA: How about listening?

ALEX. Remembering?

TEACHER. You are really getting the idea about behavior. Let's practice now and see if we can distinguish covert and overt behavior.

The teacher placed ten pictures on the chalkboard. Students were asked to observe and make a list classifying the two types of behavior. This episode provided an example of students communicating with one another as they developed the concept of behavior. The students were interacting and participating in analytic thinking. Their responses were reflective. As you review the episode, identify the teacher responses that characterize the following teaching behaviors: accepting, focusing, facilitating, reinforcing. Check yourself in the workshop section.

We have observed the development of communication skills in *each* of the teaching episodes of this chapter, yet only the last two episodes actually occurred during a "directed" English or language arts teaching period. The effective teacher often integrates subject matter fields, utilizes different types of approaches in order to vary pacing and focus, and uses large and small groups as well as individualization.

Priority 3: The Development of Decision-making Skills

The ultimate goal of education is to facilitate the individual's active participation in society. Unlike majority Amercans, some black, Puerto Rican, American Indian, Mexican-American and Asian Americans have not participated fully in citizenship responsibilities. Some have felt psychologically victimized and have responded apathetically to the process of rational decision making. Rational decision making entails six processes:

Defining the Problem. The problem is clearly defined by the individual but is subject to revision.

Valuing. The individual decides among alternatives. The individual identifies relevant values that may in turn redefine the problem, then examines the rationality of those values and refines the values, deciding on priority.

Identifying Relevant Information. The individual must select relevant information in order to make a proper inference.

Generating Trial Solutions. Using the relevant information and consistent with the values involved, the individual generates possible solutions to the problem.

Testing Solutions in Terms of Projected Consequences. The individual utilizes all previous steps to examine the evidence and predict in the light of consequences. The prediction of consequences may take the inquirer back to other steps in the decision-making process to consider new values or obtain additional information.

Deciding. The individual makes a rational decision using information, values, and predicted consequences. He chooses to act, not to act, or to act on the preference in the future.[6]

The research of Raths, Harmin, and Simon[7] emphasized the means by which the individual derives his values. The researchers call this the valuing process and defined valuing in terms of the processes of choosing, prizing, and acting. Reflective thinking assists the learner to examine alternatives and anticipate consequences. The valuing process leads to the actual decision.

Choosing. The individual chooses without coercion; he selects freely. He chooses from among alternatives and in light of consequences.

Prizing. The individual chooses happily and respectfully; the individual is willing to state his choice publicly, thereby affirming the choice.

Acting. The choice serves to direct the individual's action and pattern of life.

Krathwohl et al. recommended that students interact with one another and with a problem situation. Interaction would be at the following levels of affective involvement: receiving, responding, valuing, organizing, characterizing. Each level of involvement would suggest the following activities by the inquirer:[8]

Receiving. The learner attends to the problem by listening or observing.

Responding. The learner responds by discussing, writing, identifying value statements or relevant information.

Valuing. The learner commits himself by choosing, supporting, arguing, predicting his personal viewpoint.

Organizing. The learner compares, contrasts, systematizes information in order to make a decision.

Characterizing. The learner makes a rational decision based on organized information, relevant values, and prediction of consequences, thereby committing himself to a course of action.

Research, focused on the decision-making process, stressed the association of the cognitive with the affective. Decisions are seldom made unless the individual "values," which is another way of saying that he weighs the evidence and evaluates in terms of the consequences. The apathetic, alienated, withdrawn individual has lost the capacity to respond meaningfully. He remains uninvolved in thought and action. To the extent that any group in society is silent, chooses not to respond, or refuses to strive, that group undermines and degrades the total society. A society that is populated by a sizable group of unresponsive individuals who fail to exercise their socio-civic responsibility invites authoritarianism.

The cultural prosperity of the urban classroom provides ample opportunity for teachers to relate the oral and written history of the students with the everyday curriculum and the immediacy of urban life. For many years classroom teachers were fearful of any question asked in the classroom that began "Ought we to . . .?" "Should we . . .?" These kinds of questions reflect upon our behavior, yet what important decision does not? Disagreement over government policy, urban renewal, or social action all involve value conflicts.

Many societal (as well as urban and classroom) conflicts arise because individuals are not cognizant of the facts of a dispute (the identification of relevant information); sometimes disputes arise because of poor language when the speaker uses stereotypes that insult his listeners or emotionally laden language (value positions); sometimes the issue remains undefined and vague (problem definition). Teachers have a tremendous responsibility to teach the decision-making process. Students can be taught to examine newspaper and magazine statements, discussions, and speeches to identify and define the problem, value positions, relevant information, and possible solutions. Learning to generate alternate policies, positions, and higher values are appropriate tasks for the urban classroom. Teachers need to practice asking value questions because those are more meaningful questions for urban students. Teachers also need practice in defusing language in order to analyze objectively and to examine classroom and societal conflicts.

Shaver and Larkins[9] recommend a "flexible attitude toward words." They suggest that the following phrases ought to be avoided:

Beyond a doubt
Without exception
We can be certain
Only a fool would believe that
We have no other choice

In their place, they would suggest:

It is reasonable to believe that
The best choice seems to be

We think the most probable outcome is

Sometimes

Probably

Perhaps

Conflicts that relate to choice of language are particularly relevant to life in an urban classroom. Semantic misunderstandings sometimes arise in multicultural classrooms and may be caused by errors of translation or misinterpretation. Sometimes culturally related listening habits (Chapter 4) result in communication conflict or disagreement.

Purposeful teaching to develop students' decision-making skills will include the following teaching behaviors:

Arranging a meaningful environment

Choosing topics and setting with relevance historically, currently, culturally, and with future implications

Utilizing questioning strategies that require depth of perceptions and inquiry

Utilizing teaching strategies that provoke student involvement in controversy and conflict, cooperation, bargaining, and compromise

Providing tools of instruction (materials and media) that facilitate individual and group study

Encouraging and accepting diversity of thought and response

Small-group investigation strategies

The teaching strategies that appear in this section are specifically designed for small-group investigations and discussions. They are what the author has named "output" strategies because the student is forced to contribute and produce: knowledge, research, experience, ideas, projects. He becomes a seeking organism rather than a passive being. Objectives and procedures are defined specifically in this section so that teachers may experiment with them. All the strategies have been used by teachers in urban classrooms. The first strategy in this section is appropriate for grades 5 through 8.

WHAT DO YOU DO WHEN YOU NEED HELP?

(for grades 5–8)

Concept Statements: All people have physical, social-emotional, and mental needs. Facilities to satisfy these requirements should exist within the community.

Background: Inner city students are sometimes ignorant about publicly maintained facilities, services, and "help" agencies. They lack information about these agencies as to their function and their location. Often, they do not perceive that these agencies, even if nonexistent in their community, ought to be everywhere.

Mode of Inquiry: Integrative.

Cognitive Processes: Knowledge, comprehension, application, analysis.

Affective Processes: Responding, valuing, organizing.

Objectives:

1. During small group discussions, students will list (name) "help" facilities, social and recreational agencies needed or desired in the inner city.

2. Using a telephone directory, students will check the existence and address of the agencies listed by their group.

3. Using a city street map, students will locate the facilities and designate the type of agency using a predesigned symbol.

4. Using the street map, students will locate their own residence to use as a reference point.

5. Students will write or trace on the map with a felt pen the safest route to three vital "help" facilities, designating mode of transportation.

6. In small-group discussion, students will anticipate future needs of their community.

7. Students will locate facilities beyond the confines of the inner city.

8. Students will compare the availability of facilities for inner city residents and "others."

9. Steps 2 to 5 may be repeated for facilities outside the inner city.

Procedure:

1. Teacher *motivates* using one of the following approaches:
   A. A problems approach in which the teacher tells the story of a family living in the community and in need of emergency health care. (This can be elaborated upon depending upon the age of the students.) The family does not own a car, and does not know where to find a doctor. What would you advise this family to do? How can family members obtain help if they have no money?
   B. An experiential approach in which the teacher states: All families are sometimes in need of help. In what ways has your family needed assistance? How did your family solve its problem? (Students are given many opportunities to respond to each question.)
   C. A multisensory approach in which the teacher uses pictures, films, or filmstrips to initiate a student discussion relating to family problems, needs, and interests.

2. Students are directed to meet in small groups and focus

upon objective 1. Each group compiles its own list for further investigation and for sharing.

3. Teacher circulates to offer guidance, listens to each group's list, and suggests that they inquire further *by framing questions that conform to objectives 2, 3, 4, 5.* (How could we locate the public library if we had a city street map?)

4. Students may be directed to conjecture about future needs of their community or this may occur during the evaluation.

5. Evaluation is guided by the teacher, with all groups responding to the following types of questions:

What kinds of "help" agencies are there?

What recreational facilities exist in our community?

How can we find out what agencies or services exist?

Why should there be "help" agencies in each community?

If our community were to grow, in what ways would our needs change?

What should we do if agencies do not exist in our community?

6. Either through a whole class discussion or else in small groups, students discuss and *project* future needs of their community. Objectives 7, 8, 9 may be pursued at this time.

To Enrich or to Extend:

1. Mature students may make graphs or prepare statistics relating to population of their community and availability and ratio of doctors and dentists to inner city residents.

2. Statistics may be obtained or prepared related to other social agencies as well as recreational facilities.

3. Students may invite community leaders to the classroom to discuss their "roles."

4. Students may interview community leaders and report to class.

5. Students may role play a recreational leader, social worker, and so on.

Assume that you are the teacher of "What Do You Do When You Need Help?" Analyze the learner skills needed to achieve the objectives. Identify the learner behaviors and the teacher behaviors. Which of the three motivational approaches would you choose? Why? Reread Objectives 1 and 2. What problems should the teacher anticipate if the students are fifth graders? (eighth graders?) How will you address yourself to the anticipated problems? In what ways are these objectives related to information processing skills? Check your responses in the Workshop Section.

The next teaching strategy, "Why Vote?"[10] was designed for upper elementary and junior high school students. Most classrooms seem to need three class periods to complete the suggested procedures. The teacher may use the lesson as a motivating experience to initiate a study of the elective process.

WHY VOTE?

(for grades 5–9)

Concept Statements: Elected officials represent the people who have voted for them. Voting is a means to achieve community interest and power.

Background: A citywide campaign for the school board election is in progress in Delano. The school board consists of seven members, three of whom will remain in office. In previous years many of the poorer people in Delano did not consider it important to vote; as a result, their interests were not represented or respected by the school board.

The Issues of the Campaign: An earthquake has devastated two high schools, one in the inner city, and one in the wealthy hill district. The residents of the hill district desire a new high school with modern science and language laboratories to be rebuilt on the site of the former high school. Inner city residents want a new comprehensive high school with vocational shop training as well as modern laboratory facilities. The school district cannot afford to build two new high schools; therefore, it will have to renovate one and rebuild the other unless new funds become available or a new plan is developed. Some individuals in the city have suggested that an educational park with a modern junior-senior high school could be designed and located near the center of the city to accommodate students from the entire city. Opponents of the plan complain that an educational park would force the busing of students from at least four of the six districts into the inner city.

    Office 1 is held by a white banker who represents the hill district (A); he has already stated that he expects the old high school in the hill district to be completely rebuilt. He does not favor the idea of an educational park. Office 4 is held by a white small businessman who represents the interests of districts B and C. Office 5 is held by a white doctor who in the past has often been sympathetic to the interests of the poor people of the city. Representatives for offices 2, 3, 6, and 7 are to be chosen in the next citywide election. As residents of Delano, it is our responsibility to choose representatives for these offices who will respond to our needs.

Mode of Inquiry: Policy mode.

Cognitive Process: Knowledge, comprehension, application, synthesis, evaluation.

Affective Processes: Valuing, organizing, characterizing.

Objectives:
    1. Working in a small group, students will choose one member to represent their special needs and interests.

2. Through cooperative planning, students will write a campaign platform for their chosen nominee.

3. Students will participate in the campaign process: discussing, listening, compromising, and valuing.

4. Students will vote, thereby choosing a representative to reflect their group needs.

Procedure:

1. Teacher reads the background information to the class.

2. Having duplicated the map of the city and a list of the issues of the campaign, the teacher gives each student a copy.

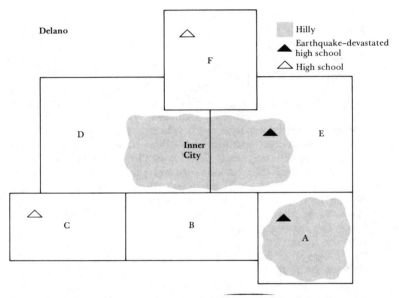

(From "Why Vote?" by Johanna K. Lemlech, *Social Studies Review,* Fall 1973, pp. 37–40.)

3. Students are divided into six districts to represent the six districts on the map.

4. Working together in small groups (districts), students assist each other as they read their issues and the Delano city map.

5. Each group discusses the issues in terms of the effect upon its district. Each district chooses a candidate to represent it. Each district writes its candidate's platform. (Teacher discusses the meaning and purpose of the platform, if needed.)

6. Teacher chooses one person from each district to act as a television interviewer.

7. Each candidate presents his "platform" on a citywide television interview program.

8. After the television program, each candidate tours the city campaigning for district support. Groups may wish to "make deals."

9. Using a secret ballot, students vote.

10. One person from each district serves on an election committee to tally the votes. The four candidates receiving the highest tally will win the election. If each group has voted for its own candidate and four winners have not emerged, then students must go back to step 8 before proceeding to a final election.

Evaluation: Teacher guides the evaluation and asks the following types of questions:

Why is it important to vote?

What would have happened if the people in districts D and E had not voted?

Why do we need to listen to campaign "promises" and the candidate's platform?

Observing the outcome of this election, what do you think will happen when the school board meets to decide the issue concerning the location for a new high school?

What are some other ways in which the people of Delano may influence their school board?

To Enrich and to Extend: Students may visit a school board or city council meeting. Discuss what happened at the meeting in terms of voting and constituent participation. Set up a meeting of the school board with the newly elected officers. Provide for constituent participation. Follow Robert's Rules of Order and have the board decide the issue of rebuilding a high school.

Assume that you are the teacher for "Why Vote?" A parent comes to you complaining that you are not teaching the basic skills. How will you justify your position? (What skill and subject areas can you identify in "Why Vote?")

The Student Council game was designed for use in grades 1, 2, or 3. The problems were identified by a second-grade child and illustrate how relevant issues in the school community or classroom problems can be utilized to develop communication skills, decision making, cooperative learning, and self-identity, particularly if entwined within a game structure. The teaching objectives were as follows:

Students will analyze and identify all facets of a problem.

Students will verbalize (or write) a rule in order to solve the problem.

Students will accept rule making as necessary to group living.

The teacher read the background information to the students, but duplicated both the rules for the game and the problem for each group. The students, working in small groups, assisted one another as they read the rules and the discussion problem. The groups were arranged so that there would be at least one good reader in each group.

THE STUDENT COUNCIL GAME

(for grades 1–3)

To Be Read to the Students: Sometimes we have rules that do not help us and so the rules need changing. Sometimes we have problems and we need a rule to assist us. Pretend that you and your friends are members of the student council and a second-grade child has told you about a problem. How will you solve the problem? What rule will you make?

Rules for the Game:
    1. Each group of students listens to or reads the problem.
    2. The group discusses the problem and decides how to solve the situation by changing the rule or making a new rule.
    3. Each group tells the other groups about the problem and how its members decided to solve it.

Group I: We have safeties and play leaders on the playground. We do not need both. There are too many and they are not doing their job. Sometimes you go to an area to play a game and there isn't a play leader there so you cannot play the game. How can we solve the problem?

Group II: You are not supposed to run on the playground. Sometimes you get tired of walking and you skip, but the safety yells "WALK." So you can't run and you can't skip. It's not fair.

Group III: In the cafeteria people are real noisy. Some people throw paper and so we don't get dismissed. How can we stop the noisy people and the people who throw papers? We are missing our lunch recess.

Group IV: Sometimes we go to the ball room to get a ball or a bean bag and they are out of them. Sometimes people take out balls and don't use them. How can we get the school to buy more equipment or else get people to return the equipment they are not using? How can we get people to share equipment?

Group V: Teachers blow their whistles on the playground to dismiss us. They do not think about the children who are near them when they blow their whistles. The whistles hurt our ears. How can we get the teachers not to blow their whistles?

The game of City Council was designed for a fourth- or fifth-grade urban classroom and is similar to the Student Council game. It was field tested in Pacoima, California. The teaching objective was as follows: Students will participate in democratic decision making as they choose a member of the city council, present a proposal, and vote.

The teacher charted both the group rules and the council rules, but duplicated all the problems so that each group would be aware of the problem distressing its neighbors. The lesson has been used to initiate a study of city government and involves only one class session.

THE GAME OF CITY COUNCIL
(for grades 4–5)

Group Rules:
1. Choose one person to be a member of the city council.
2. Discuss and write a proposal to present to the city council.
3. Choose one person to present the proposal to the city council.
4. Groups may disagree with other group proposals when they are presented to the council.

Council Rules:
1. Choose a council president to call on each group.
2. Listen to each group's proposal.
3. After you have heard all the proposed laws, discuss them.
4. You may agree with the proposal or change it.
5. Vote on each proposal.
6. The president of the council may vote.

Group I: You are living on Pine Street. It has become a very busy street. There are about 50 families living in houses and apartments on your street. There are also some businesses on the street. In the last five days there has been at least one traffic accident each day. One person was killed. There are no street lights, traffic lights, or stop signs on the corners. Some of the side streets near Pine Street are seldom used. What do you think the city council should do?

Group II: You live near Pine Street and ride in a car pool that travels down Pine Street to reach the freeway. You are very annoyed because the traffic is heavy and it slows your car pool down. How would you improve the traffic situation? What recommendation will you make to the city council?

Group III: Many people living on Pine Street are out of work. They need assistance from the city to buy food and pay rent. They are concerned that the street is not safe for their children, but they cannot afford to pay for street lights or other improvements. What should the city council do to assist them?

Group IV: The children along Pine Street have no place to play. The street is too busy. There is some empty land in the neighborhood, but there are signs posted that say, "No Trespassing." What would you like the city council to do?

Group V: You are the owner of a small business on Pine Street. Business is poor because people are afraid to walk down the street at night, and traffic is so heavy that cars are unable to park. You would like to buy some empty land in the neighborhood for a parking lot but the owner is hoping to sell it to the city for a recreational area. What could the city council do to help you?

Suggestions to Citizen Groups:
1. Read the problem confronting *each* group.
2. How will your group's proposal affect other people in the community?

In addition to the stated objective at the beginning of this strategy, what other objectives can you identify? What will the teacher be doing while the students are working? How will the teacher recognize student growth and achievement during this lesson? What kinds of evaluative questions should the teacher ask after the game has been played? The City Council and the Student Council games are more likely to elicit reflective student thinking than impulsive thought. Why? Using the last two strategies as a model, develop your own lesson for the students in your classroom.

Role-playing strategies

Similar to gaming, role-playing strategies are particularly rewarding in the urban classroom. Role playing facilitates learner involvement and interaction in the process of decision making. The research of Michaelis, Dunfee and Sagl, Massialias and Cox, and others indicated that role playing is a valid inquiry technique. In role playing the student portrays himself or others as he explores a problem situation.

Role playing as investigated by Shaftel is a problem-solving method for arriving at a decision that involves diverse interests and values.

> Role-playing, as do simulation and gaming, utilizes a symbolic model (verbal) rather than physical or mathematical. Role-playing proceeds into problem-definition, delineation of alternatives for action, exploration of the consequences of those alternatives, and decision-making.[11]

Shaftel stated that role playing assists the student to step out of his "culture shell" and become more "open" to the experiences of others. Through role playing, the student learns to explore his own values and their consequences to himself and others. Role-playing procedures are as follows:[12]

1. Teacher sets motivation.
2. Selection of players.

3. Preparing the audience to observe.
4. Setting the stage.
5. The enactment.
6. Discussion and evaluation.
7. Further enactments—new players.
8. Further discussion.
9. Generalizing.

My own research using role playing as a teaching strategy to invoke affective involvement revealed higher participant involvement using a caucus group and using the open-structured role plays.[13]

Role playing using a caucus group

1. Teacher sets motivation.
2. Students are divided into groups.
3. Groups discuss the problem and the characterization.
4. Groups choose a spokesperson.
5. The enactment.
6. Discussion and evaluation.
7. Groups offer advice, assist spokesperson, or choose a new spokesperson.
8. Further enactments.
9. Discussion.
10. Generalizing.

Open-structured role play

1. Teacher sets motivation.
2. Students portray themselves and respond freely.
3. Discussion and evaluation.

For students who have never participated in role playing, the first experience may be inhibiting if the basic procedures are implemented. It is for that reason that I experimented with the caucus group and open-structured role-play procedures. Since in neither the caucus group nor the open-structured role plays is there an "audience" watching, giggling and embarrassment are eliminated. There is greater student involvement as a consequence of the feeling of personal safety. Students participate in value clarification, problem definition, and decision making because the strategy is highly motivating and they do not feel they are "on stage."

Using the caucus group system, students are divided into small groups. Each group portrays a "role" or represents a specific segment of society. The group discusses the problem situation and decides upon the role interpretation. The group chooses one member to be the group representative for the enactment. After the first role-play enactment (5 to 10 minutes) groups caucus with their representative to decide whether or not to change their interpretation and/or their representative before the second enactment.

The open-structured role play differs from the basic or caucus system in that the whole class may take part almost like in a class discussion, without teacher participation. Each individual portrays himself; however, the situation is usually hypothetical. The situations may be created so that they begin "If you were a member of . . . how would you . . . ?" Or "Pretend that you are a . . ." During the open-structured role play, students need to face each other; no hand raising is used; students "speak out." The situations must represent a real conflict for the students; otherwise, it will not be motivating. The open-structured role play usually begins slowly and hesitantly, then builds in intensity as value conflicts emerge and as students accept the safety of the hypothetical relationship.

Both the caucus group and the open-structured role plays are more effective when the situations relate to current events, school problems, or community affairs. The short social problem that usually includes an unfinished story or situation is more effective using the rules for the basic procedures role play.

Caucus group. An example of role-play strategy using the caucus group occurred in a high school classroom. The teacher passed out copies of a newspaper article entitled: "Chicanos Criticize Saxbe on Alien Deportation Proposal."[14] After the students read the article, the teacher divided them into the following groups: Mexican-American activists, farmers, Justice Department, alien workers, Chicano workers. Each group caucused and discussed the article from the viewpoint of the role they were to characterize and the questions the teacher posed. The teacher wrote the following questions on the board:

> Should alien workers be deported?
>
> Do Mexican aliens deprive American workers of jobs?
>
> Do you believe that Mexican aliens drain our economy by sending money back to Mexico?

During the course of the enactments, the students explored the following issues:

> Unscrupulous employers.
>
> Exploitation of aliens because of lower pay and poor living conditions.
>
> United States gain because of tax dollars paid by aliens.
>
> Deprivation of other workers resulting from unemployment.

Aliens are consumers and spend most of their salary in the United States.

Aliens often fulfill jobs other workers would refuse to take.

Economic, historic, and geographic relationships were explored in successive sessions using a variety of teacher strategies, but the motivation for the sessions resulted from the first classroom session initiated by the role play.

Role playing as a teaching strategy develops self-concept, communication skills, and decision-making skills. Since it is an "action" strategy, it is particularly effective in the urban classroom. A variation on the role-play strategy is the incorporation of "props" in the form of puppets and student script-writing. The following strategy was used in a junior high school classroom.

Puppeteering. Students designed animal or people puppets with cultural emphasis. They wrote and produced their own shows. Puppeteering as a teaching strategy encourages students to create stories and plays that are realistic and meaningful. Student-written manuscripts are easily read by classmates and provide a safe medium for students to express personal feelings. Some teachers give students a problem or a story line and then assign a group of students to write the script. One urban teacher suggested the following situation:

Pretend that you are sixteen years old and that you are searching for a summer job. Who will you meet? What will you tell a prospective employer? What are your capabilities?

Using puppets, students discovered their own learning needs: The need for standard English in order to express themselves to others, the need for job competencies, and the need to make relevant decisions. These students became self-motivated and designed their own learning objectives. Puppeteering developed self-concept, communication skills, and decision-making skills.

Priority 4: The Development of Process-oriented Behaviors

Through the years a great number of teachers and researchers have developed "how to think" teaching strategies. These strategies have sometimes been called "problem solving," "inquiry," "inductive thinking," "deductive thinking," or "critical thinking." Examples of problem-solving or inquiry-oriented strategies appeared in the first three sections of this chapter. Sometimes they are also called small group or group investigation models.

Process-oriented strategies are designed to teach "how to think" competencies. They are designed to teach "thinking" and "if . . . then" types of skills. Chapter 4 revealed that urban students are deficient in information-processing skills; however, researchers verified that methods of information processing using task instructions *can* be taught. Therefore, the purpose of this section is to suggest some techniques for teaching information-processing skills.

Adkinson and Sanders define *information* as data that are arranged and ordered in a useful form. "Information may be thought of as relevant knowledge, produced as output of processing operations, and acquired to provide insight in order to achieve specific purposes or enhance understanding."[15] When Mr. Blakely planned his series of teaching strategies, he identified basic knowledge needed by the students to function within his planned curriculum (Chapter 2). Specifically, he identified *concepts*. A concept is a high-level abstraction and as such it has little transferability from teacher to student. Therefore, students need opportunities to "build" their own concepts; this occurs in the classroom when students are provided with experiences that yield ideas and data. The "best" experiences for students are those which are sequential, progressive, provide continuity, develop understandings through a variety of experiential means, and involve "input" and "output" activities.

Information-processing strategies

Concept formation skills are taught in a variety of ways. In one urban classroom I visited, the teacher provided small groups of students with pictures of the following items: radio, chair, car, television, couch, train, phonograph, bed, airplane, taperecorder, bus, movie projector, table, boat, chest. The instructions were to arrange the items into three groups. After about 10 minutes each group shared the identified categories. The teacher asked each group: "Why did you put those items together?" Or, the teacher asked the class as a whole, "What can you tell about the things in Bob's first group?" The students would then identify the common attributes for each developed category. Each developed category would be described. Finally, the teacher asked, "What is different about each group?"

The teacher in this episode could also have provided the students with already developed categories for them to analyze:

radio	chair	car
television	couch	train
phonograph	bed	airplane
tape recorder	table	bus
movie projector	chest	boat

In this case, the teacher would ask the following questions:

What can you tell about the things in each group?

Why were the things in the first column put together? second column? third column?

What is different about each group.

The teaching of mathematics yields many opportunities to facilitate concept development. A group of fourth-graders studied the following example. The teacher allowed a great deal of time for the students to discuss their concepts.

$$5 \times 4 = 20 \qquad 8 \times 4 = 32$$
$$4 \times 5 = 20 \qquad 4 \times 8 = 32$$
$$20 \div 4 = 5 \qquad 32 \div 4 = 8$$
$$20 \div 5 = 4 \qquad 32 \div 8 = 4$$

Their concepts included these:

There are number families.

Division "undoes" multiplication.

When you multiply two numbers, the first number can be obtained when you divide the answer by the second number.

Teaching visual and auditory discrimination is an extremely important task for primary level elementary school teachers. A great deal of success has been achieved by teachers utilizing concept attainment games. In a nongraded primary classroom, one teacher went about the task in this way:

A large piece of tagboard was displayed. The tagboard had the large letter M in manuscript at the top. Then appeared a number of pictures: monkey, mouse, motor, mountain, chicken, house, mitten, milk, rabbit, cookie, melon. The teacher said to the children: "Let's read our chart." (In chorus the children said the name of each picture.) Then the teacher said, "What's wrong with this chart? The children responded: "Some things don't belong." The teacher then had the students identify the pictures that "did not belong."

Lists of words are used also to induce students to analyze the attributes of a category. The following are examples:

night	should	read
might	could	weed
kite	hood	bead
light	would	lead
right		

The teacher using this strategy asked the students to look at the lists and decide if all the words belonged together. The students replied both in the positive and the negative. The teacher pretended to be mystified. Then the teacher asked the students, "Can you decide what concept is being taught, if I give you a clue?" This time the teacher wrote beside each word in two of the columns either "yes" or "no." The lists appeared as follows:

night (yes)	should (yes)	read
might (yes)	could (yes)	weed
kite (no)	hood (no)	bead
light (yes)	would (yes)	lead
right (yes)		

The students were immediately able to identify that the concept was words that are spelled alike. The teacher asked the students to identify with either a "yes" or "no" the third group of words in order to prove the attainment of the concept as well as the visual and auditory discrimination skills.

The Taba strategy

Many successful urban teachers have implemented the inductive teaching strategies of Hilda Taba because their specificity facilitates student understanding of "what to do next." Taba designed three sets of strategies to develop inductive thinking. The first set of strategies induces concept formation; the second set focuses on interpretation of data; the third set develops the application of principles.

In the first set of strategies (concept formation),[16] students are taught to enumerate and list, group, label, and categorize. *They are taught to do this with specific eliciting questions. The steps are sequential.*

Concept formation

Overt activity	Covert activity	Eliciting questions
1. Enumeration and listing	Differentiation	What did you see? hear? note?
2. Grouping	Identifying common properties, abstracting	What belongs together? On what criterion?
3. Labeling, categorizing	Determining the hierarchical order of items. Super- and sub-ordination.	How would you call these groups? What belongs under what?

SOURCE: From Hilda Taba, *Teachers' Handbook for Elementary Social Studies* (Reading, Mass.: Addison-Wesley, 1967), p. 92.

To illustrate the Taba strategy, examples will be drawn from "What Do You Do When You Need Help?" In the first procedural objective, the students are asked to differentiate among "help" facilities, social, and recreational agencies. If the students were to have difficulty, the teacher would elicit the appropriate task analysis through the following questions and clarifying responses:

1. If you saw a fire, what would you do? (Wait for student response.) If a member of your family needed surgery, where would you go? The fire department and a hospital can be called "help" facilities. What other "help" facilities can you name?
2. If your family were planning a picnic, where would you go? If you and your friends wanted to see a movie, where would you go? If you were walking along the sidewalk and heard the sound of many people dancing, what would you look for?

The teacher would facilitate "grouping" behaviors through the following teaching tasks and questions:

1. The teacher would write on the chalkboard a list of the following items: clinic, theater, YMCA, park, police station, unemployment office, water and power plant, market, skating rink, bank, playground, hospital, clothing store.
2. The teacher would then say to the students, "If you were to make two groups, what would you put together?" Next the teacher would say, "Why did you put these items together?"

Labeling and categorizing could be taught by asking the students to "name" their two groups using the procedural objective terms: help facilities and social and recreational agencies or facilities. Hierarchical categorization would also be taught by asking the students to identify common attributes and then to label and categorize these attributes into specific groupings. If the students had identified park, playground, and skating rink as places to play, they could be encouraged to label this group as "recreational."

Grouping and categorizing can be taught in a number of ways. Teachers using "What's for Breakfast, Lunch and Dinner?" might ask the students: "Why are these items in the refrigerator?" (To keep cold and/or they will spoil without refrigeration.) "Why are these items in the cupboard?" "What other items would you keep in the refrigerator? in the cupboard?" A variety of categories would also be developed as the students identify snack foods, party foods, and so on.

Taba's second set of strategies[17] involved the interpretation of data. These strategies elicited interpretation, inference, and generalizing behaviors.

Interpretation of data

Overt activity	Covert mental operation	Eliciting questions
1. Identifying points	Differentiating	What did you notice? see? find?
2. Explaining items of identified information	Relating points to each other, determining cause and effect relationships	Why did so-and-so happen?
3. Making inferences	Going beyond what is given, finding implications, extrapolating	What does this mean? What picture does it create in your mind? What would you conclude?

SOURCE: From Hilda Taba, *Teachers' Handbook for Elementary Social Studies* (Reading, Mass.: Addison-Wesley, 1967).

Again utilizing the strategy in "What Do You Do When You Need Help?" the teacher might facilitate the interpretation of data as in the following examples:

The students have categorized "help" agencies, service facilities, recreation and social facilities. Using the yellow pages of the telephone directory, the students located markets, health services, hospitals, social service and welfare organizations, and so on. Next they used a city street map to locate the agencies and facilities.

It was at this point that the teacher facilitated further identification by asking: "What do you notice about the location of service facilities?" (None existed within the school community.) Or, "What did you find out about doctors' offices?" (None, within the immediate community.)

Next, the teacher might ask: "Why do you think this has happened?" (It is more profitable for businesses to cluster together in shopping centers; doctors tend to locate near large health facilities; shopping centers are dependent upon transportation.)

Finally, the teacher would ask: "If there are no markets, clothing stores, drugstores, or hardware stores in this community, what does that mean for the people who live here? What do the people of this community do when they need these services?"

The third set of strategies[18] facilitates the application of principles and involves predicting consequences, explaining or supporting hypotheses, and verifying the prediction.

Application of principles

Overt activity	Covert mental operation	Eliciting questions
1. Predicting consequences, explaining unfamiliar phenomena, hypothesizing	Analyzing the nature of the problem or situation, retrieving relevant knowledge	What would happen if . . . ?
2. Explaining and/or supporting the predictions and hypotheses	Determining the casual links leading to prediction or hypotheses	Why do you think this would happen?
3. Verifying the prediction	Using logical principles or factual knowledge to determine necessary and sufficient conditions	What would it take for so-and-so to be generally true or probably true?

SOURCE: From Hilda Taba, *Teachers' Handbook for Elementary Social Studies* (Reading, Mass.: Addison-Wesley, 1967).

To induce the application of principles, the following situation might occur in the classroom when students discover that there is only one market in their community.

The only market located in this neighborhood is Martin's. The prices at Martin's are higher than at markets in other communities.

The teacher might ask: What would happen if the people in this community decided not to shop at Martin's for their food? Student responses: People would have to travel further; Martin's would go out of business; Martin's would lower their prices.

Next the teacher might respond: "Why do you think Martin's might go out of business?" Or, "Why do you think that Martin's would lower its prices?"

Finally, the teacher might ask: "Do you think it would be a good idea for the people in this community to shop elsewhere?" "Would you rather that Martin's went out of business or that it lowered its prices?" "What do you think this community could do to get Martin's to lower its prices?"

The objectives for "What Do You Do When You Need Help?" provide examples for cognitive tasks involving the application of principles. The teacher would elicit appropriate thinking operations by asking:

What would happen if the people of this community decided that they pay more for services and recreation than do people in other communities?

Why do you think these services might cost more here?

Why do you think that these services do not exist in this community?

What would happen if the people of this community got together and developed a cooperative market or a buying service?

Another example occurred in a high school government class in which a sophisticated type of information processing was taught to facilitate rational decision making. The issue the teacher chose was relevant to the students involved. Each student was furnished with a copy of the following article, which appeared on September 20, 1974, in the *Los Angeles Times*.

ACCORD REPORTED NEAR IN URBAN RENEWAL CASE
100 FAMILIES, BANK TELL OF PROGRESS ON RESETTLEMENT ISSUE
A settlement was reported near Thursday in a controversy over the relocation of more than 100 low-income families from a downtown neighborhood slated for urban renewal by the Bank of America.

Representatives for both the bank and the community activists who had opposed the building project reported that "substantial progress" has been made in negotiations to set up a relocation project for residents of the Temple-Beaudry neighborhood.

The neighborhood is a three-block area just west of the Harbor Freeway bounded by Temple and Mignonette Sts. and Beaudry Ave. More than 300 persons, most of them Mexican American, still live in the area.

Presently owned by the Beaudry Plaza Co., the property is to be purchased by the Bank of America which wants to build a $32 million data processing center there.

Residents of the area assisted by activist Mexican Americans and attorneys have threatened to stall the building project until the buyers, sellers and city government develop a relocation plan to help them move.

The opposition of the residents has put the property sale in jeopardy. Mayor Tom Bradley has stepped into the controversy as a mediator between the residents and the property owners.

Thursday, in a news conference at the Greater Los Angeles Press Club, representatives of the United Neighbors to Save the Temple-Beaudry Community gave the first public indication that a settlement to the controversy is near.

Rosalio Munoz, chief organizer for United Neighbors, said that "an implied agreement in principle was reached on major points by all parties."

In general terms, Munoz said, the bank negotiators offered a cash settlement "after ground was broken" for the bank project.

Negotiators for the residents "wanted the people in new homes before ground was broken."

Joe Angello, vice president in charge of urban affairs for Bank of America, confirmed that a possible agreement is near except for "some mechanics that have to be worked out."

Angello said the proposed agreement involves a cash settlement through which area residents will be helped in paying the costs of relocation to new homes.

A key issue in the controversy has been who should bear the costs of relocation. Since the bank project is a private development, area residents do not qualify for the relocation assistance normally provided in publicly financed urban renewal.

Both Angello and representatives of United Neighbors declined to give further details of the proposed settlement.

However it was learned that the proposed agreement involves a cash settlement in six figures.[19]

The teacher instructed the students to chart their information and to respond sequentially to each group of questions. The questions were listed on the board. Each student worked with a partner. The questions were as follows:

Group I
1. List people or institutions involved in the dispute.
2. Identify the feelings or dispute position of each person, group, or institution involved in the dispute.
3. Group together the individuals, groups, or institutions who share similar positions.

Group II
1. Identify factual information contained in the article.
2. Why did the dispute occur?
3. What does the dispute mean in terms of law and city government?

Group III
1. What do you anticipate will happen if the dispute remains unresolved?
2. Why do you think the above will occur?
3. In what ways could the dispute be resolved?

During the evaluation, the following discussion occurred:

ROGER AND TED. We don't see why the bank should pay the cost of moving for the residents. We don't believe that they will.

MARY AND SUE. But the article says that the bank has promised to do that.

ROGER AND TED. Where does it say that?

LUANNE AND SHEILA. It doesn't exactly say that they've promised.

TEACHER. Can you find the information related to relocation?

MARY AND SUE. This paragraph—"Angello said the proposed agreement involves a cash settlement through which area residents will be helped in paying the costs of relocation to new homes."

JIM AND ROSANNA. That doesn't say "promised"; it says "proposed." Besides that, what it really says is that money will be provided to sort of compensate the community for the inconvenience of having to move.

TEACHER. Why do you think the bank expressed willingness to compensate the residents?

JERRY AND MABEL. They have to. Otherwise this community is not going to let them go ahead and build.

TEACHER. Is there any precedent for compensating the residents?

PETE AND WILL. Sure there is.

TEACHER. Can you find it? Review your factual information.

PETE AND WILL. Yeah, under our factual information we found that when a city decided to rebuild an area they compensate the residents who will be relocated. It doesn't say it exactly like that, but that's what it means.

The discussion continued with the students verifying opinions with factual statements from the article. Anticipated problems were also discussed. On the following day, the teacher gave the students another article out of the newspaper. On this occasion the teacher had the students analyze the series of questions and why they were important to the decision-making process.

JOE. Do you mean that any dispute could be analyzed this way?

TEACHER. What do you think Pete?

PETE. Well it sure was effective yesterday when all you had to do was look for the facts. Only you had to be sure it was a fact and not an opinion.

TEACHER. Rob?

ROB. I guess the problem with most disputes is that people fail to separate their feelings from the real facts. It was kinda' fun to decide which were feelings and which were facts.

JEAN. Once you did that you sure could guess what would happen next.

TEACHER. Let's try it again with today's article.

This time the students worked quickly and efficiently. The room buzzed as teams developed their charts. At the end of the period, the teacher suggested that instead of a discussion they would take sides and debate the dispute, using their charts for data. The teacher, when interviewed by me, stated that he also chose historical problems and in this way designed a curriculum in which the students would examine the structure of American government. Once the students had learned the system for analyzing issues or disputes, the teacher could use a variety of teaching strategies to motivate further learning.

Strategies without names

The strategies thus far presented have included large-group directed discussions, teacher controlled; small-group discussions, teacher observed; small-group investigation; gaming; role playing and puppeteering; and information processing. These strategies have been reviewed within the framework of four teaching priorities for the urban school. The intent was to demonstrate the range of teaching options available to accomplish urban teaching goals. Each of the teaching approaches may be used to achieve a variety of goals. (The strategy was not exclusive to the teaching priority.)

Some teaching strategies defy typical strategy labels, yet are used often by teachers. For instance, language specialists may use the following procedures to develop language fluency skills.

1. The teacher chooses to do one of the following:
   Act as a model to read a script, story, or teacher-prepared material of a substantive nature.
   Prepare a narrative-style tape for student listening.
   Choose appropriate media—record, film, or filmstrip—for student listening and observation.
2. Students listen and observe the teacher's presentation or participate in the use of the chosen media.
3. From the presentation, the teacher selects vocabulary or dialog to conduct a language drill. The drill is presented to the whole class or to small groups waiting to use the tape recorder.
4. Students work in small groups to discuss the questions posed by the narrative. To practice speaking skills, the students, in sequence, may respond to the question and ask the question of their neighbors in the group.
5. After small-group discussions, students participate in an activity related to the original narrative or problem focus. Activities may include working with puppets, playing "culture" games, constructing dioramas, working with blocks, creating murals, participating in extemporaneous dramatizations or pantomimes. Students with highly developed auding and speaking skills may write short plays or skits and present them to the other students.

City games, culture games. Games assist children bridge the gap between the land of make-believe and reality. On the playground, student languaging is different from in the classroom. Both language and games are different on city streets than at school. Life away from school is considerably more important and realistic to students. The use of after-school games to motivate school activities has been extremely effective. An urban teacher comparing the life of American Indian children to the life of the young urban child could begin with a study of games. The following plan will illustrate initiating activities for a unit that compares Indian life in early California to urban life today. The activities and questions are designed for primary-age children.

Concepts: Play, group work.

Cognitive Levels: Knowledge, comprehension, analysis, evaluation.

Affective Levels: Responding, valuing, characterizing.

Specific Objectives:
    Students will participate in the playing of "culture games."
    Students will identify, verbally, favorite playtime activities.
    Students will identify family members or companions in playtime activities.
    Students will distinguish between "fun" and "work."
    Students will be involved in the process of valuing as they choose and discuss favorite games.
    Students will compare Indian children's playtime activities with their own.

Activity A:
Teacher's question focus:
    When do you play games?
    Why do you play games?
    With whom do you play?
    What are some of your favorite games?
    What makes some games more fun than others?
    Do you feel the adult members of your family should play games with you? why?
Use the whole class in a discussion formation (students facing one another and teacher seated with them). Begin with the question focus. When students mention specific games, note whether or not the games are related to the school culture or the neighborhood culture.
Allow students to play two or three neighborhood culture games rather than school games. If children are reticent about discussing neighborhood games, the teacher might ask whether or not they have ever played games such as stoop ball, wall ball, or punch ball. City Street Games may serve as a reference for these activities.
    Evoke valuing responses from the children by asking the following types of questions:

Why do we sometimes play games at home that are different from the games we play at school?

What happens when you play a game with a group of children?

What makes a game "fun?"

How do you feel if you are left out of a game?

When can we play games?

Should we play games anytime we feel like it? why?

Activity B:

(There are two parts to this activity—B-1 and B-2.)

Teacher's question focus (to be used *after* activity B-2):

What kinds of games did the Indian children play?

How were their games different from ours?

How were the games similar to ours?

When did the Indian children play their games?

Do you think Indian children could play games anytime they wanted to? Why do you think so?

B-1, teacher information: Indian children enjoyed playing many games using a large hoop (somewhat similar to our hula hoop) and a stick (pole) about 3 feet long. A variation of one of their hoop games may be played in this way: Two teams of children line up facing one another and standing about 15 to 20 feet apart. The first person on team 1 rolls the hoop across to the person facing him on the other team (team 2); that person attempts to catch the hoop with his stick (pole). If he is successful in catching the hoop, his team (team 2) gets a point. The hoop is then handed to player 2 on team 2 to roll to the person facing him on team 1. Each team makes points for catching the hoop with the stick. After all players have had a turn, the team with the most points wins the game. Many variations of the game may be played by increasing the number of hoops or by allowing the hoop to be caught by hand instead of with the stick.

B-2: Using media (note suggestions), students observe and generalize about Indian children at work and play. Evaluate students' conceptual development using the question focus.

Extended Activities:

1. Students may dramatize Indian children at work and play.
2. Additional "culture games" may be played and discussed.
3. Pictures may be made depicting Indian children at work and play.
4. Stories may be written by the students or by older students to accompany student pictures.
5. Books may be written for later listening and reading activities.
6. Questions may be evoked: "What we would like to know about Indian children . . ."
7. Indian songs and dances may be performed. Students may create their own.

8. Songs and dances (Mexican, Japanese) may be performed and compared with the Indian songs and dances.
9. Students may participate in craft activities.

Media:
Books
The Story of Tohi, A Chumash Indian Boy, by Elsa Falk, would supply interesting information about Indian family life at work and play (Chicago: Melmont Publishing, 1959).
Ames, Jocelyn, and Lee Ames: *City Street Games* (New York: Holt, Rinehart & Winston, 1963).
Records
Folk Songs of California and the Old West (12" LP and filmstrip, Bowmar, Glendale, California).
California Indian Songs (LP, Arthur Barr, Pasadena, California).
An Indian Dance & Drum Beats (AED10, Phoebe James Co.).
North American Indian Songs (LP–B515, Bowmar Publishing Co.).
Music of American Indians of the Southwest (4420, Folkways Records, New York).
Little Indian Drum (LP–YPR15006, Young Peoples Records).
Natay, Navajo Singer (LP–C6160, Canyon Records).
Songs of the Indians (LP–C6050, Canyon Records).
American Indian Tales for Children, Vols. I and II, told by A. M. Pellowsky (CMS 500, CMS 501).
16mm Films
Indian Boy of the Southwest (15 minutes, Bailey Film Associates, Santa Monica, California).
Indian Family of the California Desert (15 minutes, Educational Horizons).
Indians of California, Part 1, Village Life (15 minutes, Arthur Barr, Pasadena, California).
Hupa Indian White Deerskin Dance (11 minutes, Arthur Barr, Pasadena, California).
Filmstrips
Indian Cultures of the Americas—Indians of the Southwest (Encyclopedia Britannica Educational Corporation).

Language strategies. Students from kindergarten through the high school years often have difficulty differentiating among language absurdities, standard (school) English, jargon, and neighborhood language (culture-influenced dialect). Many interesting motivating activities can be planned to assist students to differentiate between correct and incorrect usage and appropriateness related to time, place, and circumstance.

One high school teacher working with a group of black students began by dividing his students into two teams. The teams were asked to pantomime the following expressions, which they drew from a box:

Carry a person to church
Get hat
Main squeeze
Give 'em some sugar
Psyched your mind
Wear threads
A mess of greens
Have a hustle
Drop a dime

The students were asked to write their own favorite expressions on slips of paper to include in the box for the continuation of the game.

Next the teacher presented the following common expressions and asked the students to work with a partner to write an example using the expression.

Hold your horses
Skate on thin ice
One foot in the grave
Six of one and half a dozen of the other
Smell a rat
Stab in the back
Step in the right direction
Stew in one's own juice
Tilt at windmills
Threadbare excuse
Touch and go
Tongue in cheek

On successive days the students discussed and researched the meaning and origin of the expressions and developed a list of their own.

Another system for initiating a study of language usage is to assign students to develop a comic strip. Working in small groups, the students may be asked to develop a strip that reflects their own cultural orientation. Their characters must speak a foreign language, in dialect, or use a dialog that is consistent with the speech pattern of their own group.

An elementary teacher concerned that his students missed the humor and absurdity of language read the following books to his class: Jaslin Sesyle, *What Do You Say Dear?* and Beatrice De Regniers, *May I Bring A Friend?* Then the teacher assisted the students to identify the "silliness" in each of the books. Students may also be encouraged to draw "silly" or absurd pictures or find them in magazines.

Summary

Urban teaching problems are complex, and no text can cover all the problems. Each child is unique (in the city or elsewhere); therefore, the effective teacher differentiates instruction. No formula or package will suffice for all situations, all classrooms, or all children. Teachers who have a "bag of tricks" readily available for use are accomplishing noteworthy goals.

The urban classroom may have disruptive students, students who often fail to attend school three consecutive days, or slow learners; still, *many urban teachers are effective* and develop teaching strategies that motivate students to learn. They are effective in changing disruptive behavior, encouraging attendance, and adapting teaching to learning styles because they have learned to observe, listen, accept, recognize, diagnose, and prescribe. If progress occurs inch by inch, it is still progress and it must be identified, appraised, and recognized in order to mediate continuous growth.

The teacher's "bag of tricks" must include a range of teaching strategies varied to motivate and reinforce learning. The strategies described in this chapter were intended to suggest options and to present a format for teachers to develop their own approaches. Another intent was that the greater number of strategies presented be representative of action-oriented activities that would encourage social participation, languaging, and decision making.

If the strategies have seemed to ignore negative classroom behavior, it is not because I do not recognize the existence of such behavior, but rather because it is the perspective of this text that negative classroom behavior can be curbed through appropriate classroom planning. Student misbehavior often occurs because lesson planning was inadequate and inappropriate for the intended group. If students do not have the necessary skills (or think that they do not) to accomplish a task, then they become frustrated and irritable; feelings of inadequacy become reinforced instead of the positive feelings the teacher desired and intended.

The competent teacher designs strategies to detect needs (a teaching strategy may serve as a pretest), to motivate, to provide data and experiences, to teach a skill, to serve as practice or follow-up, and to evaluate progress. Strategies in urban schools are most effective when they are action-oriented, when they are about the people and life styles that are real to the students, clearly defined in terms of student behaviors and tasks, sequentially organized, and process-oriented to facilitate continuing discussions and thinking.

The majority of teaching strategies and episodes in this chapter have been "field tested." They have proved to be effective, but the beginning teacher should realize that teaching strategies are designed for specific students and must be adapted for use with other students. Also, if a teacher is trying a strategy for the first time, he must exercise patience; both teacher and learner need practice to develop competence.

Notes

1. HENRY D. KASIN, "Let Me Live in My House (By the Side of the Road)," 1965.
2. ANDREW WILKINSON, "Oracy in English Teaching," in *Language and the Language Arts*, ed. Johanna S. DeStefano and Sharon E. Fox (Boston: Little, Brown, 1974), p. 64.
3. WALT WOLFRAM, "Sociolinguistic Alternatives in Teaching Reading to Nonstandard Speakers," *Reading Research Quarterly*, fall 1970, pp. 9–33.
4. IMOGENE RAMSEY, "A Comparison of First Grade Negro Dialect Speakers' Comprehension of Standard English and Negro Dialect," in *Language and the Language Arts*, ed. Johanna S. DeStefano and Sharon E. Fox (Boston: Little, Brown, 1974), p. 482. Emphasis added.
5. Los Angeles Unified School District, *Developmental Reading*, Amidon & Associates. St. Paul, Minnesota 1975, p. 2.
6. Statewide Social Sciences Study Committee, *Social Sciences Fducation Framework for California Public Schools, Kindergarten and Grades One Through Twelve* (Proposed, Sacramento, California State Board of Education, 1968), pp. 19–21.
7. LOUIS E. RATHS, MERRILL HARMIN, and SIDNEY B. SIMON, *Values and Teaching* (Columbus: Merrill, 1966).
8. DAVID R. KRATHWOHL, BENJAMIN S. BLOOM, and BERTRAM B. MASIA, *Taxonomy of Education Objectives: The Classification of Educational Goals, Handbook II: Affective Domain* (New York: McKay, 1964).
9. JAMES P. SHAVER and A. GUY LARKINS, *Decision-Making in a Democracy* (Boston: Houghton Mifflin, 1973), p. 425.
10. The strategy "Why Vote" by Johanna K. Lemlech was published in the *Social Studies Review*, fall 1973, pp. 37–40 (Sacramento: California Council for the Social Studies).
11. FANNIE R. SHAFTEL and GEORGE SHAFTEL, *Role-Playing for Social Values* (Englewood Cliffs, N.J.: Prentice-Hall, 1967), p. 9.
12. *Ibid.*, pp. 65–66.
13. JOHANNA K. LEMLECH, "Affective Involvement in Inquiry Methodology Using Role-Playing in Teacher Education" (Unpublished doctoral dissertation, University of Southern California, 1970), p. 201.
14. FRANK DEL OLMO, "Chicanos Criticize Saxbe on Alien Deportation Proposal," *Los Angeles Times*, November 8, 1974.
15. LEON ADKINSON and DONALD H. SANDERS, *Study Guide to Accompany Computers in Society* (New York: McGraw-Hill, 1973), p. 2.
16. HILDA TABA, *Teachers' Handbook for Elementary Social Studies* (Palo Alto: Addison-Wesley, 1967), p. 92.
17. *Ibid.*, p. 101.
18. *Ibid.*, p. 109.
19. FRANK DEL OLMO, "Accord Reported Near in Urban Renewal Case," *Los Angeles Times*, September 20, 1974.

Workshop V

The workshop section for Chapter 5 focuses on teaching objectives, teacher and learner behaviors, teacher responses, and the design of teaching strategies.

It is desirable to refer back to the designated strategy or section before attempting each exercise in order to familiarize yourself with the specifics of the strategy or a similar exercise. Practice designing strategies may be achieved by altering and varying the problems or with slight variations of the rules. The Student Council game and the City Council game are workable strategies to use as models.

The information-processing strategy for high school students using the article entitled "Accord Reported Near in Urban Renewal Case" is a good strategy to use to practice your own skills in the identification of relevant information, values, and decision making. Use of the same article would be appropriate to develop a role play. Identify the groups and viewpoints for each group. Use the section on role playing to assist you. Decide what questions you will pose in order to initiate the first enactment. Students who develop good inquiry skills usually have teachers who are good inquirers.

Teacher/Learner Behaviors, Teaching Objectives

OBJECTIVE: Identify teacher and learner behaviors.

1. Review the teaching strategy entitled, "What's for Breakfast, Lunch and Dinner?" Identify the teacher and learner behaviors for the strategy.
2. List the teaching objectives for the strategy.
3. Identify the school success oriented behaviors in this teaching lesson.

(Continued on Page 255)

Answers

Teacher behavior

1. Constructed 3 charts and cut-outs.
2. Displayed charts.
3. Divided children into small groups.
4. Recited information in Spanish and then in English.
5. Gave directions.
6. Provided groups with paper cut-outs.

Learner behavior

1. Matched printed label in picture with item.
2. Discussed assignment in a small group.
3. Listened and compromised with group peers.
4. Made a group decision and pasted cut-outs on newsprint.
5. Shared with whole class the group decision.

Answers

Teacher behaviors	Learner behaviors
1. Planned the strategy.	1. List, group, categorize help, social and recreational facilities.
2. Gathered maps, telephone directories, pens.	
3. Motivated the lesson.	2. Locate facilities in a telephone directory using categories established in No. 1.
4. Divided the students into groups.	
5. Gave instructions.	3. Locate facilities using a city streets map.
6. Observed, listened, took	

(Continued on Page 256)

What Do You Do When You Need Help?

OBJECTIVE: Identify teacher and learner behaviors.

Identify the teacher and learner behaviors throughout the strategy.

Teacher objectives

1. Development of self-concept through listening to Spanish prior to the secondary language.
2. Forced involvement and decision making through group interaction.
3. Development of visual, auditory, and semantic (readiness) skills related to functional literacy through listening and manipulation of corresponding pictures and labels (development of analytic skills).
4. Development of decision-making skills through listening and sharing with others, identifying the problem, the alternatives, and the choices.
5. Development of communication skills through listening and sharing with others, identifying the problem, the alternatives, and the choices.
6. Development of reflectivity through process-oriented problem solving and interactive encounters.
7. Development of information-processing skills as students classified foods into categories.

(Possible Answers continued from Page 254)

---

7. Circulated among groups.	6. Listened to conflicting decisions.
8. Listened to group discussions.	
9. Evaluated by facilitating discussion in which each group shared its point of view and its production.	7. Debated decisions in terms of rationality.
	8. On successive days, classified foods into categories.

(Continued from Page 254)

Questions for Strategy Analysis

OBJECTIVE: Analyze two teaching strategies.

The purpose of these questions is to assist your review of some of the strategies in this chapter. There is no one right answer to the questions. Your responses should depend upon your perceptions, your desired teaching style, the community in which you expect to teach, and the needs and interests of your students.

In the strategy "What's for Breakfast, Lunch and Dinner?" how did the first-grade teacher provide for students who could not read? How did the teacher encourage students to talk and interact with one another? What was the purpose of setting a limit to the number of items that the mother would buy at the market? If you were the teacher, how would you initiate the evaluation?

In the strategy "What Do You Do When You Need Help?" how would you motivate the lesson? If students do not understand the concept of "help" agencies, what illustrations could you use to assist them to develop the concept of social agencies? What insights about their community will students gain when they designate the mode of transportation to a help facility? What are some problems that young children might encounter when they research social (governmental) agencies in the telephone directory? What resources would you anticipate that capable students might need to use for research purposes in order to project future community needs? In what way are you satisfying student "needs" by inviting community leaders to the classroom?

Questions for Strategy Analysis

OBJECTIVES: Analyze teaching strategy; anticipate events that would inhibit students' success; plan factors to develop successful behaviors; using chapter strategies, design new strategy.

Why do people living in the inner city have such a poor voting record? In what ways do politicians respect pressure groups? Why is it important to involve the urban poor in the process of democracy?

In the strategy "Why Vote?" how did the teacher develop democratic decision making? If you were the teacher, how would you motivate this lesson? How could you develop composition skills as a part of the campaign process? How can you facilitate the "campaign" process so that students do not become unruly? How will you encourage cooperative voting so that each group does not persist in voting for its own candidate, thereby necessitating a run-off election? What other problems do you anticipate?

How will the strategy of Student Council develop students' ability to express themselves? How can you redesign this game to be relevant to the students with whom you work? How does the strategy provide for cooperative team learning?

In the City Council strategy, why is the concept of *rules* important? As a teacher, how can you assist the students to realize that decisions which affect one group will also affect all other groups? How will you facilitate group interaction as students listen to conflicting proposals?

Teacher Responses

OBJECTIVE: **Identify teaching behaviors.**

Refer to the directed discussion strategy, elementary school teaching episode, third grade. Identify the teacher responses that characterize the following teaching behaviors: accepting, clarifying, reinforcing, focusing, facilitating.

(*Continued on Page 258*)

Answers

Accepting:	You are good observers. That is very good thinking, class.
Clarifying:	Fighting and playing are both examples of what scientists call "behavior." It sounds like you agree that behavior is "doing." Juan was trying to describe covert actions.
Reinforcing:	That is very good thinking, class. Now I have another puzzle for you. What kinds of actions or behavior can you describe? Juan has brought up something very important. Let's look at two new words. You are really getting the idea about behavior.

(*Possible Answers continued from Page 257*)

Let's practice now and see if we can distinguish covert and overt behavior.

Focusing: What are these pictures about?
What do you think is meant by the word behavior?
Can you think of another word to use for "doing?"
What kinds of actions or behavior can you describe?
Can you think of some other covert actions?

Facilitating: Explain that, Juan.

The City Council Game

OBJECTIVES:

1. Identify additional objectives for this strategy.
2. Identify possible evaluative questions the teacher could ask.
3. Design your own City Council game by changing the problems.

Answers

Objectives

1. Students will assume leadership or membership in a group activity.
2. Students will discuss a group problem and propose means to alleviate the problem.
3. Working with others, students will cooperatively write a proposal for a law or suggest means to alleviate a problem, anticipating the consequences of their proposal.
4. Working in a group, students will choose one member to represent their point of view.
5. Students will listen to other group's proposals and debate them.
6. As members of the city council, students will vote agreement or disagreement or propose modifications to the proposals.
7. Students will evaluate as a class the proposals, the game, and their own performances.

Teacher's evaluative questions

1. What was your group's problem?
2. Why was it a problem?
3. What were some of the possible solutions to your problem?
4. How did your proposal solve the problem?
5. How did your proposal affect others?
6. How did you feel about the council's action?
7. What can citizens do if they are not pleased with the actions of their city council?

(*Continued on Page 259*)

(*Teacher's evaluative questions continued from Page 258*)

8. What pleased you about your group's work and proposal?
9. How could each group improve its performance?
10. If we were to play this game again, how could we make it more realistic?

Design Your Own Game

OBJECTIVE: To design a game strategy.

Follow these guidelines to design your own game:

1. Decide who is to play the game.
2. Identify your teaching objective.
3. Is the game to be a board game or a simulation?
4. Will you design the game or are the students to do it, as in the Immigrant game?
5. Decide on the situation and conditions. Will there be voting? Will there be movement as on a game board? What resources will be needed?
6. What will be the object of the game? Will there be scoring? How will the students know when the game has been completed?
7. Decide on rules and any other constraints that will affect behavior.
8. Set a time limit so that students will know when they must be finished.

Design a Concept Attainment Game

OBJECTIVE: To design a strategy to teach a concept.

1. Decide who will play the game.
2. What is the teaching objective? (Identify the concept.)
3. Who will do the listing and grouping, you or the students?
4. How will the students analyze the attributes of a category?
5. How will the students develop the concept?
6. How will you reinforce the concept?

Refer to the section on concept formation for assistance.

Language Lesson

OBJECTIVE: Plan a language lesson to develop fluency skills.

DIRECTIONS

1. Write a short narrative appropriate for student listening.
2. Tape your presentation.
3. Select vocabulary for a language drill.

4. Decide whether the drill will be conducted with the whole class or whether students will use tape recorders or language masters to practice the drill exercise.
5. Design questions about the narrative that involve the vocabulary drill.
6. Design an "active" lesson as a follow-up to the drill and discussion.

For assistance, refer to the section with suggestions for a basic procedure to develop language fluency skills.

Dialect and Reading

OBJECTIVES: Read to gain knowledge about: the controversy related to dialect training in reading, the language-experience approach to reading instruction.

The dialect and reading research of Goodman indicated that teachers should accept the student's primary language and/or dialect and develop it further. Read his article and contrast his approach with the work of Rystrom. As you read the two articles, consider the following questions:

1. How could teachers develop a formal reading program for black English speakers? What kinds of sociolinguistic data would be needed?
2. What would be the advantages and disadvantages of such a program?

Goodman, K. S.: "Dialect Rejection and Reading: A Response," *Reading Research Quarterly*, 5 (1970), 600–603.
Rystrom, R.: "Dialect Training and Reading: A Further Look," *Reading Research Quarterly*, 5 (1970), 581–599.

Mainstreaming: a construct for teaching all children humanely

Special Education

Is special education obsolete and unjustifiable? Should individuals with exceptional needs be removed from the regular classroom? Have minority children been victimized?

Chip Sutton was in the third grade at the Franklin School when his teacher requested that he be tested by the school psychologist. Chip's first- and second-grade teachers had noted that his motor skills were poor. Chip's third-grade teacher stated that his oral language skills were restricted; he became frustrated easily when performing simple tasks or else he appeared disinterested and withdrawn. The school psychologist administered the Wechsler Intelligence Scale for Children and the Bender Visual Motor Gestalt test. The Vineland Social Maturity Scale was administered by the counselor in an interview with Chip's mother.

At a late afternoon conference, Chip's parents, his teacher, the school counselor, and the principal conferred to discuss Chip's case. Chip's verbal and performance skills on the WISC classified him as a borderline retradate; his performance on the Bender revealed delayed visual-motor development. Chip's social quotient (SQ), assessed through the Vineland interview technique, correlated closely with his IQ score. Although Chip could have continued in the regular classroom, the school counselor and the teacher recommended that he be placed in a special education classroom. After consideration and a great deal of discussion, the parents agreed that Chip might perform better in a classroom with fewer children and more teacher assistance. At least they were willing to try it. ·

Chip's new teacher was one of 136,000 teachers holding an advanced credential in special education or at the very least having had some extra training that qualified him to teach children with special needs. (Although most school districts require extra training or an advanced degree, some employ teachers to teach special education without advanced preparation.) The United States Office of Education statistics for 1970 reveal that of those 136,000 teachers employed by the public schools, 54,000 of them teach classes for the mentally retarded. When compared to 1967–1968 statistics, only 32,000 teachers were identified as teaching retarded children, an indication of the increase in the population identified as retarded. The remainder of the teachers were employed in the following special education categories:

Speech	35,100
Learning disabled	27,900
Emotionally disturbed	11,300
Hard of hearing	2,000
Deaf	2,300
Partially sighted	800
Blind	500
Crippled	1,800
Mentally retarded	54,000
Total	136,000

Special education is usually interpreted to mean special facilities, special opportunities for learning, special resources, special assistance for children who have special needs. But for many children, special education has meant labeling (emotionally handicapped, learning disabled, mentally retarded, behavior disordered) or "pigeonholing" and exclusion. The single most striking feature of the special education classroom is the overabundance of minority students. This overrepresentation is of great concern to minority communities as well as to concerned educators.

The most stunning example of the effect of the labeling process occurs in the classrooms for the mentally retarded. (Over one-third of all special education teachers teach the mental retardates.) The purpose of labeling in essence has been to enable the school to recognize and deal with learner differences. But the category system has become rigid, and students assigned to a special classroom for special opportunities, that is, retarded, fail to emerge from the special classrooms. A child once labeled "retarded" is seldom reevaluated even though he may be performing well. Statistics for students assigned to retarded classrooms indicate that only 10 percent will ever return to a regular classroom. Chip Sutton's placement in a classroom for the mildly retarded in all probability will be permanent. In San Francisco, with a black school population of 28.5 percent, the educable mentally retarded (EMR) population for black students is 66 percent. Similar mislabeling and overrepresentation has been documented for Puerto Rican, Mexican, and American Indian students in New York; Washington, D.C.; Philadelphia; Tempe, Arizona; San Diego, California; and Massachusetts. A 1966 study in California disclosed that of 85,000 children labeled retarded, 26 percent had Spanish surnames, although Spanish surnames accounted for only 13 percent of the school population. Dunn observed in a 1968 article that 60 to 80 percent of the children in retarded classrooms were from low socioeconomic status backgrounds.[1]

Other researchers corroborated Dunn's statement. Grotberg[2] questioned the disproportionate number of minority students in mentally retarded classes while so few minority students were in classes for children with learning disabilities. Franks worked in 11 Missouri school districts and studied the ethnic and social status characteristics of children enrolled in EMR and LD classes in grades 1–8. His study supported Dunn and Grotberg: the data revealed overrepresentation of black children in the EMR classes and surprisingly few in the learning disability classes. Although Franks did not find a conscious conspiracy to assign the black children to the EMR classes, he felt that further investigation was warranted to examine whether low socioeconomic status children were disregarded when they had learning disabilities.[3]

Children enrolled in special education classes are often called "exceptional." This term encompasses all types of handicapped designations as well as the gifted programs. There are approximately 7 million children of school age who are in need of special services. (Approximately 10 percent are handicapped and 1 to 2 percent are gifted.) It is estimated that only 3 million of those children receive an effective education. One million receive no education at all.

Kirk provided a definition of the exceptional population:

> The exceptional child is the child who deviates from the normal or average child 1) in mental characteristics, 2) in sensory abilities, 3) in neuromuscular or physical characteristics, 4) in social or emotional behavior, 5) in communication abilities, or 6) in multiple handicaps to such an extent that he requires a modification of school practices, or special education services, in order to develop to his maximum capacity.[4]

Ms. Coombs, Chip's second grade teacher, conscientiously believed that Chip would profit from an experience that would remove the pressures of the normal classroom. The sorting or tracking of youngsters begins in the kindergarten as teachers observe motor development, sensory capacity, linguistic skills, ability to follow directions, eye-hand coordination, shoelace tying, attention span, relations with other children, and so on. The observation skills of elementary teachers who detect the majority of exceptional differences is to be applauded, but the dilemma occurs after the initial detection. To examine the issues involved, the first section of this chapter focuses upon the following questions:

1. In what ways will special placement affect the child?
2. To what extent will the stigma attached to categorizing the child affect him?
3. Should the child be tested and if so, by what means? Who will administer the test? How will adaptive behavior be determined?

Effectiveness of special education classrooms

A number of research studies have questioned whether handicapped children make more progress when placed in special education classrooms as compared to children's progress in the regular classroom. Since the teachers for the handicapped in most cases have had special training and receive extra supplies and equipment, many have assumed, as did Ms. Coombs, that the handicapped child would profit from the assistance of the specialist. Yet a great body of literature concludes that there is no evidence that special programming is beneficial.[5]

Typical of the efficacy studies conducted was one by Welch, who compared the self-concept and achievement of educable retarded children in special classrooms with others in regular classrooms for at least one-half of the school day. The children integrated into normal classrooms for at least half of the school day improved in reading and had a higher self-concept than those children segregated into special classrooms.[6] Another study by Zito and Bardon compared the achievement motivation of three groups of black adolescents: one group in a special education program, one group in a regular classroom, and a third group of normal intelligence. The researchers concluded that special education placement affected the youngsters by making them more cautious and less likely to anticipate success in school tasks even though the achievement motivation was comparable to the students of normal intelligence.[7] Despite the results of these and other similar studies, some researchers state that there are too many variables to differentiate satisfactorily between exceptional and regular classroom placement.

Labeling

The largest group of children bearing exceptional status are those designated mentally retarded, and since minority children are consistently overrepresented in this category, further discussion will focus on the children labeled "mental retardates."

In a now classic study in Riverside, California, Mercer questioned why there was a disproportionate number of persons from low socioeconomic groups and from minority backgrounds labeled retarded. Mercer distinguished between a clinical and a social system perspective in referring to the categorization of mentally retarded. In the clinical system, individual pathology exists, diagnosed or not; therefore, explanations are related to biological terms. Once labeled mentally retarded from this perspective, the individual can then be expected to have physiologic components that limit behavioral expectations. The individual with this disease will perform in expected ways and in a restricted manner. "The diagnostician begins with the definition and moves to the empirical world to identify cases."[8] The sociologic perspective "defines mental retardation as an achieved status which some persons hold in some social systems. The role of retardate consists of the behavior expected of persons occupying the status of mental retardate."[9]

The Mercer premise is that it is possible to study how an individual achieves the status of mental retardate just as it is possible to study how other roles in society are achieved. Mercer hypothesied that there is an interactional relationship between sociocultural factors and the referral and labeling process. From the social system point of view, if students have not been designated "mental retardate" and if they are functioning in a regular classroom, then they are *not* playing the role of mental retardate and in fact are not mentally retarded *because they are perceived by others as normal*. Since a clinical prerequisite for mental retardation is low IQ (below 80), those individuals with IQs below 80 are what sociologists describe as the "population at risk."[10]

If the student is functioning in a regular classroom and playing the role of a normal student even though he possesses the low IQ, then Mercer hypothesied that other factors lead teachers to refer the child for further study. In the Riverside research, Mercer and her associates discovered that for most Anglo children (majority population) in the population at risk, those eligible for mental retardation designation actually did acquire the status of mental retardate. Teacher observations and evaluations seem to be more accurate with the Anglo child and *referrals* occur more often. The Anglo retardate appears to be more physically disabled than the Mexican or black retardate; the Anglo retardate is "more visibly different." In the case of minority children in the population at risk, there are many who have not acquired the designation. Therefore, it was possible to study the minority child eligible for the status in order to differentiate between the eligibles and those who had acquired the status of mental retardate and thus isolate the selective factors.

Mercer and associates examined three variables: the characteristics of the child during individual testing and evaluation; the characteristics of the child's family; and the characteristics of the school system. The researchers differentiated between minority eligibles and minority retardates:

1. Eligibles scored higher on verbal performance skills on the WISC, particularly in arithmetic and information subtests and on the digit span subtest.
2. There was no distinction between the two groups in educational aspirations, self-concepts, emotional adjustment, attitudes toward school, or any social psychological variable.
3. There was no distinction between the two groups in family backgrounds.
4. There was significant difference between the two groups in terms of teacher's perception and comments on cumulative records.

    The children who were placed [in mental retarded classrooms] and the children who were eligible but not placed had three characteristics in common which differentiated them from other children in the classroom: they were less often described as having high mental ability, less often described as academically competent, and more often described as poorly adjusted. However, on every variable the eligibles received more favorable comments and fewer unfavorable comments than the children who were placed.

    Mental retardates in special education received significantly more comments about their poor adjustment and their low mental ability and fewer comments about being liked by peers than the eligibles. In addition, the children assigned the status of mental retardate were more often described as incompetent in the use of English. Those with low IQ who were not placed were more frequently described as easy to manage.[11]

The researchers concluded that low academic competence + poor adjustment + low competence in English + few friends = perceived low mental ability = mental retardation. The major difference in teacher perception between the two groups hinged upon English language skills, peer rapport, and manageability. Although low IQ is a prerequisite for the label, other sociocultural factors are of paramount importance.[12]

Using the social system perspective of mental retardation or any other categorized label for exceptionality, the Mercer research indicated that deviant behavior *as perceived* by one group of teachers or others in professional positions defined the attributes of those designated atypical. But the attributes perceived are not necessarily accurate or inherent in the individual assigned the deviant status nor will all individuals assigned to the status behave in similar ways.

Haywood summarized the reasons for classification and labeling:

1. Scientific faith that description and classification aids in the process of explanation.
2. Categorization reduces the number of problems to be solved in dealing with deviant behavior.
3. Diagnosticians assume that naming a problem or disease will lead to treatment of it.

Classification and labeling can be seen as a system devised for "social convenience."[13]

Dunn's analysis of the labeling process led him to conclude that disability labels probably did children more harm than good. He saw the diagnostic process as one in which people searched for causation and then quit when something was found wrong; the label served as a self-fulfilling prophecy and to reduce the teacher's expectancy for student success. Furthermore, it was Dunn's estimate that the labeling process isolated the child by removing him from his peer group and "regular" classroom, thereby affecting his self-image and contributing to feelings of inferiority.

The testing dilemma

Many educators have questioned whether or not testing minority youngsters should be discontinued. Their concerns relate to test bias, sociocultural factors, the examiner, administrative procedures, and environmental situation factors. Since the school "labels" more individuals than any other institution, and since the school relies primarily on IQ test results rather than corroborative medical diagnoses, the test results are crucial for low socioeconomic individuals, particularly those of minority status. Although some sociologists, linguists, and educators have related the overrepresentation of minority students' assignment to special education classrooms to the aforementioned concerns, other researchers, most notably Arthur Jensen, cite genetic reasons.

Mental deficiency as defined by the American Association on Mental Deficiency (AAMD) has two components: low IQ and inability to adapt to new environmental situations. Although there are many IQ tests available, there are few tests of behavioral adaptation; thus, it is understandable that the school relies primarily on IQ scores. To add to the dilemma, test designers and the AAMD do not agree on the cutoff score for mental retardation. Mercer in the Riverside study identified individuals with low IQ and impaired adaptive behavior and compared them with individuals designated "quasi-retarded" because they had low IQ but normal adaptive behavior. The researchers developed their own test of adaptive ability. From the results of their study, they concluded:

1. The cutoff level for subnormality should be an IQ below 70. (Most school districts use below 79.)
2. Mental retardation must be defined using two measures: IQ score and a measure of adaptive behavior.
3. The IQ tests presently being used in the schools are culturally related and therefore biased.

Mercer stated: "IQ tests are Anglocentric. . . . They measure the extent to which an individual's background matches the average cultural pattern of American society."[14]

The Mercer study demonstrated a relationship between degree of acculturation and success on an IQ test. Similarity of life style between the student and the test-standardized population (Anglo characteristics) was the crucial factor. Implications of the Mercer research that must be considered by prospective teachers include these:

The designation of exceptional status can handicap the individual for life.

The "handicap" may exist only in the eyes of the perceiver.

Minority groups are heterogeneous; subgroups have diverse values; labels lack precision.

Test bias. A number of researchers have noted culturally biased test items. For instance, Briere, a linguist, noted that the use of a yellow banana as a test item confused poor children whose mothers would buy the very ripe almost brown banana because it was cheaper; Mexican children newly arrived from Mexico would be used to the green banana that is cooked or baked in the Mexican home. Hewett and Massey took exception to the picture of a comb with a missing tooth as a picture-completion item on the WISC, believing that ghetto children may not see anything wrong with an incomplete comb.[15]

The effect of cultural background on IQ scores when social factors are equalized was elaborated by Garcia with the following example: In Israel first-generation children of Oriental Jews had a mean IQ of 85, whereas first-generation children of European Jews had a mean IQ of 105. When both groups grew up in a kibbutz nursery and were tested after four years, the mean IQ scores of both groups was 115.

Garcia theorized that there are facets of intelligence that are invisible to IQ tests, that life on the kibbutz made the children "test-wise."[16]

Some educators and researchers have recommended *translating* tests into the student's native language in order to eliminate language bias. However, Bransford cited the following problems with translated tests:

> IQ tests have not been standardized to or adjusted for ethnic sub-groups. Students often speak a dialect rather than a formal language. (Minority groups are heterogeneous.)
>
> Native language development often halts after the child enters school; the child may be handicapped in both languages.[17]

Jensen recommended testing potential learning abilities by using tests that provide direct measures of present learning abilities. Jensen concluded from his total work that the IQ test is not a valid measure of ability for Mexican American children because inherent learning ability is not the only basis on which the IQ test discriminates. Mexican American children may not have acquired, prior to school experience, the requisite knowledge, skills, and habits necessary for IQ testing.[18]

Roessel studied the achievement on IQ tests of American Indian children. He concluded that American Indian children experience language or verbal handicaps when tested, and that achievement on tests varies among tribes and within tribes depending upon degree of acculturation.[19] Sattler,[20] in an extensive review of testing problems, cited other researchers who noted that American Indian children were more successful on the WISC performance scale than on the verbal scale. The children also appeared to have less self-confidence and greater testing fears than white children.

Culture-free tests, described in the past by some researchers as a testing panacea, have not provided accurate information concerning learning potential. Black Americans are often bicultural and bidialectical; nonverbal tests have been found to be as difficult for black children as verbal tests. Sattler in his review of intelligence testing of minority children cited the investigations of several researchers who noted that nonverbal tests are not culture-free because they are dependent upon analytic thinking. If the black student's cognitive style is relational (note Chapter 4), then he or she will have difficulty with the nonverbal test. Similar problems have been noted for Mexican American children.[21]

The Davis-Eells test of general intelligence or problem-solving ability is a nonverbal test; Stablein, Willey, and Thomson investigated its use with Spanish-speaking children aged ten and Anglo children aged nine. The investigators found that the Spanish-speaking children had as much difficulty with the Davis-Eells test as with any test of verbal intelligence.[22] Sattler's review of testing ethnic minority group and culturally disadvantaged children concluded that none of the investigations had verified the applicability of a so-called culture-free intelligence test.

Test examiner and the testing environment. Children react to the test examiner in different ways. For instance, American Indian children have been found to speak softly or not at all to the examiner, which has resulted in misinterpretation. Labov (note Chapter 4), investigated the differing performance of black children using black and white adult interviewers. He also noted the difference when the interviewer sat down and when the interviewer towered over the child.

Hewett and Massey noted language difficulties between a white examiner and black examinee if the child used phrases that had meanings unknown by the examiner. Other researchers have noted that black children express fear and discomfort when tested by a white examiner.[23] Some research investigators believe that the examiner's language may be as important as the examiner's skin color; both may provide cues to the children that motivate or destroy testing rapport.

Palomares and Johnson invesigated Spanish-speaking and English-speaking test examiners as they tested Mexican American children. They discovered that the English-speaking examiner recommended a greater number of children for EMR placement (73 percent) than did the Spanish-speaking examiner (26 percent).[24] Sattler also reported research relating to the testing environment. Some research indicated that low socioeconomic students might perform better in an individual testing situation than a group situation which is more distracting.

Recommendations. Sattler noted that many psychologists suggest a moratorium on testing. (A 1975 California court ruling required a moratorium on testing of black students.) Some researchers caution that testing should occur only if a wide range of mental tasks are given. Others suggest that for Spanish-speaking youngsters, testing should occur sometime after bilingual programs have been initiated and the students have demonstrated greater language ability and pride. Mercer suggested the following procedures:

Information should be provided that gives a sociocultural index about the child.

A test reflecting adaptive behavior at home and in the community should be included in the child's assessment.

A standard IQ test should be given to measure academic readiness to be interpreted against standard norms in order to determine whether the child can succeed in a regular public classroom without additional assistance.

A standard IQ test should be given and interpreted within the child's ethnic norms to provide information concerning the child's learning potential.[25]

In this first section, three issues concerned educators about special education:

Ambiguous results from comparisons of exceptional students' progress in special classrooms and in regular classrooms

The stigma of the labeling process and the ultimate effect of the classification system

Cultural bias of test instruments, the test examiner, and the testing situation

The Right to Education

Change in our society occurs most frequently through judicial decisions and legislative enactments. Public policy influences how groups act and how individuals feel about themselves and others. While educators debated the validity of special education classrooms and researchers challenged the sanctity of the IQ test, parents had their day in court. Court litigation has affected the rights of children previously excluded or segregated in special education classrooms. The second section of this chapter examines the court decisions and the legislative enactments that will affect special education in the next decade.

State compulsory attendance laws have been used by many school districts in the United States to exclude children with handicaps. Often state laws provide that students with certain body or mental conditions are excluded from attendance (Alaska, Nevada) or, as in California, educational services were postponed until the child reaches eight years of age. The Fourteenth Amendment to the Constitution guarantees equal protection of the laws to all people. In the last several years, using the equal protection clause, handicapped individuals are achieving change as educational institutions are forced to examine equal educational opportunities.

Judicial decisions

One of the most important court victories occurred in Pennsylvania when the Pennsylvania Association for Retarded Children and thirteen retarded children who represented all other school-age retarded children in the state brought a class action suit against the Commonwealth of Pennsylvania. The suit charged the state with failure to provide access to free educational opportunities for school-age mentally retarded children. Evidence was presented through expert testimony. The witnesses indicated the following:

> All mentally retarded persons are capable of benefiting from a program of education and training.
>
> The greatest number of retarded persons, given such education and training, are capable of achieving self-sufficiency, and the remaining few, with such education and training, are capable of achieving some degree of self-care.
>
> The earlier such education and training begins, the more thoroughly and the more efficiently a mentally retarded person will benefit from it.
>
> Whenever a training program is begun at any point in life, the mentally retarded person will benefit from such education and training.[26]

The court concurred that it was the obligation of the state to place each mentally retarded child in an appropriate free public program of education and that placement for education and training was *preferable in a regular public school class* rather than placement in a special public school class, but that placement in special education was preferable to placement in any other type of program. Other provisions of the decision required

> Automatic reevaluation of any educational assignment other than to a regular class
>
> Annual reevaluation at the request of the child's parent or guardian
>
> Opportunity for a hearing concerning the reevaluation
>
> The child must be entered in school no later than age 8 and until age 17
>
> School districts must provide preschool education to retarded children whenever such a program is provided for other children of the same age
>
> Supervision of educational programs and institutions in the state

The Pennsylvania court order went into effect October 13, 1971, when each plaintiff child was to be reevaluated. The result was that school districts would no longer be able to postpone, deny, or terminate access to a free public education for retarded children.[27]

The next court victory having great impact occurred in Washington, D.C. (*Mills* v. *Board of Education*), when a class action suit was brought against the District of Columbia Board of Education, the Department of Human Resources, and the mayor of the city. The suit charged that the district failed to exercise its legal and moral responsibility to educate all children. The court decreed the constitutional right of all children, regardless of handicap, to a free public education.[28]

Another landmark decision occurred in California (*Larry P.* v. *Riles*). The suit filed in behalf of six black elementary children in San Francisco claimed:

That the children were not mentally retarded

That placement in EMR classes had been made on the basis of tests which were biased against the culture and experiences of black children

That irreparable injury had resulted from placement in EMR classes because of minimal curriculum offerings; as a result of low teacher expectation; from subjection to ridicule by other students; because of acquired feelings of inferiority resulting from EMR placement; and from the notation of EMR placement on the students' permanent record, which is given to colleges, employers, and the armed forces.

The court agreed that students wrongfully placed in EMR classes did suffer irreparable harm. The plaintiffs were required to demonstrate that the IQ tests were the primary basis for placing students in EMR classes; they did this by demonstrating the disproportionately high number of black students placed in EMR classes in San Francisco (9.1 percent of all school age children in California are black, yet 27.5 percent of black school-age children were placed in EMR classes). The court shifted the burden of proof to the school district to justify the use of IQ tests. The San Francisco school district did not dispute that IQ tests are culturally biased.

The court concluded that the school district did not demonstrate "that IQ tests are rationally related to the purpose of segregating students *according to their ability to learn* in regular classes, at least insofar as those tests are applied to Black students."[29] The court ruled that

Black students may not be placed in EMR classes on the basis of results attained primarily with an IQ test, if the consequence of use of the IQ test will be racial imbalance in the composition of EMR classes.

For students already placed in EMR classes, there must be yearly reevaluations.

In an earlier California case (*Diana* v. *State Board of Education*), it was the aim of the plaintiffs to ensure that exceptional children were not placed in inappropriate programs. The facts of this case will be provided as a workshop activity so that you may compare your perceptions with those of the court.

Legislative enactments

Judicial decisions have influenced many state legislatures and school districts across the country. New York City has banned group IQ tests and instead relies on achievement test results and teacher evaluations. In Massachusetts, a psychological assessment of potential EMR students is required; IQ testing is not specified as a factor in the psychological assessment. Precipitated by the *Diana v. State Board of Education* case, new sections of the Education Code in California specified:

> EMR placement must be based upon a psychological examination by a school psychologist.
>
> The credentialed psychologist must investigate developmental history, cultural background, and school achievement to substantiate individual test scores.
>
> The examination shall include estimates of adaptive behavior. (Adaptive behavior scales are to be developed, normed, and approved by the California State Board of Education.)
>
> Until adaptive behavior scales are available, the school psychologist or an administrator in the school system is to visit the student's home to interview members of the student's family.
>
> Consideration is to be given to family mobility; occupational history; status of parent; sibling relationships; isolation of home, family, and child within the environment; developmental materials in the home; and other environmental factors.[30]

In 1973 the following states passed legislation on behalf of exceptional children: Arkansas, Arizona, Colorado, Illinois, Kansas, Louisiana, Maine, Maryland, Mississippi, Missouri, North and South Dakota, New Jersey, New York, and Nevada. Comprehensive legislation for the education of the handicapped has been enacted by nearly 30 states. The 93rd Congress passed the Education Amendments of 1974 (PL 93–380) to the Education of the Handicapped Act. The amendments specify criteria for funding special education programs with federal monies through fiscal 1977. Major provisions include the following:

> Establishes a goal to provide *full educational opportunities* to all handicapped children.
>
> Provides procedures to expend funds to accomplish this goal.

Priority established to expend funds for children not receiving an education.

Procedural safeguards established for handicapped children, parents, or guardians in regard to the identification, evaluation, and placement of the children.

Ensures that parents or guardians will be notified if educational placement of the child is to be changed by a state or local agency.

Provides for a due process hearing for parents or guardians to examine records with respect to the classification or placement of the child.

Allows parent or guardian to obtain an outside independent evaluation of the child.

Provides procedures to protect the rights of a child who is the ward of the state, including the appointment of an individual to act as a surrogate for the parents or guardian.

Provides procedures for a due process hearing to ensure impartiality subject to administrative or judicial appeal.

Provides procedures to assure that, to the maximum extent appropriate, handicapped children in public or private institutions or other care facilities *are educated with children who are not handicapped* and that removal from the regular classroom occurs only when the handicap is of such severity that educational services cannot be achieved satisfactorily.

Provides procedures to ensure that testing and evaluation materials utilized for the classification and placement of handicapped children will be *selected and administered so as not to be racially or culturally discriminatory.*[31]

The reassessment of state and local special education programs continued; the combined clout of the courts and federal funding is apparent in the directions of the new programs. The California plan provides an example of the new philosophy and goals that guide exceptional programming. California initiated special education programs in 1860. It was one of the first states to do so. The impact of both judicial decisions and federal law influenced the California State Board of Education to develop and implement a new Master Plan for Special Education (1974). The Pennsylvania decision and the Diana case focused on two directions for special education: mandatory rather than permissive programming for exceptional children; and identification, classification, and placement standards and procedures.

The California plan identified special education students as "individuals with exceptional needs." Four subclassifications were identified for the purpose of data collection and reporting:

Communicatively handicapped

Physically handicapped

Learning handicapped (excluded are children whose needs are derived from unfamiliarity with the English language or cultural differences)

Severely handicapped

The California plan identified two strands and eight program components:

Supportive:
1. Identification, assessment and instructional planning
2. Management and support services
3. Special transportation services
4. Capital outlay

Instructional:
5. Special classes and centers
6. Resource specialist program
7. Designated instruction and services
8. Nonpublic school services

Three components of the plan are pertinent to the discussion in this chapter. Component 1, the identification, assessment and instructional planning element, is indicative of the new trends in special education. In this component, the procedures for identification, assessment, and instruction are specified. The needs of preschool children are included. A school appraisal team is provided for; the team is to include the school administrator, a resource specialist, designated instruction teachers and specialists, regular teachers, and a program specialist. Participation of other specialists is provided for as need arises. These individuals may be the school psychologist, social worker, nurse, or counselor. A second-level team is also identified: professional specialists representing health, psychology, social work, language services, management services, and diagnostic teaching. This team is designated the educational assessment service and provides the following services: reviews referrals, recommends program components, recommends needed additional assessments, confers with parents, and develops instructional goals for each student.

Component 5, special classes and centers, describes the grouping procedures to be utilized. The special classes and centers are to concentrate on students with intensive needs. Whenever possible, these programs are to be maintained in conjunction with regular programs. Regular program teachers are to receive support to facilitate the integration of exceptional students into the regular program. Other centers and state schools are also provided for in this component, as well as teacher-pupil ratios in the special programs. Instructional aides are provided in each special classroom.

Component 6, the resource specialist program, is unique to the plan. The description is as follows:

> The resource specialist program should provide instructional planning, special instruction, tutorial assistance, or other services to exceptional individuals in special programs *and/or in regular classrooms of each school.* This program is to be coordinated by a resource specialist, who is a special education teacher with advanced training in the education of individuals with exceptional needs.[32]

It is this component that provides for "specialist" teacher consultant services to the regular classroom teacher. The specialist is responsible for the interpretation and implementation of the psychological assessment and the individual instructional goals. This component focuses on

The integration of the exceptional child into the regular classroom

Resource services to regular teachers and to parents

Coordination, interpretation, and implementation of psychological findings and educational planning

An evaluation system as well as a financial model are included in the master plan program for California. The allocation of fiscal resources for special education has been extremely influential in reinforcing old practices or encouraging new services. For instance, in Georgia and in Texas, school districts receive funds for retarded children as an integral part of the funding formula for regular education. In some states, funds are received according to a weighted equivalency formula, which necessitates the isolation and segregation of the retarded child in order to be eligible for funding. The greater the number of hours the child spends in the special education classroom, the greater is the reimbursement. In the Georgia and Texas models, districts are encouraged to integrate the handicapped child at least half of the school day into the regular education program.

Special educator Lloyd M. Dunn has been held responsible by the educational community for initiating the dialog regarding the validity of special placement, the effects of the labeling process, and the fairness of the testing tools used in the identification and placement of children in special education classrooms. All three aspects of the dialog have had major implications for teaching in the urban school, because low socioeconomic status youths and/or minority children have borne the brunt of the education system's equivocal practices. Dunn argued that self-contained special education classrooms were unjustifiable because of changes in the modern school which facilitate and accommodate greater flexibility: variable plans for the organization of classrooms, team teaching, flexible groups, differentiation of instruction, resource personnel, and sophisticated teaching tools. Dunn suggested a "blueprint for change," the result of which has been a number of educational models that emphasize the concept of *main-streaming.*

Mainstreaming

The third section of this chapter considers the construct of mainstreaming as an alternate system for exceptional children. As you read the definition of mainstreaming, consider the following questions: What would a classroom teacher need to know about the concept in order to integrate the exceptional child with normal peers? What skills would the classroom teacher need in order to implement the concept?

What is mainstreaming? Kaufman, Gottlieb, Agard, and Kukic have defined it thus: "Mainstreaming refers to the temporal, instructional and social integration of eligible exceptional children with normal peers, based on an ongoing individually determined educational planning and programming process and requires clarification of responsibility among regular and special education administrative, instructional, and supportive personnel."[33]

There are three elements in the definition on which the authors elaborate: integration, educational planning and programming process, and clarification of responsibility. Using the example of Chip Sutton, the eight-year-old borderline retardate, the three components can be illustrated as follows.

Integration. If the concept of mainstreaming were to be implemented at the Franklin School, Chip would probably participate in his "regular" classroom activities half of each school day. The other half of the school day would be spent in a special education classroom. Chip's special education teacher would be responsible for the diagnostic workup and the individual program planning. The plan would be communicated to child, parents, and "regular" teacher. Coordination for the program as well as continuous evaluation would be the responsibility of the special teacher. In the special classroom, Chip would experience a learning center approach to meet his skill needs. In the regular classroom, Chip would undergo some peer teaching. Since Ms. Coombs is a responsible professional as well as sympathetic and knowledgeable about Chip's problems and instructional goals, she has assessed her own teaching performance in terms of teaching style and personality. She has also observed Chip's learning style, along with the special teacher. Together the teachers decided to utilize an individualized academic skill program. Chip will experience individualized assistance from his regular teacher, the instructional aide in his special classroom, and peers in his regular classroom.

When Chip's special teacher developed his individual educational profile, it was necessary to use the psychological assessment prepared by the school psychologist and the evaluations and observations of Ms. Coombs, Chip's first- and second-grade teachers, and Chip's parents. Interpreting all of the information, the special teacher decided that Chip's program must provide him with the opportunity to develop social relationships with his peer group. Since Chip had already been described as sometimes frustrated and sometimes withdrawn, the teacher was sensitive to the need to build into Chip's program opportunities for ego-satisfying and group-satisfying activities. The learning center approach was particularly related to developing Chip's ego strength, with activities planned to induce success and to commence "intervention" strategies to deter regression and Chip's complete withdrawal. Next, the special teacher working with Ms. Coombs designed a number of small-group activities that would allow Chip to be a contributor as well as a follower. Both teachers were aware that if Chip did not have the opportunity to participate meaningfully with his peers, he would not experience peer approval or learn to communicate, which was essential for his language development. Thus, the group activities would be another intervention strategy to promote social, emotional, and academic growth.

Educational planning and programming process. The educational planning process refers to the assessment of Chip's educational needs and the detailing of them in terms of specific goals and objectives. The specialist teacher assessed Chip's academic, social, and emotional development. Then long-term and immediate goals were formulated. The goals and objectives are related to the "what" (content) of curriculum. With Chip's third-grade teacher, specific behavioral objectives were established for the teaching of reading, arithmetic, spelling, and handwriting; additional objectives were formulated for language, social studies, health, physical education, music, and art.

Whenever possible, the plan for Chip was to provide individual and group activities within the context of the normal classroom, but if Chip's needs conflicted drastically in any area with the regular program, then he would be provided with educational services in the special classroom. For instance, as Chip's assessment progressed, the specialist realized that Chip needed a program which emphasized language development, auditory training, and fine motor coordination exercises. The special classroom had a listening center Chip could use to listen to stories and read them simultaneously out of a paperback book; there was also a tape in which letter sounds were repeated and Chip could practice making the sounds and tracing the letters. Although the regular classroom also had a listening center, it would have been embarrassing for Chip to trace letters or listen to stories at a level far below his peer group; therefore, in order to plan for Chip's ego needs as well as his academic needs, the special classroom would provide these services. In the special classroom Chip used a number of materials that developed experiences for storytelling: the instructional aide recorded Chip's experience stories he would later read. These activities foster language development.

CHIP SUTTON'S DAILY PROGRAM

Regular Classroom	*Special Classroom*
9:00–9:40 Individualized mathematics	
9:40–10:00 Individualized spelling	
10:00–10:20 Recess	
	10:20–12:00 Individualized program: pictures, concrete materials, experience story writing, listening center —reading, skill activity—reading, motor coordination exercises, mathematics manipulative activities
12:00–1:00 Lunch	
1:00–2:00 Small group and whole class activities: language, science, social studies, health, or art	
2:00–2:20 Team play, physical education	
2:20–2:40 Music, whole class	
2:40–3:00 Handwriting	

Chip's educational plan and program reflected continued change. As Chip's progress was evaluated, the specialist teacher recorded new information and new programming directions that would be used by all supportive personnel as they worked with Chip.

Clarification of responsibility. Since Chip was working in two classrooms, it was vital that an organizational structure exist which clarified each person's responsibility in the mainstreaming process. At the Franklin School, it was understood that the specialist teacher (who performs the functions of assessment, interpretation, planning, programming, and evaluation) would have exclusive responsibility for Chip's educational program. Although Ms. Coombs exercised personal authority and Chip was expected to be responsive to her authority, it was the specialist teacher who was expected to exercise overall responsibility.

Implementation of the concept

Research, professional dialog, court decisions, and legislative enactments all emphasized the need for educational programs that would integrate the exceptional child into the mainstream of the educative process. Programs vary from theoretical proposals to university training models to alternate systems in the public schools. The public school programs range from highly structured behavior modification models to open classrooms with team teaching. In most of the existing programs severely handicapped children have not been accommodated, but in some states crippled and hard-of-hearing children have been mainstreamed whenever feasible.

The Israeli model

An innovative program in Israel described by researchers Feurstein, Krasilowsky, and Rand has important implications for mainstreaming in urban schools of the United States. Under the jurisdiction of the Child and Youth Immigration Department, Youth Alliyah was created in Israel as an education agency responsible for a total care program for Israeli youth.

After World War II, the agency was confronted with hundreds of teenaged youths assessed and described by psychologists and teachers in the following ways:

Socioculturally deprived

Language problem (Arab-speaking youths demonstrated a developmental gap of three to five years as compared to European Israeli agemates.)

Retarded as indicated by IQ, developmental culture-free, and culture-fair tests

Twelve to sixteen years of age

Illiterate

Limited conceptual-abstract thinking ability

Devoid of basic learning skills

Impulsive, aggressive

Unable to accept delayed gratification

Poor future orientation

The researchers in cooperation with Youth Alliyah supervisors and field workers were convinced that their present means of assessment did not provide them with knowledge about the levels of cognitive functioning, modifiability, or adaptive behavior.

> In coping with uprooted youngsters coming from conditions of life and countries where regular educational processes were almost nonexistent, one had to be able to discriminate between a low manifest and a retarded level of functioning and the capacity of the individual to function given appropriate instruction.[34]

Their first step was to construct the Learning Potential Assessment Device (LPAD). The purpose of the device was to teach cognitive operational principles (analogistic and syllogistic thinking and classification); then the youngster would be asked to apply what he learned to a new task that would be a variation of the original operation. The youth would be observed as he applied himself to the new task. His ability to use the newly acquired experience in a different situation was used as an index of change (modifiability). During the testing situation, *the examiner worked as a teacher,* offering encouragement and feedback.

> Process orientation was substituted for product orientation. . . . This method of assessment enabled us to demonstrate the educability and modifiability of many people who otherwise would have been considered mentally deficient.[35]

The second step in the program was to provide individual and group training to correct cognitive deficiencies. The training was provided by teachers who received special preparation. Each youngster received about 400 hours of individual or group assistance in cognitive functioning exercises. The theory underlying the Instrumental Enrichment Program was the assumption that cognitive improvement is possible at any level of individual development. Goals for enrichment included the increase of the individual's capacity to gather, extend, and process information.

> Instrumental Enrichment is an active modification approach which considers the functioning of the retarded performer as an open system, subject to modification. Active modification is concerned with the building of capacity rather than accepting retarded performance in a passive way.[36]

The third element of the program was to place the adolescents in normal peer groups. The researchers utilized four principles in their mainstream program:

> *Unconditional Acceptance.* The exceptional youth was placed in a group and made to feel that he belonged.

Reduction of Anxiety. Effort was made to restore the individual's sense of power as he worked within a group of agemates and encountered success.

Induced Regression. The individual was allowed to fulfill infantile needs in relationships with teachers and peers.

Planned and Controlled Relationship with the Normal Peer Society. The researchers defined this principle as the essence of the treatment. "The use of the total environment as a means of continuous, controlled, and regulated interaction with a benevolent reinforcing society."[37]

Results reported by the researchers included IQ scores higher than the average obtained by the total sample of Youth Alliyah graduates, few signs of delinquency, no signs of negative behavioral contagion among peer group, and mental hygiene enrichment for the total group. The researchers concluded that the technique was economical, feasible, and successful for use with disturbed adolescents and high-risk populations. Although the researchers described and claimed only cognitive goals, their components appear to emphasize total cognitive and affective development.

An open education approach

Knoblock, a Syracuse University special educator, studied inner city children labeled disturbed and disturbing. He created an open education approach for working with the students, utilizing the following identified principles:

(a) respecting and valuing the individual rights of each person,
(b) viewing the learning environment as a community in which those who are directly involved have control over what happens to them, and
(c) guaranteeing equal opportunity without bias against the skills, viewpoint, or goals of each learner in the environment.[38]

From his observations of teachers working with troubled youth, he identified the following typical behaviors of teachers in open classroom settings:

Teachers and other adults in the open classroom work as partners to facilitate children's learning; the adults are inclined to be responsive to individuals and small groups of children.

The adults facilitate children's use of learning resources by organizing the materials, identifying resource persons, and making the materials available to the children.

The adults design learning activities and motivate the children to participate in the desired activity.

The teachers ask problem-solving questions and encourage children to respond.

The teachers perceive themselves as "resources and catalysts" for learning.

The teachers encourage the children to commit themselves to reasonable goals and to schedule the appropriate amount of time to accomplish the goals.[39]

Open education was found to be advantageous because it provided teachers with opportunities to do the following:

Integrate affect and content

Acknowledge and respond to feelings and behaviors

Respond to readiness levels of children

Relate learnings to the individual as a person

Utilize a learning environment that facilitates teachers' diagnostic behaviors

Knoblock's research in urban settings allowed him and his associates to identify five core concerns of troubled children and the responses of open education to those concerns. The children's concerns related to power needs, self-concept, interactional relationships with adults, the need for emotional and environmental control, and self-definitional needs. The response of open education included the following:

The development of an environment in which the children actively participate in planning and defining own goals

Nonauthoritarian adults who open up communication lines with the children and respond to the emotional needs of the children

Planned activities which facilitate self-evaluation by the children.[40]

The experiences of Knoblock and his associates with inner city children and their teachers seem to indicate that exceptional children would profit from open classroom environments.

Teaching Humanely

The Franklin School where Chip Sutton was enrolled provided special education services such as assessment, parent conferences, and educational planning. The faculty demonstrated professional behaviors. Yet current thinking advises that the practice of placing a mildly retarded child in a special classroom, segregated from his peermates, is inappropriate and unjustified.

Society is composed of disparate cultures; individuals represent a wide range of interests and abilities. For schools to accomplish meaningful goals, the student population must reflect human variability. Students and teachers should be able to demonstrate the importance of human dignity, individuality, and individual integrity. Heterogeneous rather than homogeneous classrooms provide opportunities for curriculum experiences to be focused on the learner and designed to enhance mutual respect. Mainstreaming is a goal to ensure full educational opportunities to handicapped students, but there are several professional tasks essential to its accomplishment. In essence, these tasks require new role assumptions for classroom teachers. These new tasks are the focus of this last section of the chapter:

The need for expanded assessment procedures

Techniques to integrate newly mainstreamed children into the regular classroom

The development of a collegial team

Expanded assessment of each child's needs

Purpose of assessment. An assessment of a child's needs provides data to enable the teacher to analyze and judge the appropriateness of instruction. Greater specificity in terms of accumulated data will yield an improved decision base. For this reason, prior assessment practices that sometimes depended solely on achievement and IQ tests were inadequate when used for the purpose of educational diagnosis, placement, and planning. Skilled teachers are able to gather a great deal of evidence about a child's levels of functioning. Tests provide information, but considerable data can only be procured through planned observations.

What is an expanded assessment? The expanded assessment is a means to increase the extent of the data base. It should include information about motor development, sensory functioning, communication skills, cognitive development, independence, socialization, personality, and learning characteristics. The following lists are illustrative:

Motor development
  Gross motor abilities (skipping, jumping, throwing, balancing, running)
  Fine motor skills (cutting, coloring, folding, bead stringing, drawing)
  Eye-hand coordination
  Spatial orientation
  Identification of body parts and location
  Body positioning
Sensory functioning
  Auditory discrimination
  Visual acuity, color blindness, visual discrimination

Communications skills
  Language dominance
    Spanish
    English
    Nonstandard English
    Bilingual
    Bidialectical
  Oral language development
    Creative expression
    Simple and complex sentences
    Vocabulary
    Clarity of speech
  Writing skills
  Reading skills
  Listening skills, demonstrates understanding of others
Cognitive development
  Problem solving
  Concept formation
  Number concepts
  Indefinite concepts
  Spatial concepts
  Time concepts
Independence
  Dresses appropriately
  Ties shoes
  Cleanliness
  Follows directions
  Works independently
  Plays and works safely
  Appropriate toilet habits
  Plays independently
Socialization
  Plays and works with others
  Listens to others
  Contributes to a group
  Participates in group activities
  Demonstrates appropriate manners and habits
  Shares interests
  Influences others
  Is influenced by others
  Is amenable to change
  Demonstrates cultural interests and feelings
  Expresses cultural values
  Accepts, recognizes the values of others
  Demonstrates understanding of rules

Personality
  Assertive
  Aggressive
  Withdrawn
  Social leader
  Self-assured, independent
  Shy
  Arrogant
  Introverted
  Extroverted
  Insecure-dependent, conforming
Learning characteristics
  Responds to concrete rather than abstract materials
  Responds to concrete and abstract materials
  Responds to meaningful situations, ideas, materials
  Responds to nonmeaningful situations, ideas, materials
  Demonstrates flexibility in problem solving or search system
  Demonstrates rigidity in problem solving or search system
  Demonstrates organizational ability
  Demonstrates ability to categorize
  Attention span (long, lags)
  Motivation (poor, adequate, superior)
  Memory (short, long-term)
  Analytically oriented
  Relational orientation
  Visual-perceptual orientation
  Responds to auditory stimulation
  Prefers manipulative activities, materials

These lists are not intended to be interpreted as conclusive. The
teacher is limited only by his or her observation skills. The function of
the assessment is the extension of knowledge and understanding about
the child. The single assessment instrument tends to be restrictive.

Adelman and Feshbach discussed the impact of assessment procedures to predict success or failure in school noting that children's
success or failure in the first grade depended not only on their skills
and behaviors but also on the classroom environment. They hypothe-
sized that there is a relationship between the child's skills and behaviors and the skills and behaviors required in a specified classroom
so that the greater the congruity between the child's skills and behaviors and what is required in a specific classroom the greater the likelihood for success.[41]

Adelman and Feshbach theorized that the teacher should "go
beyond the readiness model" to predict success or failure by assessing
the child's ability to cope with the tasks he will encounter. The assess-

ment would be accomplished by evaluating the child's reading relevant skills and behaviors and evaluating any interfering behaviors. Each first grade program would be evaluated to determine critical skills and behaviors needed by children to cope with the required reading tasks. Finally, an analysis would be made to determine the discrepancy between what is required of the child and the child's own skills and behaviors.[42]

Although the researchers applied their theory to the development of a model to predict reading failure in the first grade, a discrepancy analysis would prove useful in other grades and subjects as well as yield information about the teacher's personal teaching style. Ms. Coombs recognized the importance of her own teaching performance; if Ms. Coombs had been unable to utilize an individualized academic skills program, she would not have been able to accept Chip in her classroom. The discrepancy between Chip's skills and behaviors and what would be required of him to be successful in Ms. Coombs' classroom had to be compared.

Assessment by parents. Parents can contribute a great deal of information about the child that cannot be gleaned from any other source. For instance, the element of independence: Does the child dress himself? Does the child choose his own clothes? If necessary, could he make his own breakfast or lunch? Is the child willing and able to play alone? If required, what tasks can/does the child perform at home? Will the child voluntarily perform tasks or study? To what extent does the child require assistance with homework or other tasks? Does the child bathe himself? (Does he do so of his own accord?) In each element of the assessment, parents have information essential to a complete understanding of the child. It is critical that parents not be surprised by the assessment process or workup of data about the child. They should be considered partners in the assessment process.

Recordkeeping. Keeping record of student progress is a familiar and traditional task to most teachers. Developing an assessment record is just as simple. Adelman and Feshbach suggested the development of a scale whereby the teacher could rate each item within a range of 5. If 1 were the lowest point and 5 the highest, inappropirate behavior that occurred 90 to 100 percent of the time would be rated 1.

Other recording systems can be used to allow the observer to check the occurrence of the behavior. The important point is that the observer be comfortable with the system; for this reason, the best system is one devised by the teacher/observer.

Assessment conclusions. The teacher's expanded assessment may detect patterns of behavior that should be investigated by other specialists (physician, psychologist). The teacher must not assume auditory disability on the basis of poor auditory discrimination skills. The manifested behavior may have occurred by chance or may be one of many symptoms or characteristics. This is another reason for planned observations over a fairly long period of time.

The assessment process is a data-gathering operation. It must not be confused with diagnosis, which occurs sometime after the data have been analyzed and interpreted for meanings. The diagnosis should also be based upon other data, such as the child's sociocultural index, a measure of adaptive behavior, and potential for learning. Other colleagues and specialists should be involved in the diagnostic and prescriptive procedures. The diagnostic-prescriptive process as it affects exceptional children will not be discussed at this juncture; however, it is crucial to the realization of the mainstreaming goal.

Techniques to integrate newly mainstreamed children into the regular classroom

Although mainstreaming projects in the public schools have not been numerous, some educators who have experimented with mainstreaming have concluded that it is not a prescriptive plan for changing teaching goals, procedures, or behaviors. These educators believe that *not* all teachers or future teachers will be able to embrace a mainstreamed child into their classrooms. Despite the worthiness of the goal, only confident teachers who are able to utilize broad, flexible teaching strategies should be expected to work with children who in the past were considered unsuccessful in the regular classroom.

Christoplos described a pilot plan initiated in three elementary schools in Baltimore. The students were considered "learning disabled." The first technique utilized in the program was *interstudent tutoring*. Interstudent tutoring served three purposes:

> To relieve the classroom teacher so that he would not be overwhelmed by the variety of children, curricula, and materials
>
> To facilitate skill mastery by a one-to-one relationship during the learning experience
>
> To foster cooperative attitudes, mutual and self-respect

The tutor was another student in the same classroom and was not necessarily more capable or older. The only requirement for the tutoring situation was that the tutor be capable of performing the specific skill for which he was assisting.

> For example, for the skill of letter naming, the child who knows only five letters may tutor the child who knows only three. The tutor himself thus has additional and needed opportunities to overlearn what he knows or just recently learned by teaching the skill to another.[43]

The tutor also experienced tutoring by another child; in that way mutuality, cooperation, and self-respect were to be developed.

The teacher's role during the tutoring sessions was to keep track of each student's progress, decide upon new tutor-tutee assignments, and work as a tutor for the top children. The teacher also made suggestions for variations in the tutoring techniques when a child did not make progress. When the teacher tested the tutored child, the tutor was present. In that way, responsibility between tutor and tutee was strengthened.

Christoplos cited the following advantages derived from the tutoring procedures: "fluid pairing of children, no rigid classification by ability, individualized tutoring, individualized rates of progress, and total class involvement in related activities."[44] Christoplos identified other researchers who corroborated that the tutoring process has a positive effect upon the child acting as tutor;[45] therefore, it is extremely important to have *all* children experience the tutor role.

Two other techniques emerged as necessary as a result of the tutoring experiences: recordkeeping and task analysis. For *recordkeeping*, the investigator suggested graphing to be performed by the students:

> For example, the number of correct answers during interstudent drills and tutoring sessions may be graphed, and after a stipulated number of perfect drills have been recorded by one student for another, the teacher would be asked to do the final skill testing and advancement.[46]

The second technique, *task analysis*, was vital to the whole operation. To perform the technique, the teacher had to analyze the discrepancy between actual performance (the child's ability level) and the performance level goal. In a sense, the teacher's role was that of a program developer.

If these techniques proved unsuccessful, then Christoplos recommended that the teacher request a psychological assessment to diagnose the problem area in relation to the activity where the child's performance was unsuccessful. Tests would be determined by three factors: the teacher's goal, in which the teacher is unable to integrate the child; the child's level of performance; other skills or knowledge prerequisite to the goal or an area where a relationship is suspected.

The Christoplos plan had four elements in the approach for integrating the exceptional student:

Emphasis on the teacher's goals and methods

Inservice retraining and renewal for teachers

Specialists assisting the regular class teacher to develop an appropriate curriculum that facilitates multi-ability levels

Individual diagnosis only if other measures fail, and then diagnostic testing related to the specific classroom activities that precipitated failure

In another study, Glass and Meckler[47] prepared 18 elementary teachers during a summer workshop to mainstream mildly handicapped children. The workshop objectives can be translated into teacher competencies and as such considered techniques for mainstreaming. Three sets of competencies were identified: diagnostic skills, remediation-intervention skills, and interpersonal relationship skills.

For diagnostic purposes, the teachers were expected to use informal and formal testing procedures. The skills included (1) observation of children's behavior, relating the behavior to a psychodynamic and learning theory framework, and (2) diagnosis of child's preferred learning modality (auditory, visual, kinesthetic). The remediation-intervention skills included eight competencies:

1. Implementation of basic behavior modification procedures
2. The use of role playing and behavior rehearsal techniques to resolve conflict and develop appropriate classroom behavior
3. Cross-age tutoring
4. Problem-solving discussion strategy to solve classroom interaction problems
5. The use of basic life-space interviewing techniques to provide emotional support to children and to teach new behavioral tools
6. Development of a task structure appropriate for multi-ability levels
7. Application of remedial materials and procedures in basic skills and in perceptual-motor development
8. Application of diagnostic information for the modification of traditional curriculum and materials for selected children

The interpersonal relationship competencies included

1. Listening and responding empathetically to students' ideas, feelings, perceptions
2. Responding encouragingly, acceptingly, to students' feelings
3. Open-minded discussions with students concerning interpersonal relationships and human relations problems
4. Nonthreatening communication to other teachers and parents

Glass and Meckler concluded that teaching skills for mainstreaming could be learned in a very short period of time, provided the conditions emphasized the development and practice of the skills in an action-oriented setting. Whereas Christoplos used tutors of the same age, Glass and Meckler used older and more capable children. In the

Christoplos plan diagnosis occurred if failure ensued and under the direction of a specialist, but Glass and Meckler used diagnosis for behavior modification as a strategy integrated into the total plan.

Performance discrepancy and task analysis. The process of teacher discovery of a child's functioning level can on occasion happen almost in serendipitous fashion. For instance, Amos Steele was teaching third grade and for the fourth time that morning he was explaining to Henrietta the procedures she was to follow in her construction project. His voice was raised and he was ready to holler, but then he scratched his head and muttered: "It can't be; it *just can't be!*"

Steele took Henrietta by the hand and sat her down in front of a tape recorder. He had Henrietta listen to a story; then he asked her to tell the story to him. All Henrietta could tell was the last event of the story. That was how Steele discovered that Henrietta *lacked auditory memory.* Once he knew that single fact, he was able to plan a program of instructional tasks to expand her auditory memory. Steele's program included these activities:

1. Henrietta would listen to a series of words and then be asked to repeat them sequentially.
2. Henrietta would listen to oral directions and be asked to repeat them.
3. Henrietta would be given directions to listen for some specific details; then a short story would be told to her, and she would raise her hand every time she heard the specific details.
4. Henrietta would listen to a short story on the tape recorder and draw pictures about specific details in the story.
5. Mr. Steele would cut out the pictures and paste them on cardboard.
6. Henrietta would arrange the pictures sequentially and tell the story to another child.

Henrietta would not progress to the next task until each prior task was completed successfully, but each task was at a simplified level so that success was almost assured.

Steele's task analysis expanded Henrietta's auditory memory and succeeded in contributing to the development of comprehension skills. Although Steele's discovery of the child's problem happened seemingly by accident, there are many ways to determine functioning levels in skill areas.

Technical skill summary. Techniques for mainstreaming selected children appear to focus primarily on the improvement of skills and attitudes. For skill improvement, teaching behaviors include an analysis of the child's performance discrepancy (as in Henrietta's case), an analysis of the goal into modules for learning (task analysis), recording changes in progress, testing, and choosing a new goal.

To improve attitudes, the teaching strategies utilized small groups in problem-solving and role-playing tasks. The decision-making strategies and other small-group activities suggested in Chapter 5 would be appropriate. The majority of the mainstreaming programs suggested the addition of an instructional aide to assist the classroom teacher. Except for a few of the behavior modification plans, tutoring was an essential feature. The teacher's humanistic skills were considered to be an integral part of successful mainstreaming.

Chaffin reviewed both theoretical and public school mainstreaming programs and made the following suggestions for the implementation of a mainstreaming proposal:

1. A comprehensive support system should be provided for students and teachers involved in a mainstream effort.

2. Mainstreamed children should be selected by specialists familiar with the child's educational and social needs. All handicapped children will not benefit from a mainstreaming program.

3. Since mainstreaming approaches differ, a specific plan should be selected by the individuals who will be involved, not imposed upon them.

4. All personnel should participate in planning efforts.

5. Regular classroom teachers should determine the kind of support they and the child will need.

6. Inservice education should be included in the plan for regular and special teachers.

7. A communication system should be provided so that all individuals are aware of procedures and kinds of support services.

8. An accounting system should be implemented. The system should specify number of children involved, teachers, support system, duration of services.

9. Data related to student progress should be accumulated, as well as information on the variables involved, such as teacher attitudes. Follow-up studies should be initiated on a sample of the children to provide feedback on the effectiveness of the services.

10. All results of the program should be reported to all personnel, including parents and community. "Even poor results can improve morale if proper steps are being taken to remedy problem areas."[48]

The development of a collegial team

This text has focused on *successful* urban teachers; teachers whom the author has designated "specialists" in urban teaching. Explicit in that statement is the perspective that all teachers should not be expected to teach all children; correspondingly, all teachers cannot be expert in all subject areas and specialties. For this reason, professional educators are appraising models that join colleagues for consultation and support purposes.

Effective teaching is situation-based; it is related to the client being served, the community, the resources, and the services dispensed. (There are some constants: All competent teachers should be able to assess, prescribe, and evaluate.) The psychologist who spends one day a week (sometimes one day a month) in a school of necessity must confine professional chores to assessment and diagnosis. Many school psychologists have no teaching experience; therefore, it is not surprising that prescriptive teaching suggestions are seldom forthcoming from the school psychologist. Other school specialists, such as doctors and nurses, have similar deficiencies and should not be expected to perform apart from their specific professional roles.

It is sometimes useful when a new model is being considered to examine similar concepts in use, or services rendered, by other service-oriented groups. For example, large accounting firms utilize the principle of differentiated staffing. A flexible teaming arrangement may be implemented depending upon the problem. The team could be composed of staff assistants (new graduates), senior accountants, a manager, and/or a partner of the firm. Depending upon client needs, the members of the team may represent the same specialization in the accounting field, or individuals who specialize in specific areas may be consulted (taxes, auditing, small business management).

The medical model is similar. When the patient's ills encompass complex but interfaced problems or peripheral afflictions, the generalist seeks the assistance of specialists. Together they form the medical consulting team. The generalist, who may be an internal specialist or some other specialist whom the patient consulted, becomes the team leader who coordinates the diagnostic procedures, interprets the recommendations in terms of the patient's needs, and then selects the appropriate measures.

The teaching profession, particularly in the last twenty years, has utilized aspects of this team approach. Both differentiated staffing and conference teams have been implemented in many school districts. The Franklin School applied the conference team approach for Chip Sutton's parent conference. The California Master Plan for Special Education requires both an appraisal team and consultant services to be available for regular classroom teachers. Both theoretical and public school mainstreaming models have provided for a support system or a service hierarchy. No conscientious individual has proposed returning all exceptional children to the regular classroom or mainstreaming children without consultant services.

The service hierarchy concept. Chaffin investigated the Pinckney Elementary School in Lawrence, Kansas. The Pinckney School is a

Title I school, which means that a majority of the school population is in the lower socioeconomic levels. The mainstreaming project staff consisted of nine regular classroom teachers; one special education teacher; half-time specialists in physical education, music, and remedial reading; the principal (half-time basis); and an administrative intern. A school psychologist, learning disabilities teacher, and counselor were each assigned one day per week. Chaffin described the essential program elements:

> One of the major benefits of a carefully defined service hierarchy is enhanced communication between the regular and special education staff. Regular education staff know what kind of services are available and what functional behaviors of the special educators are associated with each service. The services provided in a hierarchy may vary, but it is essential that they be cooperatively developed and explicitly defined by the building staff and the assigned instructional support persons.[49]

At the indirect levels of service, the resource personnel had no contact with the child. Levels of services were provided in the following ways:

> The resource personnel may observe the child in the classroom then offer suggestions of appropriate procedures based upon personal experience.
>
> Support person will provide or suggest formal and/or informal testing measures. The purpose is to assist the regular teacher become a better diagnostician. If needed the support person will teach the class in order to release the classroom teacher for testing purposes. The support person does not work with the child.

SERVICE HIERARCHY[50]

	I–1	Consultation and Observation
Indirect	I–2	Formal and Informal Testing Assistance
	I–3	Supply Instructional Materials
	D–1	Tutorial in Regular Class
	D–2	Resource Room Random
Direct	D–3	Tutorial Regular Class (1–6 weeks)
	D–4	Contracted Services
	D–5	Resource Room Regular (6 weeks or more, 1–2 periods)
	D–6	Resource Room Regular (6 weeks or more, 2–4 periods)
		Other Alternative (e.g., special placement)

After the instructional plan has been agreed upon, the support person will locate and demonstrate the use of resource materials.

Direct levels of service contrast with the indirect in that the support personnel have contact or some interaction with the child. Levels of service included these:

Support person provides tutorial service with the child in regular classroom. Tutoring service may assist the child in skill needs or in the use of resource materials. Service is limited to about two weeks.

The student is sent to the resource room for assistance with one specific task the classroom teacher cannot provide.

Three or more students may be provided with tutorial assistance by the support person in the regular classroom. The purpose of the service is maintenance in the regular classroom. If needed at this level, additional support services are contracted.

Duration of the support services is agreed upon by regular teacher and support person. If needed, the support person locates and trains a tutor to continue the assistance.

This service is provided only when prior support has failed or is considered inadequate.

Regular resource room service is provided only when preceded by other levels of service. This is the highest level of service provided by the school.[51]

Underpinning the service hierarchy are two professional considerations: *Communication* among regular and support personnel with full knowledge of the services each can contribute, and the *variety of options* available for assuring full educational opportunity for exceptional children.

Support systems. Mercer[52] proposed a continuum of special education services and recommended that all special education programs not be abandoned, warning that minority children need help to do well in the mainstream of education with or without designated labels.

Support system services is not a new concept in public education; however, the professional interpretation has changed. In the Pinckney project three regular classroom teachers were charged with the responsibility of acting as a referral committee. The composition of the California appraisal team was discussed earlier under legislative enactments. The purpose of these teams is to recommend appropriate educational actions, including contracting for additional support services.

Traditionally, appraisal teams included experts outside the field of education, and it was not uncommon for a consulting physician to chair the committee, with the result that educational recommendations were seldom made. The trend emerging as a consequence of the mainstreaming concept is for regular classroom teachers to be responsible for assessment and diagnosis, with the specialists providing assistance for related child study (vison, hearing, neurological, speech assessment).

The collegial team approach. The emerging model with the classroom teacher as the leader of the team impels new patterns within the teaching profession. The suggested model is based upon several assumptions:

Preservice-inservice education is conceived as a continuing developmental process.

Professional education is an individual and school responsibility. The goals of a school, decided by all individuals involved, determine the direction for continuing education.

Individuals with common interests (goals) should assume responsibility for professional education.

The classroom teacher is an expert and should be held responsible for self-renewal, leadership capacity, and decision making.

The collegial team may be composed of preservice teachers, classroom teachers with varied levels of experience, instructional aide(s), and a special education teacher. The team's primary responsibility is the education of the classrooms of children involved. The team's fundamental considerations will involve what to teach, how to teach it, and how to find out whether or not learning transpired. These three considerations are fundamental to the teaching of normal and/or exceptional children in urban and suburban settings.

The team will be responsible for the total workup on each child. This means assessment, prescription, and evaluation. The collegial team will decide and contract for outside assistance or recommend consultant services outside the profession. Its members will make decisions concerning their own continuing education in terms of the goals of the school, priorities, and problems in their own classrooms. Perhaps sometime in the future, school districts (which presently have more teachers than jobs) will accept the concept that the collegial team may elect to put itself out of business for the purpose of self-renewal.

The concept of a collegial team bridges the gap that formerly constrained relationships between specialized personnel and regular teachers. The regular teacher should be the team leader because it is the regular teacher who is held responsible in the eyes of the client-community and the law for guiding normal peer relationships and full educational opportunity.

Summary: Implications for Urban Teaching

The impetus for mainstreaming originated from the concerns of educators about special education and the rage of minority Americans over the fact that minority children were overrepresented in special education classes (specifically classes for mental retardation). Judicial decisions and the legislative process acknowledged

> Educators' contradictory results concerning the effectiveness of special placement
>
> Cultural bias of IQ tests and the testing milieu
>
> Prejudicial attitudes resulting from the labeling process

A number of researchers recommended a moratorium on IQ testing, and Mercer and associates concluded that test assessment should include information that gives a sociocultural index about the child, a test reflecting adaptive behavior, a standard IQ test interpreted to predict success in a regular classroom without additional assistance, and a standard IQ test interpreted within the child's ethnic norms to provide information concerning the child's learning potential.

Evidence cited in the chapter implied that urban teachers should

> Expand their knowledge and understanding of cultural groups and the diverse values among subgroups
>
> Recognize the effect of environment upon learning
>
> Evaluate factors that affect the development and the measurement of intelligence

Legislative enactments in a number of states banned the use of IQ tests, and Congress passed the Education Amendments of 1974 (PL 93–380), which affect federal funding and establish a goal to provide full educational opportunities to all handicapped children. The congressional enactment also established procedures to ensure the placement of handicapped students, whenever appropriate, with non-handicapped peers; placement decisions also now must be based on testing and evaluation materials selected and administered so as not to be racially or culturally discriminatory. Since urban schools are dependent upon federal funding for personnel and material resources as well as breakfast and lunch programs, the congressional enactment and the judicial decisions will have impact on the ways in which the school identifies, assesses, and plans for handicapped students.

Identification procedures in the future will be based on an expanded assessment of the students' levels of functioning. The practice of discrepancy analysis (difference between goal and actual performance) will influence much of the instructional planning for exceptional children. To encourage the development of maximum potential for each child, many classroom teachers have suggested teaching to the handicapped child's strengths instead of focusing on weaknesses. New teaching approaches will try a variety of options; some teachers will attempt behavior modification techniques such as correction and intervention, and others will focus on strengths.

The integration of all children into the classroom perhaps was inspired by a new spirit for humanistic education. The new humanism may also influence professional relationships. Evolving trends impel regular classroom teachers to accept professional responsibility for observation, diagnosis, prescription, and evaluation of instructional outcomes; to develop the appropriate professional attitudes to facilitate the consultation services and support of special educators; and to self-evaluate for purposes of continuing education and self-renewal.

Notes

1. LLOYD M. DUNN, "Special Education for the Mildly Retarded—Is Much of It Justifiable?" *Exceptional Children*, 34 (1968), 5–22.
2. E. H. GROTBERG, "Neurological Aspects of Learning Disabilities: A Case for the Disadvantaged," *Journal of Learning Disabilities*, 3 (1970), 321–327.
3. DAVID J. FRANKS, "Ethnic and Social Status Characteristics of Children in EMR and LD Classes," *Exceptional Children*, 37,7 (March 1971), 537–538.
4. S. A. KIRK, *Educating Exceptional Children*, 2d ed. (Boston: Houghton Mifflin, 1972).
5. G. O. JOHNSON, "Special Education for the Mentally Retarded—A Paradox," *Exceptional Children*, 29 (1962), 62–69.
6. E. A. WELCH, "The Effects of Segregated and Partially Integrated School Programs on Self-concept and Academic Achievement of Educable Mental Retardates" (Unpublished doctoral dissertation, University of Denver, 1965).
7. R. J. ZITO and J. I. BARDON, "Achievement Motivation among Negro Adolescents in Regular and Special Education Programs," *American Journal of Mental Deficiency*, 74 (1969), 20–26.
8. JANE R. MERCER, "The Meaning of Mental Retardation," in Richard Koch and James C. Dobson, eds., *The Mentally Retarded Child and His Family* (New York: Brunner/Mazel, 1971), p. 27.
9. JANE R. MERCER, "Sociocultural Factors in Labeling Mental Retardates," *Peabody Journal of Education*, 48,3 (April 1971), 191.
10. MERCER in Koch and Dobson, *op. cit.*, p. 29.
11. *Ibid.*, p. 45.
12. *Ibid.*
13. H. CARL HAYWOOD, "Labeling: Efficacy, Evils, and Caveates" (Paper presented at the Joseph P. Kennedy, Jr., Foundation International Symposium on Human Rights, Retardation, and Research, Washington, D.C., October 16, 1971).
14. JANE R. MERCER, "IQ: The Lethal Label," *Psychology Today*, 6,4 (September 1972), 46–47.
15. FRANK HEWETT and J. O. MASSEY, *Clinical Clues from the WISC* (Palo Alto, Calif.: Consulting Psychologists Press, 1969), as described in Jerome M. Sattler, "Intelligence Testing of Ethnic Minority-Group and Culturally Disadvantaged Children," *First Review of Special Education*, Vol. 27 (Philadelphia: Journal of Special Education Press, 1973), pp. 161–201.

16. JOHN GARCIA, "IQ: The Conspiracy," *Psychology Today*, 6,4 (September 1972), 94.

17. LOUIS A. BRANSFORD, "Social Issues in Special Education," *Phi Delta Kappan*, 55,8 (April 1974) 531.

18. A. R. JENSEN, "Learning Abilities in Mexican American and Anglo American Children," *California Journal of Educational Research*, 12 (September 1961), 147–159.

19. ROBERT A. ROESSEL, JR., "Intelligence and Achievement of the Indian Student," in James C. Stone and Donald P. DeNevi, eds., *Teaching Multi-Cultural Populations* (New York: Van Nostrand Reinhold, 1971), pp. 348–357.

20. JEROME M. SATTLER, "Intelligence Testing of Ethnic Minority Group and Culturally Disadvantaged Children," *First Review of Special Education*, Vol. 27 (Philadelphia: Journal of Special Education Press, 1973), pp. 161–201.

21. *Ibid.*, citing Cohen, p. 170.

22. J. E. STABLEIN, D. S. WILLEY, and C. W. THOMSON, "An Evaluation of the Davis-Eells (Culture-Fair) Test Using Spanish and Anglo-American Children," *Journal of Educational Sociology*, 35 (1961), 73–78.

23. SATTLER, *op. cit.*, quoting Hewett and Massey.

24. THOMAS P. CARTER, "Mexican Americans in School: A History of Educational Neglect," describing the research of Palomares and Johnson, in James C. Stone and Donald P. DeNevi, eds., *Teaching Multi-Cultural Populations* (New York: Van Nostrand Reinhold, 1971), p. 219.

25. MERCER, *op. cit.*, p. 96.

26. *Pennsylvania Association for Retarded Children* v. *Commonwealth of Pennsylvania*, 334, Federal Supplement 1257, 1971.

27. *Ibid.*

28. *Mills* v. *Board of Education of the District of Columbia*, 348, Federal Supplement 866, 1972.

29. *Larry P. et al. Plaintiffs* v. *Wilson Riles et al. Defendants*, 343, Federal Supplement 1306, 1972, p. 1314. Emphasis added.

30. *Ibid.*, pp. 1311–1312.

31. Education Amendments of 1974, pp. 93–380.

32. *California Master Plan for Special Education* (Sacramento: California State Department of Education, 1974), and p. 30.

33. MARTIN J. KAUFMAN, JAY GOTTLIEB, JUDITH A. AGARD, and MAURICE B. KUKIC, *Programmed Re-entry into Mainstream Education, Mainstreaming: Toward an Explication of the Construct* (Washington, D.C.: Office of Education, Bureau of Education for the Handicapped, Intramural Research Program, Project No. IM–71–001, March 1975), p. 9.

34. REUVEN FEUERSTEIN, DAVID KRASILOWSKY, and YAACOV RAND, "Innovative Educational Strategies for the Integration of High-risk Adolescents in Israel," *Phi Delta Kappan*, April 1974, p. 557.

35. *Ibid.*, p. 557.

36. *Ibid.*, p. 558.

37. *Ibid.*

38. PETER KNOBLOCK, "Open Education for Emotionally Disturbed Children," in Grace J. Warfield, ed., *Mainstream Currents* (Reston, Va.: Council for Exceptional Children, 1974), p. 54.

39. *Ibid.*

40. *Ibid.*, p. 56.

41. HOWARD S. ADELMAN, and SEYMOUR FESHBACH, "Predicting Reading Failure: Beyond the Readiness Model," *Exceptional Children*, 37,5 (January 1971), 350.

42. *Ibid.*

43. FLORENCE CHRISTOPOLOS, "Keeping Exceptional Children in Regular Classes," in Grace J. Warfield, ed., *Mainstream Currents* (Reston, Va.: Council for Exceptional Children, 1974), p. 204.

44. *Ibid.*

45. *Ibid.*, citing F. C. Niedermeyer and P. Ellis, "Remedial Reading Instruction by Trained Pupil Tutors," *Elementary School Journal*, 71 (1971), 406, and R. L. Croth, R. J. Whelan, and J. M. Stables, "Teacher Application of Behavior Principles in Home and Classroom Environments," *Focus on Exceptional Children*, 1 (1970), 7.

46. *Ibid.*, p. 205.

47. RAYMOND M. GLASS and ROY S. MECKLER, "Preparing Elementary Teachers to Instruct Mildly Handicapped Children in Regular Classrooms: A Summer Workshop," in Grace J. Warfield, ed., *Mainstream Currents* (Reston, Va.: Council for Exceptional Children, 1974).

48. JERRY D. CHAFFIN, "Will the Real 'Mainstreaming' Program Please Stand Up! (Or . . . Should Dunn Have Done It?)," *Focus on Exceptional Children*, 6,5 (October 1974), 17.

49. *Ibid.*, p. 13.

50. *Ibid.*

51. *Ibid.*

52. MERCER, *op. cit.*, p. 96.

Workshop VI

The observation activities in this section, although focused on so-called exceptional children, are appropriate for developing teacher skills in the behavioral observation of all students.

As you apply the exercises in this section, it is sometimes useful to consider these points:

When did you first notice the onset of the behavior?

Under what conditions did the behavior occur? (How was it provoked?)

Was the behavior appropriate or inappropriate?

How often does the specific observed behavior occur?

Additional activities in this workshop section emphasize knowledge competencies for prospective teachers, pedagogical decision making (methods for teaching), and the development of professional decision making as the reader-participant develops a teaching strategy in conjunction with peer-colleagues.

Community Agencies for Exceptional Children

OBJECTIVES: To identify community agencies (national, state, local) devoted to the assistance of the exceptional child; to obtain materials and to gain knowledge about the exceptional child.

DIRECTIONS: Identify national, state, and local organizations or social agencies that will provide information or furnish speakers about the exceptional child. The following are examples:

Council for Exceptional Children, 1920 Association Drive, Reston, Virginia 22091

National Association for Retarded Children, 2709 Avenue E East, Arlington, Virginia 76001

American Association for Gifted Children, 15 Gramercy Park, New York, New York 10003

Bureau of Education for the Handicapped, United States Office of Education, Department of Health, Education, Welfare, Washington, D.C. 20202

Association for Children with Learning Disabilities, 2200 Brownsville Road, Pittsburgh, Pennsylvania 15210

Diana v. State Board of Education

OBJECTIVE: Thoughtful analysis of the issues involved.

Judicial considerations:

1. Should all children be tested in English?
2. Should the board of education have the right to label children as retarded?

3. Did the plaintiffs prove that Mexican-American students are over-represented in EMR classrooms?
4. If the plaintiffs have proved overrepresentation, is it the responsibility of the board of education to prove the justification of the IQ test?
5. Should tests be standardized for particular populations?

Plaintiffs:

Nine Mexican-American students, 8 to 13 years of age.

Spanish primary language spoken in home.

All nine children designated retarded: IQs range from 30 to 72.

When tested in Spanish, seven of the children scored higher than the cutoff points for retardation; one scored three points below the cutoff score.

Plaintiff charges:

Testing procedures prejudicial because of the emphasis upon English language verbal skills.

Questions biased because of cultural base.

Tests standardized on white, native Americans.

One-third of the Spanish-surnamed students in Monterey County are designated educable retarded although only 18.5 percent of the population is composed of Spanish-surnamed students.

Observation of Selected School Success-Related Behaviors

OBJECTIVE: To observe and rate a primary-age child in a group activity in a classroom or elsewhere.

DIRECTIONS: Rate the child's behavior on a scale of 1 to 5 for inappropriate behavior and 6 to 10 for appropriate behavior, with 1 representing the lowest point on the scale. Decide upon additional school behaviors to observe.

Answer

Judicial Decision:

1. Students are to be tested in primary language and if a bilingual examiner is unavailable, then an interpreter may be used.
2. Mexican-American and Chinese students segregated in EMR classes are to be retested and reevaluated.
3. Efforts are to be made to facilitate the readjustment of previously segregated students into the regular classroom.
4. California must begin to develop and to standardize appropriate IQ testing instruments.

Behavior	Inappropriate 1–5	Appropriate 6–10
1. Responds to distractors		
2. Suppresses tendency to wander around classroom (or elsewhere)		
3. Suppresses tendency to speak out of turn		
4. Suppresses tendency to touch others		
5. Demonstrates willingness to wait his turn		
6. Responds to questions		
7. Asks questions		
8. Listens to others during a discussion		
9. Will continue a task to completion		
10. Can tolerate cessation of work period even if task is incomplete		
11. Demonstrates willingness to share materials		
12. Demonstrates willingness to clean up own materials		
13. Demonstrates willingness to assist others to clean up		
14. Can retell a story providing the sequence of events		

Assessment

OBJECTIVE: Plan a course of action to gather data about a child.

DIRECTIONS: Read the short vignette about Lee. Decide what kind of information you need about Lee to plan a teaching strategy. Will you require assistance?

Lee was one of five children. He was born in Hong Kong and did not speak English. When he was seven years old, his family came to the United States; they were extremely poor. At age ten he was in the fourth grade and having difficulties. His teacher commented that his motor development was poor; he could not read; he appeared to dislike school; he was absent frequently. If you were Lee's teacher, what would you do?

Expanded Assessment

OBJECTIVE: Develop an observation chart; perform an assessment.

DIRECTIONS: Reread section related to the expanded assessment. Choose three categories, such as motor development, socialization, learning characteristics. Develop a chart of possible behaviors, tally the occurrence of the behavior, and describe the circumstances. Check the example below.

Motor, cognitive development	Activity, circumstances	Number of times
Gross motor abilities (Add additional competencies)	(Rhythms) Child could not hop on one foot; child failed to skip	Monday and Thursday during rhythms; playground game activity on Friday; all occurred during same week
Indefinite concepts	Social studies: Failed to understand "long ago" "few," "many," "several"	Class discussion on Monday
Concept formation	Social studies: Failed to give an example of the concept ' change"	Class discussion on Monday

SUGGESTION: In each chosen category, designate all the possible competencies for observation.

Answer

Lee is probably experiencing linguistic and cultural problems. You would need a complete assessment of his levels of functioning, particularly oral language development, sensory functioning (hearing), specific motor development skills, learning characteristics. It would be wise to obtain the assistance of a colleague to verify observations. A medical colleague should check sensory functioning.

Interaction Exercise 3

OBJECTIVE: Tally interactions, learner/teacher.

DIRECTIONS: Review interaction exercises 1 (Chapter 1) and 2 (Chapter 2). In this exercise, observe an adolescent student; record her or his behavior and the teacher's response. Tally the number of times behavior occurs. Check the example below.

Adolescent behavior	Teacher response
Speaks out	Gestures—"quiet"
Slugs another student	Speaks quietly to student
Gets up and sharpens pencil	Ignores
Assists another student	Praises
Follows directions	Smiles encouragingly
Begins to read assignment	Pats on shoulder

Behavioral Disabilities

OBJECTIVE: To observe individuals exhibiting selected behaviors.

The medical model for classifying individuals tends to identify individual pathology. The result of this has been that educators concentrated on the individual's weaknesses instead of strengths.

Quay identified four dimensions to describe behavioral characteristics of children suspected of having behavioral disabilities. Although individuals are seldom "all one way," Quay's dimensions provide a basis for observation and classification.

Lloyd M. Dunn, ed., *Exceptional Children in the Schools* (New York: Holt, Rinehart and Winston, 1973), pp. 248–249, describes the Quay dimensions.

DIRECTIONS: Study Quay's dimensions. Can you identify these kinds of behaviors? What might the individual be doing in the classroom to exhibit these behaviors? Think about the question: To what extent will all children exhibit some of these behaviors?

1. Conduct disorder, attention-seeking behaviors (What will a child do to seek attention?)
2. Anxious-withdrawn, lacking in confidence, "underbehavior" rather than misbehavior (How is underbehavior exhibited?)
3. Inadequate-immature, lack of interest, sluggish, daydreaming (Can you identify the immature learner?)
4. Socialized delinquent, delinquent acts, gang activities, truancy (When does the teacher see evidence of delinquent behavior?)

Integration Strategy for Mainstreamed Children

OBJECTIVE: Identify "permissible" regressive behavior.

The Israeli mainstreaming project identified the principle of induced regression to allow the mainstreamed student the opportunity to fulfill infantile needs in the classroom. What kinds of regressive behaviors could a classroom teacher permit? How can you provide constructive means for regressive behaviors?

Integrating Mainstreamed Children

OBJECTIVES: Infer relationships between behavior, desired behavior, learning activity, teacher behavior, classroom environment.

DIRECTIONS: Choose desired behavior, learning activity, and preferred environment to accomplish the desired behavior. *Review strategy, learning environment, and teacher behavior material in Chapter 2.*

Research at the Stanford Research Institute reported by Jane Stallings and Richard Maricano of the institute in the *Los Angeles Times*, July 23, 1975, "Teaching Study Findings Told," indicated the following relationships:

Teacher behavior and classroom environment	Emphasis	Learner behavior
High teacher control High structured environment Positive reinforcement and praise	Textbooks, workbooks	High scores in reading and math; acceptance of responsibility for failure; less independence
Low teacher control Low structured environment (flexible classroom)	Exploratory materials, student independence	High scores on nonverbal reasoning; willingness to work independently; acceptance of responsibility for success; lower absence rate

Answers

The mainstreamed primary child may require emotional regressive behaviors. The teacher can provide for it by accepting the following behaviors: a hug on the way to the playground, hand-holding on the way to the library, a kiss after school, a surprise smile provided by teacher, an affectionate pat provided by teacher, a momentary rest, as child puts head down upon tabletop. There are many acceptable responses to this problem. For instance, if you asked a mainstreamed child to do something and he retorted, "Don't want to," you could express acceptance of his negative response without condemnation.

Complete the following chart:

Teacher behavior and classroom environment	Learner behavior	Desired behavior	Learning activity
Low control, open environment	Shy, withdrawn	Independent, outgoing	Small-group activity, acting as a tutor
	Aggressive Assertive Fearful Delinquent Fails to complete work Anxious Lack of interest	Self-control	

Team Planning for Small-Group Teaching

DIRECTIONS: Form a collegial team. Read the performance objectives. The learners may be in a classroom, play activity, club activity. As you formulate your plan, study and respond to the questions under teacher behavior and learner behavior.

Performance Objectives:

1. Each team member will participate in planning a teaching-learning activity for a small group of students.
2. Each team member will implement the planned activity by guiding the learning experience of a small group of students.
3. Each team member will evaluate his own teaching performance in terms of learner interest, learner participation, and the achievement of the teaching objective.

Teacher behavior	Learner behavior
What do you want to teach?	What does he want to learn?
How will you develop sensitivity and understanding of your students' needs and interests?	
How will you motivate learner interest?	How will he observe?
How will you provide for student planning?	How will he participate?
How will you provide for learner creativity?	

How will you challenge student thinking?

How will he solve problems?

How will you provide for physical activities?

How will he explore?

How will you provide for the expression of student feelings?

How will you provide for the acquisition of skills?

What materials and equipment will you need?

What materials and equipment will he need?

How will you progress step-by-step through your activity?

How will you know if you have achieved your purpose?

How will he communicate?

Suggested Readings

Beery, Keith: *Models for Mainstreaming* (San Rafael, Calif.: Dimensions Publishing, 1972).

Birch, J. W.: *Mainstreaming: Educable Mentally Retarded Children in Regular Classes* (Minneapolis: University of Minnesota Press, 1974).

Kreinberg, N., and S. Chou, eds.: *Configurations of Change: The Integration of Mildly Handicapped Children into the Regular Classroom* (Berkeley, Calif.: Far West Laboratory for Educational Research and Development, 1973).

Meyen, E. L., G. A. Vargason, and R. J. Whelan: *Alternatives for Teaching Exceptional Children* (Denver: Love Publishing, 1975).

Warfield, Grace J.: *Mainstream Currents* (Reston, Va.: Council for Exceptional Children, 1974).

Index